ENGLISH HOME-LIFE

OTHER BOOKS BY CHRISTINA HOLE

ENGLISH CUSTOM AND USAGE

A description of the traditional customs and ceremonies which still exist in England, together with an account of their origin and history. Fully illustrated from photographs and old prints.

Demy 8vo. *Second Edition*

ENGLISH SPORTS AND PASTIMES

Their origin in medieval times, and their development through the centuries. Illustrated by 80 contemporary prints, paintings and old photographs.

Demy 8vo.

HAUNTED ENGLAND

An attempt to collect and classify the richly diversified ghost-lore of England. Illustrated from the brilliant and macabre drawings of John Farleigh.

Demy 8vo.

ENGLISH FOLKLORE

A record of the folklore and traditions of England as they affect the lives of the people, fully illustrated from photographs, prints, and drawings.

Demy 8vo. *Second Edition*

ENGLISH FOLK-HEROES

A record of the principal legends of the English national folk-heroes—Arthur, Robin Hood, St. George, etc. Illustrated from woodcuts by Eric King.

Demy 8vo.

BATSFORD BOOKS

Frontispiece

I "The First Ear-ring"

From the painting by Sir David Wilkie

Reproduced by courtesy of the Trustees of the Tate Gallery

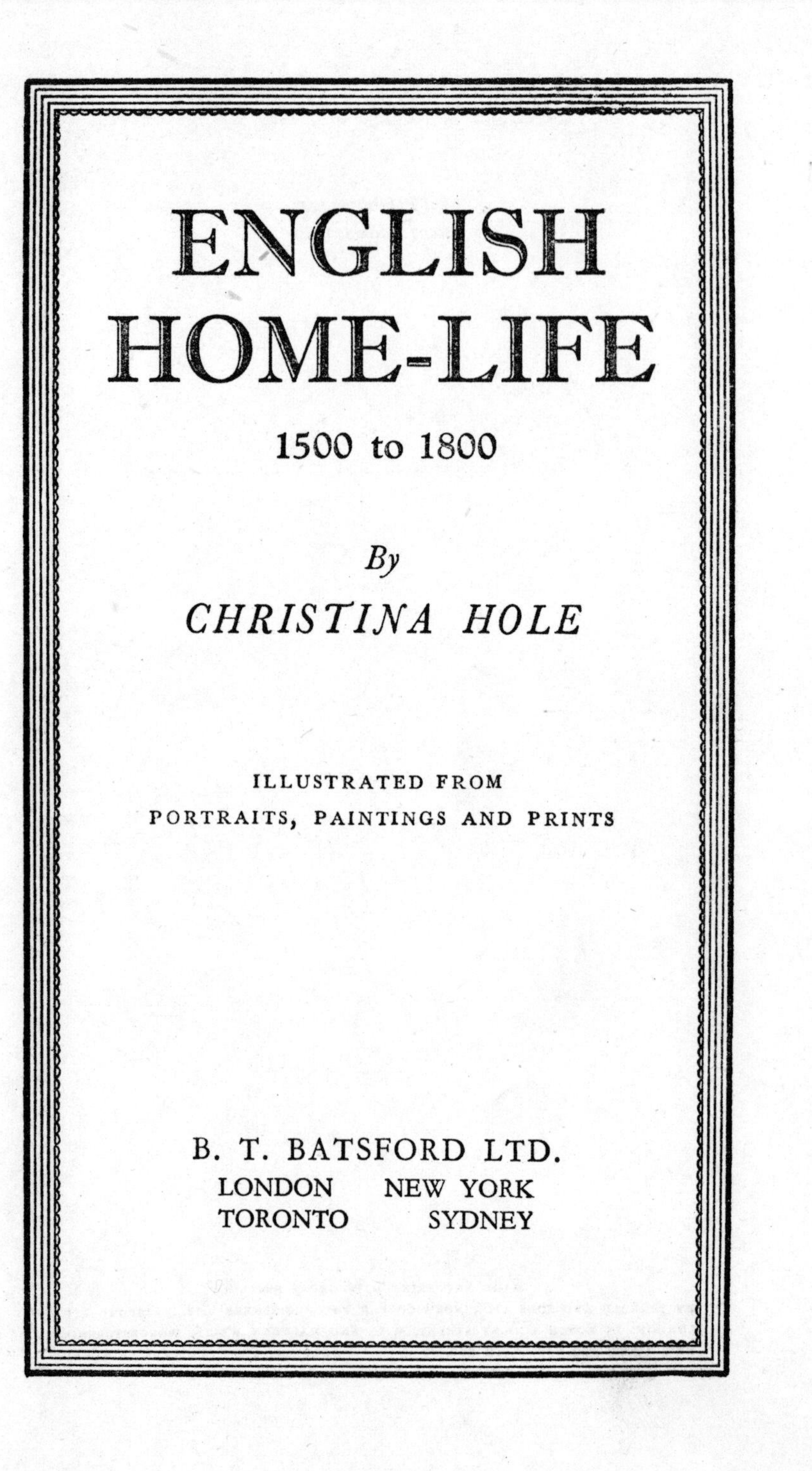

ENGLISH HOME-LIFE

1500 to 1800

By

CHRISTINA HOLE

ILLUSTRATED FROM
PORTRAITS, PAINTINGS AND PRINTS

B. T. BATSFORD LTD.
LONDON NEW YORK
TORONTO SYDNEY

First Published, 1947
Second Edition, 1949

MADE AND PRINTED IN GREAT BRITAIN
BY JARROLD AND SONS LTD., NORWICH FOR THE PUBLISHERS B. T. BATSFORD LTD.,
LONDON: 15 NORTH AUDLEY STREET, W.1 AND MALVERN WELLS. WORCESTERSHIRE
NEW YORK: 122 EAST 55TH STREET TORONTO: 480-6 UNIVERSITY AVENUE
SYDNEY: 156 CASTLEREAGH STREET

PREFACE

IN this book I have attempted to describe some aspects of the ordinary home-life of country-dwellers in England during the sixteenth, seventeenth, and eighteenth centuries. It is necessarily a record of small and familiar things, of those daily habits, thoughts, superstitions, and prejudices which form the groundwork of existence for most of us. I have not dealt with any of the great events which make these centuries so important a period in our history; they are mentioned only in so far as they affected family life and modified the habits of those who lived through them. What is recorded here is the simpler and more intimate side of living—the day-to-day routine, the shape and furnishing of houses, the hours of meals and what was eaten at them, and the customary duties of householders and servants in simple country dwellings.

Home-life, however, does not consist entirely of the domestic round. It is made up quite as much of thoughts and ambitions, of sacrifices made in the cause of education or religion, of courtships, marriages, amusements, and illnesses, as it is of more immediate concerns. For this reason I have gone beyond the kitchen and the stillroom to the church, the school, the high road, and the holiday-resort. These things together add up to something rather more than a mere chronicle of simple family customs. They are the essential stuff of our national life, the continuous background against which are played out the serious dramas of kings, statesmen, and reformers. Rightly understood, they enable us to perceive more clearly the real springs of those great happenings about which we learn in our history-books, and trivial as they sometimes are in themselves, they are still worth our study for the sake of the small clear light that they shed upon the lives of our ancestors.

Many small and all-important details have been preserved for us in the diaries and letters of country gentlemen, yeomen, clergymen, and their womenfolk. From such contemporary writings we see how different from our own were the customs of our forefathers, and yet how similar the feelings and ambitions which inspired their actions. In the home more than any other place the real continuity of living can be seen. Tools may differ from age to age, but the same duties must be regularly performed, and the same order, comfort, and contentment, striven for and

achieved. In three centuries which saw far-reaching changes everywhere, the home changed also, a little more slowly than the outside world. But through all the religious and political upheavals of Tudors and Stuarts, through the economic revolutions and protracted wars of the Hanoverians, the old pattern endured. Beds must be made and children cared for, though the master of the house has ridden away to fight for a doomed king, or the plague-cart rattles over the cobbles outside the door. Rooms must be swept and meals prepared, though Bonaparte's armies are massing across the Channel, even, indeed, though house and family may be obliterated by a German bomb before another day has dawned. Nor can education be neglected or religion forgotten simply because the world has gone awry in some way or another. The running of the home, the training of children, the care of the aged, birth, marriage, and burial—these are the eternal concerns of mankind that have survived all the cataclysms of the past and will endure so long as humanity endures, whatever troubles or blessings the uncertain future may hold for us. And in the study of such matters as our ancestors saw them, we may perhaps learn a little of our own roots, and the manner in which we became the men and women that we are.

CHRISTINA HOLE

Oxford,
September 1947.

CONTENTS

Page

PREFACE v
ACKNOWLEDGMENT viii

PART I (1500–1700)

Chapter I. HOUSE AND HOME 1
II. THE DAILY ROUND 15
III. FARTHER AFIELD 27
IV. HORNBOOK AND GOWN 40
V. MARRIAGE 55
VI. SICKNESS AND DEATH 66
VII. THE THINGS OF THE SPIRIT . . . 78

PART II (1700–1800)

Chapter VIII. THE GEORGIAN HOME 91
IX. KITCHEN AND DINING-ROOM . . . 103
X. GROWING UP 117
XI. PASTIMES AND PLEASURES . . . 130
XII. HOLIDAYS AND TRAVEL 142
XIII. DISEASE AND ITS CURE 155
XIV. TO CHURCH ON SUNDAY 165

BIBLIOGRAPHY 178
INDEX 181

ACKNOWLEDGMENT

THE Publishers gratefully acknowledge their indebtedness to the owners of the originals of the illustrations for permitting their reproduction in this book. Figs. 2 (from Windsor Castle), 13 (from Windsor Castle), 19 (from Windsor Castle), and 20 (from Hampton Court Palace), have been reproduced by gracious permission of H.M. The King. The provenance of the other illustrations is as follows: Viscount Bearsted, fig. 43; Lord Camrose, fig. 41; Glasgow City Art Gallery, fig. 34; The Earl of Inchester, fig. 73; Lord Leconfield, fig. 24; Viscount Lee of Fareham, fig. 36; A. T. Lloyd, Esq., fig. 54; The Marylebone Cricket Club, figs. 69 and 70; The Metropolitan Museum, New York, fig. 62; The National Gallery, London, fig. 35; The National Gallery of Canada, Ottawa, fig. 84; The National Portrait Gallery, London, figs. 25 and 35; Col. Richard Roundell, fig. 63; The Trustees of the Royal Holloway College, London, fig. 40; The Marquis of Salisbury, fig. 21; Sir Osbert Sitwell, fig. 39; Messrs. Spink & Son, Ltd., fig. 23; Isidor Strauss, Esq., fig. 33; The Tate Gallery, London, figs. 1 and 80; Frank Travers, Esq., fig. 55; The Victoria and Albert Museum, London, figs. 38, 58 and 60; The Wallace Collection, London, fig. 59. The Publishers are also grateful to Messrs. W. T. Spencer, of New Oxford Street, London, for lending the originals of some of the prints.

PART I (1500–1700)

Chapter I

HOUSE AND HOME

THE winds of change blew steadily over England throughout the Tudor and Stuart periods, and nowhere more strongly than in the home. The old, haphazard mediaeval house, with its central Hall (3), its inner courtyard, its moat and fortified gatehouse, was gradually passing away and giving place to a new form of dwelling in which for the first time convenience and appearance mattered more than safety. In the Middle Ages easy defence was the primary consideration in house-planning and, though in the course of centuries the original simple house was greatly amplified and improved, no real change in design was possible so long as any householder was liable to armed attack from without. Doors and windows had to be small and placed where they were least vulnerable; whenever possible the rooms faced inwards on to a courtyard, and gardens were luxuries tucked away in whatever space was available inside the protecting walls. The strength of gatehouse, moat, and outer wall, was more important than comfort, and such details as adequate light, air, and sleeping-space, were cheerfully sacrificed to the overriding claims of safety.

But when under the Tudor kings a strong central government put down lawlessness and private armies, ideas on domestic architecture changed. Men were no longer willing to live as hard as their ancestors had done, and greater security and wealth made it unnecessary for them to do so. Beauty and comfort were what they now desired in their homes and these they set themselves to achieve by the building of many new houses and the improvement of old ones. The Tudor period, for all its troubles, was a time of hope and broadening ideas when an urge for new and better things was making itself felt in almost every department of life. New learning, new ways of living, new notions of beauty and convenience were all the fashion, and the lovely houses that sprang up in every district were only one indication of the hopeful spirit that then prevailed. Old houses were pulled down to make room for others in which the fresh young conceptions of the Renaissance could be expressed, haltingly at first and with a strong admixture of old styles, and then with an ever-increasing certainty of touch that culminated in the beautiful buildings of the later seventeenth century. Those who could not afford to rebuild altogether added new rooms, new chimneys, or

new gardens to the original house and spent their money on a host of improvements undreamt of by their forebears.

The standard of comfort was steadily rising, and though the early Tudor house was a draughty and poorly furnished place when seen through modern eyes, it must have seemed a heaven of luxury to those who remembered their grandparents' homes or the conditions under which their remoter ancestors were forced to live. There was a growing desire for privacy which resulted in more rooms and in the consequent shifting of the centre of household life from the Hall to other apartments. Furniture was more plentiful and better designed, and few families were without their collections of silver, gilt, or pewter plate. Standing houses were altered out of recognition by the addition of chimneys, the glazing of windows, and the sweeping away of narrow, twisting stone staircases in favour of fine wooden stairs. Side fireplaces and chimneys had become fashionable in the fifteenth century but they were then beyond the reach of smaller householders who continued to use the open hearth in the centre of the room. In the following century they became more general, and Harrison remarked upon the increase in their numbers as one of the three notable changes of his time. This was an improvement which did not meet with universal approval. Leland regarded it as a sign of degeneracy, and Harrison complained in 1577 that

> Now have we manie chimnies, and yet our tenderlings complain of rheumes, catarhs and poses. Then had we none but reredosses, and our heads did never ake. For as the smoke in those daies was supposed to be a sufficient hardening for the timber of the house, so it was reputed to keepe the good man and his familie from the quacke or pose, wherewith as then verie few were oft acquainted.[1]

But these were the familiar plaints of men looking back to their youth through a golden haze of memory. It is unlikely that many young housewives agreed with them, nor can it be supposed that an atmosphere laden with smoke escaping slowly and inefficiently through a hole in the roof was really very healthy, however "hardening" its effects may have been upon rafters and beams.

New houses were built with many more windows, both for the sake of extra light and air and to obtain a symmetrical effect from the outside. In existing houses the window openings were filled with glass whenever the family finances permitted it instead of the thin horn or wooden lattices that had formerly been used. In the *Furse Family Book* we read how in 1583 Robert Furse

[1] William Harrison, *A Description of England*, 1577.

"glaste all the windoes" in his house, and at the same time built a new porch and put a ceiling in the hall. Glass was at first an expensive luxury which only the wealthy could afford, and it was still far from universal in private houses at the beginning of the seventeenth century. Aubrey, who was born in 1626, remarks that in his youth it was denied to copyholders and ordinary poor people, but by the time he wrote in 1671 its use had spread so widely that "now the poorest people upon almes have it".[1]

Both windows and chimneys were long regarded as personal property, distinct from the rest of the house, and they were often mentioned separately in wills. The word "chimney" in this context presumably means the movable fireback and grate which preceded the stationary fireplace we know, since a real chimney could hardly be detached from its position. Windows presented no such difficulty, for they were often made so that they could be taken down and stored in a place of safety during the absence of their owner. In 1556 an official of Alnwick Castle reported that the windows were being badly damaged by the wind and advised their removal, adding

> . . . and at such time as either his Lordship or any other should lie at any of the saide places, the same might then be set up anewe with small charge to his Lordship; when now the decaye thereof shalle be very costlie and chargeable to be repayred.[2]

In the fifteenth century it was not unknown for departing tenants to carry off the windows with the rest of their baggage, and in the Paston Letters we read how the Parson of Oxnede removed both windows and doors when he left the Rectory. The legal position was defined in Henry VIII's reign when the judges decided that windows were part of the house and should not be so removed, but the practice of bequeathing them as separate items went on for many years afterwards and was still not uncommon in the reign of Charles I.

At the beginning of the sixteenth century, furniture was sparse even amongst the wealthy, but it gradually became more plentiful as the standard of living rose. "The furniture of our houses also exceedeth, and is growne in maner even to passing delicacie," wrote Harrison in his usual slightly critical style, and he goes on to say that even "inferiour artificers and manie farmers . . . have for the most part learned to garnish their cupbords with plate, their joined beds with tapistrie and silke hangings, and their tables with carpets and fine naperie."[3] This, like many later

[1] J. Aubrey, *Natural History of Wiltshire*, 1671.
[2] T. H. Turner and J. H. Parker, *Domestic Architecture in England*, 1877.
[3] W. Harrison, *op. cit.*

writings about "modern times", was somewhat exaggerated, for silk hangings were rare in farmers' houses, and their plate often consisted only of a dozen Apostle spoons and some pewter bowls, with perhaps a silver salt as the most precious piece in the collection. But much more attention was certainly paid to such matters than formerly, and farmers and yeomen, as they increased in wealth, were quick to advertise their improved status by a more lavish expenditure upon the furniture of their houses.

In Elizabeth's reign rushes were still strewn on the floor in most houses, and Thomas Platter noticed them even in the Queen's own quarters when he visited Hampton Court Palace in 1599. When newly laid and mixed with herbs, they formed a warm and sweet-smelling carpet, but they decayed quickly and became offensive if, as often happened, they were left down too long. They were gradually superseded by rush-mats, a cheap and much cleaner form of covering which remained popular throughout the seventeenth century. There were also a few rugs, but the carpets so frequently mentioned in household accounts of the time were generally laid on seats and tables rather than on the floor. Small Persian rugs or pieces of tapestry were used for this purpose, as well as carpets made of Turkey work, in which bright wools were worked upon canvas in treble cross-stitch and cut to give the effect of a close pile.

In the principal rooms the walls were hung with tapestry or panelled in oak, cedar, or pine wood, which was often ornamented in linenfold patterns or decorated with coloured designs (32). Panelling became increasingly popular as the sixteenth century advanced, being a means, as Harrison observes, "whereby the rooms are not a little commended, made warm, and much more close than otherwise they would be." Tapestries were imported from Flanders or made at the famous Mortlake factory established in James I's reign. A cheaper form of hanging much used in bedrooms was the painted or "steyned" cloth made of canvas painted to look like tapestry. Occasionally the walls of smaller rooms were decorated with pictures of Biblical subjects or conventional designs of flowers painted directly on to the plaster. Such a room is still to be seen in Oxford in a house that was formerly the Crown Tavern, where Shakespeare used to stay with his friends, the Davenants. Wallpapers printed on wooden blocks appeared in the seventeenth century, and in Queen Anne's reign were being manufactured in great variety in London, but they were considered suitable only for bedrooms and did not become generally popular until well into the eighteenth century.

All these hangings, carpets, and decorations, combined to

bring a vivid colourfulness to ordinary rooms unknown in our more sober age. Centuries of use had not yet darkened the wall panelling, tapestries were still fresh from the loom and glowing in soft and lovely tints. Bright-hued carpets covered tables and seats, and there were numbers of embroidered cushions everywhere, made necessary by the fact that upholstered chairs were unknown in the sixteenth century and still scarce and expensive throughout the seventeenth. Furniture was often inlaid with coloured woods, chests and rails were painted in reds and greens, and heraldic designs let into the windows threw deep-hued patterns on to the floor whenever the sun shone. And to all this colour were added the beautiful pieces of needlework wrought by the patient fingers of housewives, the gilded ornamentations of the more expensive beds, and the fine displays of silver and gold plate of which our ancestors were so proud.

The Hall (3) remained the principal room in the house for most of the Tudor period, though its importance steadily declined as private dining-rooms, withdrawing-rooms and parlours became more common. In simple houses, hall and parlour were the chief living-rooms, the latter often serving as a bedroom as well and housing that valuable article of furniture, the best bed. Greater houses contained a library, study, winter parlour, and Great Chamber in addition to the Hall, and often a Long Gallery in which the family kept most of their finest possessions. The kitchen department was made up of a number of rooms where the vast work of a busy household was carried on—kitchen, still-room, buttery, pantry, laundry, dairy, and brewhouse, and sometimes a servants' hall for the large staff of servants then employed. On the bigger estates the outbuildings often included a slaughter-house, for much of the meat eaten was home-produced, and there might also be a carpenter's shop, a smithy, a sawpit and wood-yard, as well as the stables and ordinary farm buildings needed for the care of horses, cattle, and poultry. A great house then looked outside only for luxuries; ordinary food and other necessities it provided for itself, and this was true in a lesser degree of most country houses above the rank of cottage.

At one end of the Hall stood a low dais, often with a bay window behind it; at the other a carved screen separated the room from a broad passage leading to the kitchen quarters and the entrance porch. It was this screen and passage that made the Hall a habitable living-room; its decline into the mere entrance lobby of modern times began in the early seventeenth century when the main outer door was first made to open directly into it. On one side a vast fireplace capable of taking enormous

logs provided what was probably rather inadequate heating—much of the warmth must have escaped up the wide chimney or have been lost among the rafters of the unceiled roof.

On the dais stood a joined table for the use of the family; servants and dependents ate at trestle tables which were put up at meal-times and afterwards removed. Guests sat on the dais with their hosts unless there were too many to be accommodated there, when some would sit at the upper end of a trestle table divided into upper and lower halves by a large salt. Chairs were scarce and reserved for master, mistress, and principal guests; children and lesser visitors sat upon stools, and servants upon benches. Further seating was provided by chests, of which every house contained a great many. At the end of the Hall were two or three court cupboards on which the family plate was displayed, and there were smaller cupboards along the walls for wine or table linen and for the servants' livery allowances. Here also hung pikes, swords, and fowling-pieces, and such armour as the householder possessed. At night the room was lighted by candles set in iron or wooden chandeliers hanging from the roof, or in latten or silver candlesticks placed upon the tables. The latter form of lighting became more common during the seventeenth century and gradually replaced the chandeliers for ordinary use, as they in turn had superseded the earlier torches set in brackets along the walls.

The parlour was a smaller and more intimate chamber, furnished with stools, a chair or two, some chests, a draw-top table for meals, and one or two inlaid cabinets of oak or walnut. In small houses it was the only withdrawing-room and frequently a bedroom also; in it the spinning-wheel was usually kept and the best bed, which was used as seat during the day. It was probably the most comfortable seat in the house for, in spite of many cushions, the average chair or stool was not very restful, and even the day-beds that came into fashion towards the end of Elizabeth's reign were somewhat stiff and angular when compared with the settees and couches of to-day.

The great four-poster beds of those days were frequently very valuable and ranked amongst the most highly prized possessions of their owners (32). In the sixteenth century they were often heavily carved, gilded, or inlaid, with squat bulbous pillars that gradually gave place to the lighter and more graceful shafts supporting a higher roof of the Stuart fashion. The tester and ceiling were made of tapestry or carved wood, the hangings and valances of silk or embroidery. A criss-cross of ropes fixed to the framework supported a feather mattress, under which a

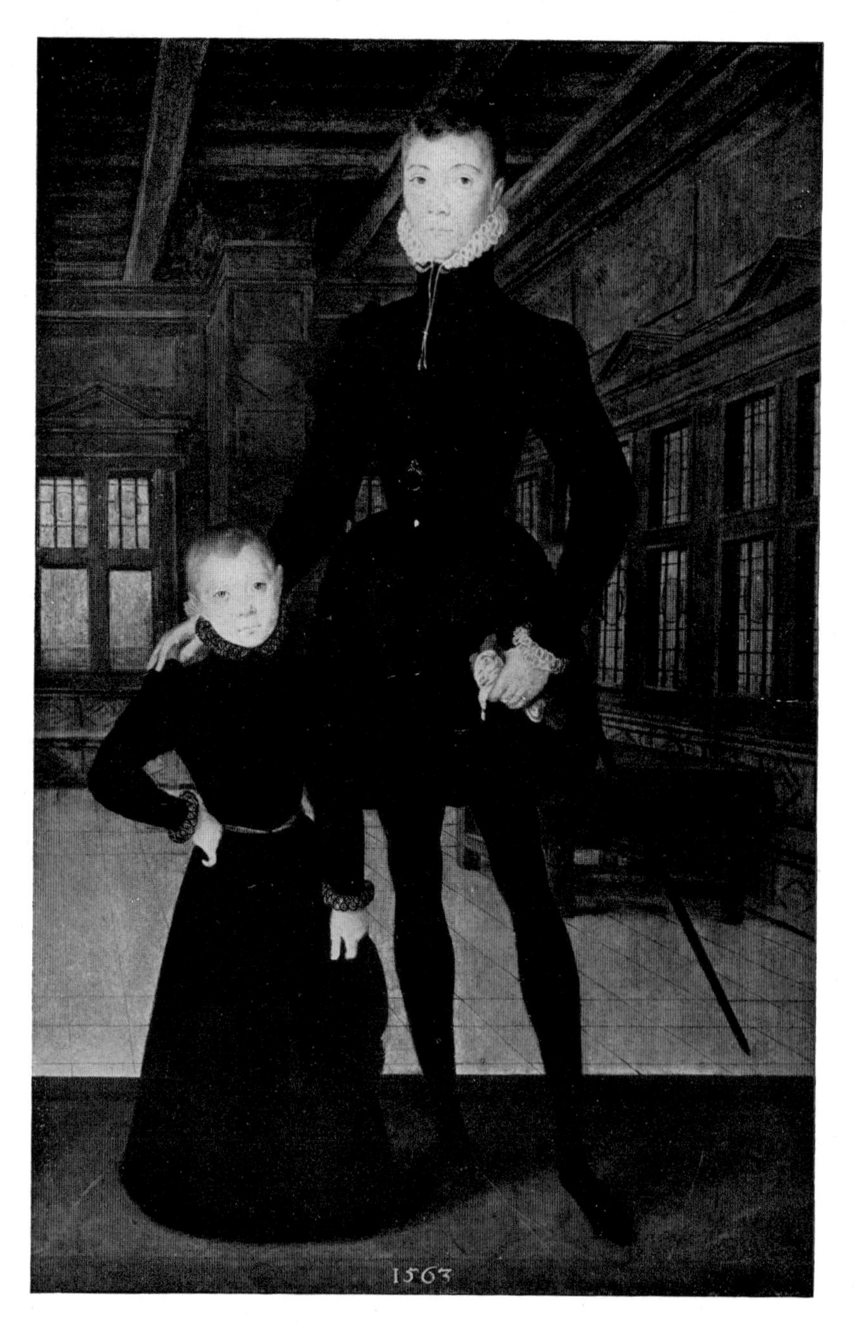

2 Two Brothers of the mid-sixteenth century: Henry Stuart, Lord Darnley, and Charles Stuart

Reproduced from the painting by Hans Eworth, by gracious permission of H.M. The King

3 The late mediaeval Great Hall: Little Mitton, Lancashire

From a drawing by J. C. Buckler

straw or wool pallet was sometimes placed for greater firmness. When the bed was made the mattress was first smoothed down with a staff and then covered with linen sheets, blankets, pillows and headsheets, and a coverlet of silk or needlework. Fur rugs were sometimes used, and in wealthy houses a strip of ermine covered the linen headsheet over the pillows. At night the curtains were closely drawn all round and occasionally pinned together, so that the sleeper lay in a sort of inner room of silk or tapestry, completely protected from the night air which was then thought to be so dangerous.

The total cost of a really good bed was considerable, and when special hangings or bedding were used it was sometimes enormous. The bed provided for James I when he visited Knole cost £8,000, being entirely hung with gold and silver tissue, and £1,000 was not an unheard-of price, even without the excuse of a royal visit. Ordinary beds for everyday purposes naturally cost much less, but even these were often finely carved and ornamented, and furnished with silk, velvet or embroidery. In 1608 Francis Fitton bequeathed to his niece a down bed with a canopy of yellow silk taffeta and a quilt to match, and in a list made after the Restoration of goods taken from Corfe Castle we read of

> A furniture of a bed of french green cloth embroyder'd; 6 curtains and valences, with changeable taffity, teaster head-cloth and fringe, all of the same taffity; 2 carpets of cloth embroyder'd, and Indian quilt of white wrought with yellow to the bed.[1]

Small householders usually possessed only one four-poster, and not always that, but even secondary beds were considered sufficiently valuable to be mentioned in wills, as were also the sheets, bolsters, and pillow-covers, that went with them. Less important beds were not curtained and were more plainly furnished. In farmhouses of the simpler sort the old-fashioned trestle bed, put together with pegs, was sometimes used, with flock instead of feather mattresses. Personal servants often slept on truckle-beds which had very low frames upon castors, and could be stowed away by day under a bigger bed and brought out to its foot at night. These were generally provided with a pair of sheets and a pair of blankets, but very little else.

The improvement in bed-furnishings seems to have been very marked in the sixteenth century, for Harrison tells us that old men living in his day could remember the time when linen was a luxury and down mattresses were found only in very wealthy households. Pillows were then thought fit only for women in

[1] J. Hutchins, *History of Dorset*, 1774.

childbirth, and poor men slept upon straw pallets with only thin, coarse coverings of dagswain or hop-harlots above them. It is probable that labourers still did so when he wrote, and for many years afterwards, but no family of any pretensions was without at least two or three feather-beds and a quantity of homespun sheets and pillow-covers. Young girls filled their marriage-chests with linen of their own spinning, and hangings embroidered by themselves, and only the poorest Elizabethan or Stuart bride was forced to go to her new home without a good store of napery for table and for bed.

The other furniture of a bedroom was but slight. In the Great Chamber and other important rooms the walls might be panelled or tapestried but elsewhere the cheaper painted cloths were used. Dressing-tables were few, and chests of drawers and wardrobes did not become fashionable until the seventeenth century was fairly well advanced. Where they were absent, clothes were kept in presses and mirrors or cosmetics were set out on small tables or on the tops of coffers. Mirror-glass was not common before the end of Elizabeth's reign, and polished metal was still used by Tudor ladies as it had been in the Middle Ages. Wall mirrors were rare until well into the Stuart period, and the average looking-glass before which women dressed their hair and applied the many essences, paints, and perfumes then in vogue, were small and not very clear. A flat-topped cupboard on a shelf supported the ewer and basin of latten, pewter, brass or silver, and towels hung on a roller fixed to the wall above. In the larger rooms there was usually a fireplace with tongs and bellows. Boorde recommended that a fire be lit night and morning "to waste and consume the evil vapours of the chamber, for the breath of man may putrify the air",[1] which, in an age when ventilation was little regarded, was probably true enough. A stool or two sufficed for seating, except in the Great Chamber which was also used as a reception room and might contain some chairs, and occasionally cushions were heaped upon a long chest to form a couch or serve as an additional bed.

The finest furniture was usually found in the Long Gallery (4, 5) on the first floor. This room was a characteristic feature of Elizabethan houses, and remained popular until Charles I's reign when changing ideas of comfort caused it to disappear from the designs of contemporary architects. It was very long and comparatively narrow, with panelled walls, a handsome fireplace, and windows all down one side and sometimes at both ends as well. The loveliest inlaid cabinets, buffets and tables

[1] A. Boorde, *The Dietary of Helth*, 1542.

were kept in it, and the most treasured curios, china and Venetian glass, with perhaps a chiming clock, or one that showed the phases of the moon, set upon a bracket on the wall. Chairs were few even here, but they were the best in the house, and window-seats, stools, and the inevitable chests made up the deficiency, with an occasional day-bed covered by a loose mattress. The size and shape of the Long Gallery made it an awkward room for sitting, and it seems to have been used principally for dancing and music, and for exercise when the weather was too bad for outside activities. Virginals, flutes, viols, and sometimes a little organ, were often kept in it, for music-making was then an integral part of every cultured man's life. Lord Lauderdale, who told Pepys he "had rather hear a cat mew than the best musique in the world", was decidedly an exception to the general rule of his time; there is an engaging honesty about his added remark that "the better the musique the more sick it makes him".[1] In later years the Long Gallery was frequently cut up into a number of small rooms which were less imposing but easier to keep warm. But in its day it must have been a pleasant place to walk or sew in on a fine spring morning, and pleasanter still at night when the soft light of numerous candles gleamed on its inlaid panels and furniture and the moving figures of dancers dressed in the splendid silks and velvets of that colourful age.

In the kitchen, spits turned by dogs or young boys stood before the huge open fireplaces, and cauldrons for stewing and boiling hung from a complicated system of rods and chains above the hearth. Baking was done in brick ovens; sauces and small made-up dishes were cooked over braziers or the basket-like tops of tall and-irons. There was usually a good supply of pots and pans, chafing-dishes, pestles and mortars, cooking-knives, bowls, sieves and other utensils needed for the preparation of the heavy meals then eaten. In the dairy stood the churn and its attendant milk-bowls, tubs, and crocks, with vats and presses for cheese in

Frying Fish, *c.* 1590

[1] *Pepys's Diary*, ed. H. B. Wheatley, 1893-9.

districts where cheese was made. The bakehouse contained querns and moulding-boards and all the paraphernalia of bread-making on a large scale. In small houses it was sometimes used as a brewery as well, but in larger establishments there was a separate brew-house, where great quantities of ale were made once or twice a month. In cottages and humble farmhouses there were no separate kitchens, and cooking was done in the Hall or main living-room which was sometimes known simply as "the House", a term which still survives in the word "house-place" applied to the kitchen living-room of many northern farms.

The sanitary arrangements even in a great house were elementary. In the Middle Ages privies were built with drains discharging into moats or streams running near the walls, or, if these were lacking, into deep walled pits. But in the sixteenth and seventeenth centuries even this primitive device had disappeared. Ordinary pails were used and emptied as often as not out of a window, to the danger of any passer-by who happened to come within range. This simple custom obtained even in towns, where streets and rivers were regarded as the natural dumping-places for rubbish. Dustmen, scavengers, and the constantly reiterated regulations of the municipal authorities struggled to keep the narrow streets clean, but without much success, and in London and the bigger towns the roads stank like an Oriental slum. In the country, with its purer air and less congested housing, these carefree habits did not matter quite so much. "Houses of easement" existed in most dwellings larger than cottages, though it was rarely considered necessary to provide more than one, even in mansions. They were usually to be found in the cellars, on the leads, or in a corner of the courtyard. Occasionally they were furnished with a double seat so as to accommodate two persons at a time. In John Russell's *Book of Nurture*, servants are instructed to keep the master's privy clean, to cover the seat with green baize and a cushion, and to see that there is a sufficiency of linen, cotton, or blanket for his use. This book was written in the fifteenth century but the instructions probably held good for most of the two following centuries, during which there was little improvement in such matters. In 1594 Sir John Harington invented a water-closet differing little in essentials from those in use to-day. He installed it in his own house and published an account of it, but his contemporaries regarded it as a mere affectation. Queen Elizabeth, it is true, was sufficiently impressed to have it copied in Richmond Palace, and much later, in Queen Anne's reign, there was a little closet with water sluices in Windsor Castle. But in spite of royal

4 The Long Gallery at Knole Park, Kent

5 The Long Gallery, Haddon Hall, Derbyshire

From lithographs by Joseph Nash

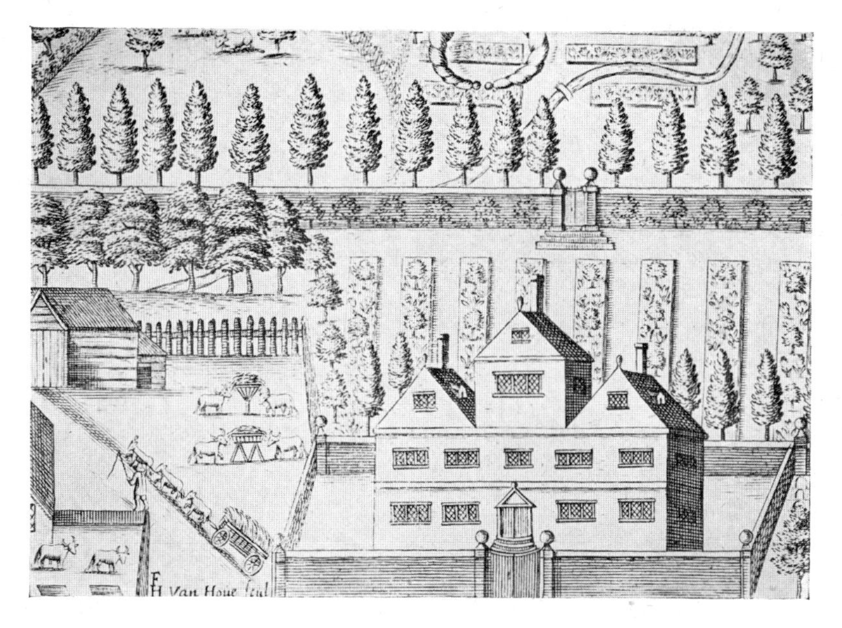

6 The lay-out of a late seventeenth-century Garden

7 A Tudor Travelling Carriage

From a lithograph by Joseph Nash

approval the idea was too novel for ordinary people, and it was not heard of again in private houses for two hundred years or more.

Bathrooms did not exist until the late seventeenth century and then only in the houses of the nobility. Celia Fiennes saw one very magnificent "batheing room" at Chatsworth, with blue and white marble walls and a deep bath fitted at the upper end with "two locks to let in one hott, ye other Cold water to attemper it as persons please."[1] Most people, however, took their baths in wooden tubs before the bedroom fire. Perfumed soap was often used, and the water scented with sweet herbs. In Tudor times personal cleanliness was a more important matter than it became in the following century. Towns then had public baths which were much used, but these declined in popularity in later years because it was thought they spread infection. Sir John Harington urged the cleansing of the whole body every day and begged his readers to "love you to be cleane and well apparelled, for from our cradles let us abhor uncleannes, which neither nature or reason can endure."[2] But this advice was not always followed when bathing meant carrying tubs of water about the house, and scent sometimes tried to do the work which soap would have performed better.

It is not certain when toothbrushes were first introduced. They existed during the Commonwealth, but they cannot have been common until much later, and most people cleaned their teeth by rubbing them with cloth or using toothpicks of ivory, silver, or gold. Mouth-washes were known at least as early as 1602 and probably before. One such lotion is mentioned by William Vaughan in his *Naturall and Artificiall Directions for health.* It was compounded of vinegar, rosemary, myrrh, "the water of the mastick tree (if it may be easily gotten)", dragon's herb, boll armonack, allum, honey, cinnamon, and spring water, and, according to Vaughan, was "better worth than a thousand of their dentifrices". When Paul Hentzner visited England in 1598 he remarked that many Englishmen had blackened teeth, and this he ascribed to their too great use of sugar. But in spite of primitive hygiene and the prevalence of scurvy, most people retained their teeth until they were old, and dental caries appears to have been a much less common trouble than it is to-day.

Outside the house the same enterprising spirit that was responsible for so many improvements within began to show itself in the gardens. In the Middle Ages gardens were cultivated mainly

[1] Celia Fiennes, *Through England in a Side Saddle in the Reign of William and Mary.*
[2] Sir John Harington, *The Englishman's Doctor or The School of Salerne*, 1608.

for utilitarian purposes, and far more attention was paid to herbs and fruit than to flowers, lawns, and arbours. Such pleasure gardens as existed were little more than turfed enclosures with a grassy mound to sit on and a few flowers grown more for their usefulness as medicines or flavourings than for their beauty. Space did not permit of broad walks or shrubberies, and even the necessary herb plots and orchards were comparatively small except on the monastic estates, which were less troubled by defence considerations than the contemporary manor-houses and castles.

But in the sixteenth century gardening came into its own and as much attention was paid to the lay-out of the grounds as to the design of the houses. Here as in the house symmetry was the key-note of design. Straight walks, pleached alleys, groves, and terraces, were all the fashion. Intricate "knot" flower-beds edged with box or thrift and filled with bright flowers or, when these failed, with coloured stones, gave the effect of a brilliant, geometrically patterned carpet. Statues, fountains, and sundials, were common in large gardens; covered walks and arbours provided shelter from heat or rain, and yews clipped into fanciful shapes added variety to wide lawns and the hedges which divided the different sections of the grounds. Small householders who could not spare so much space had simpler gardens, but these were usually well filled with plants, and even cottagers had much the same bright plots as they have now.

Much more attention than formerly was paid to the cultivation of flowers, and a number of new varieties were imported, as well as herbs and fruits hitherto unknown in this country. "If you look into our gardens annexed to our houses," wrote Harrison, "how wonderfully is their beautie increased, not only with flowers . . . and variety of curious and costlie workmanship, but also with rare and medicinable herbs sought up in the land within these fortie yeares; so that in comparison of this present, the ancient gardens were but dunghills and laystows to such as did possess them."[1] Larkspur, syringa, white lilac, laburnum, passion flowers, Christmas roses, and many other flowers, were introduced in the late sixteenth century, and so were such curious exotics as tobacco and olives, both of which seem to have been grown with a certain amount of success. Tobacco was first brought to England in 1565 by Sir John Hawkins, and in a few years became so popular that James I was moved to protest most vigorously against the universal habit of smoking. Not only regular tobacconists but innkeepers, grocers, chandlers, and

[1] W. Harrison, *op. cit.*

apothecaries, all sold it, and in *Sylva Sylvarum* Francis Bacon describes it as a profitable plant to grow, though he adds that "English Tobacco hath small credit, as being too dull and earthy." Sweet potatoes arrived in the same year and were regarded as luxuries "more delicious than any sweet apple sugred."[1] The ordinary potato followed later, but more than two hundred years were to pass before it was grown as a regular food crop and became the popular vegetable that it is to-day.

The herb garden was still a necessary adjunct to every house and was the particular province of the housewife who looked to it for all the herbs needed in cooking and medicine. In the kitchen garden grew the beans, carrots, cabbages, peas, parsnips, pumpkins, onions and salad herbs that served the tables of that time. Vegetables were gradually coming into greater use though, with the exception of salads, they were long regarded as materials for soup rather than accompaniments to the main fish or meat course. Apricots, apples, pears, quinces, cherries, peaches, and mulberries, were all popular, and under the Stuarts oranges and lemons were sometimes grown in boxes and brought outside during the summer. Celia Fiennes noted at Woburn "all sorts of pots of flowers and Curious greens, fine orange, Cittron and Lemon trees and mirtles, striped ffileroy and ye fine aloes plant."[2] Large quantities of fruit were grown in both private and market-gardens, but in spite of this, there was a lingering prejudice against it in certain circles owing to the fact that it was supposed to cause fevers. In 1569 the sale of fruit in the streets was forbidden for fear of the pestilence, and ninety-six years later cherries, melons, and gooseberries, were amongst the foods thought dangerous during the plague epidemic in London. Pepys evidently felt the same nervousness, for in 1661 he recorded how he

> in the afternoon had notice that my Lord Hinchinbrooke is fallen ill, which I fear is with the fruit that I did give them on Saturday last at my house; so in the evening I went thither and there found him very ill, and in great fear of the smallpox.[3]

Great landowners had parks round their houses, but these were usually little more than rough grasslands which ensured greater privacy for their owners and permitted the preservation of game. It was not until the beginning of the eighteenth century that they were brought into the general scheme of design and related to the house itself by the opening up of vistas and the planting of

[1] R. Hakluyt, *The Principall Navigations . . . of the English Nation*, 1598–1600.
[2] Celia Fiennes, *op. cit.*
[3] *Pepys's Diary.*

avenues and groves. The Tudor or Stuart builder thought a park necessary to any house of considerable size and pretensions, but it was upon the inner gardens that all the care, trouble, and expense, were lavished. What could be achieved there under good direction is shown by John Evelyn's description of Lady Clarendon's garden at Swallowfield, which seems to have struck that connoisseur of gardens as particularly admirable. He tells us that

> there is one orchard of 1,000 golden and other cider pippins; walls and groves of elms, limes, oaks and other trees. The garden is so beset with all manner of sweet shrubs, that it perfumes the air. The distribution also of the quarters, walks, and parterres is excellent. The nurseries, kitchen-garden full of the most desirable plants; two very noble orangeries well furnished; but, above all, the canal and fish ponds, the one fed with a white, the other with a black running water, fed by a quick and swift river, so well and plentifully stored with fish, that for pike, carp, bream, and tench, I never saw anything approaching it.[1]

[1] *Diary of John Evelyn*, ed. W. Bray, 1859.

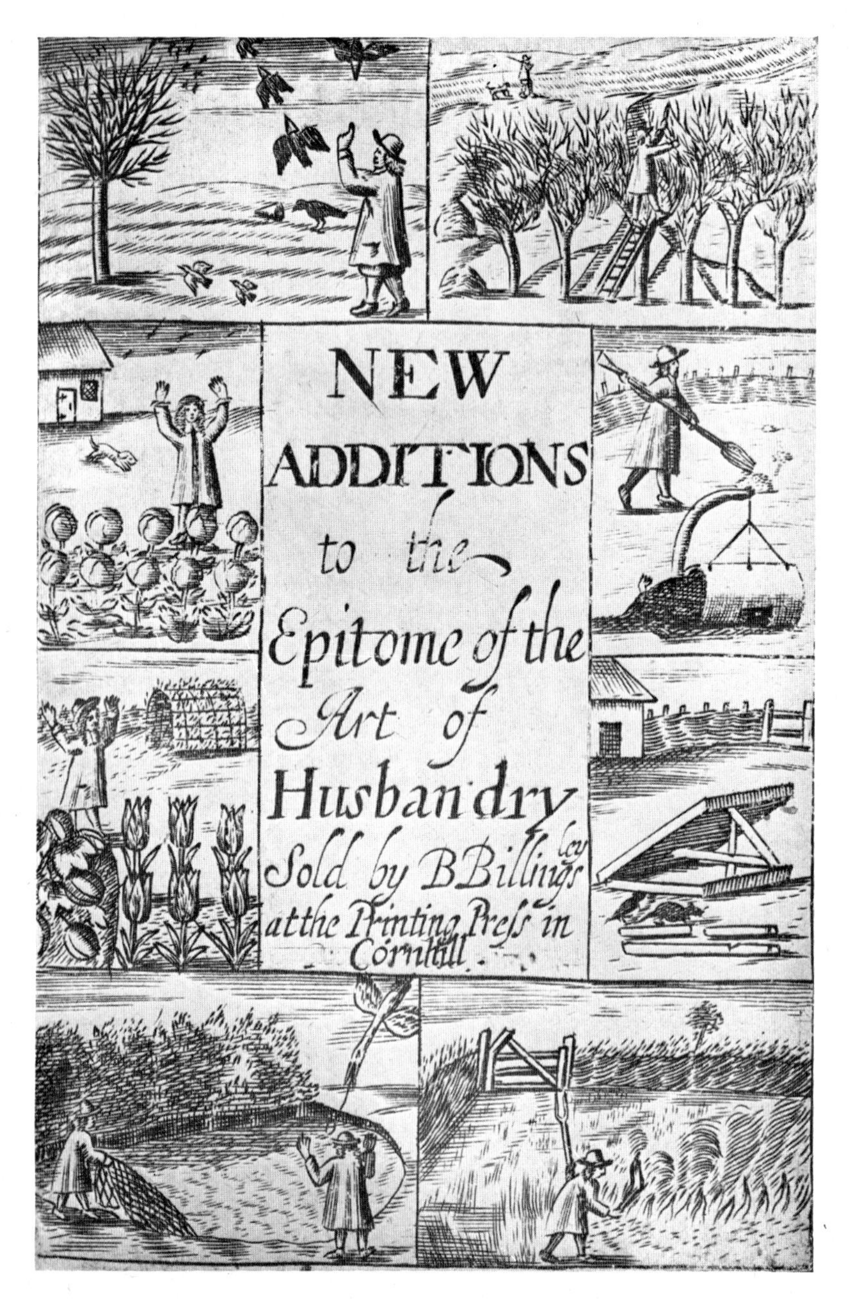
NEW
ADDITIONS
to the
Epitome of the
Art of
Husbandry
Sold by B Billingsley
at the Printing Press in
Cornhill.

8 Work on the Farm, as illustrated on the frontispiece to a Manual of Husbandry (1685)

9 Spinning with a Distaff

10 Cheese-making in the Dairy

From early seventeenth-century engravings

HOUSEHOLD PURSUITS

Chapter II

THE DAILY ROUND

A GENTLEMAN'S wife in the sixteenth and seventeenth centuries was expected to have a wide practical knowledge of domestic matters and to be an extremely capable organizer. A country house was then almost entirely self-supporting, producing its own fuel and lighting, its linen, clothes, and medicine, and relying for the bulk of its food upon its own fields and stock-yards. The winter stores had to be carefully planned and prepared beforehand, for a remote house might easily be cut off for weeks together in bad weather when the atrocious state of the roads made the transport of goods almost impossible. The work involved in running such an establishment was constant and very varied and there were no labour-saving devices to help in it or handy shops to supply a sudden deficiency. Everything had to be done by hand from beginning to end, and everything that was done had to be directed by the mistress who needed far more than theoretical knowledge to keep the wheels of her large household turning smoothly and well.

In their due season hams were smoked and bacon cured, fish was salted down and fruit laid by in lofts or made into syrups. Herbs were dried for seasonings or medicine, vegetables were pickled, roses, violets and cowslips made into conserves. Bread had to be baked and butter churned all the year round; ale was brewed once a month or oftener, and in some houses cider, perry or mead was made as well. In the kitchen, fats were saved for the candlemaker who came at regular intervals to make dark yellowish tallow candles with rush wicks for the servants and finer waxen ones with cotton wicks for parlour and hall. Soap was sometimes bought, but quite as often made at home from fats and lye and delicately scented with herbs or rosewater for toilet use. Feathers from the poultry-yard were cured for mattresses and pillows, and the spinning-wheel was kept constantly turning to supply flax or woollen thread for napery and clothes. Dresses for great occasions were made by the tailor, but more ordinary garments and nearly all the house-linen was spun and sewn by the mistress and her maids, only the weaving being done by a visiting weaver or on some cottage loom in the village. In the laundry a vast wash took place every three months or so when the accumulated dirty linen was pounded and beaten with wooden

bats by the vigorous arms of laundrymaids. And with all this went the ceaseless cleaning of the house, and such additional tasks as the care of the herb-garden and poultry-yard, the fetching of letters from the nearest town, and the continual mending and renovating necessary in every considerable household.

All these activities had to be directed by the mistress who was expected to know at least as much about them as the most experienced of her maids. She had other responsibilities as well. The upbringing of the children naturally devolved upon her, and so did the moral and physical welfare of her servants. She had to know how to cure simple ailments and, when necessary, to set a broken limb or dress a burn if, as frequently happened, there was no doctor within reach. Most housewives kept books of herbal remedies in which were written the cordials, physics, and purges handed down to them by their mothers or collected from their friends. Many of these were strange and semi-magical prescriptions, the ingredients for which had to be gathered only in certain aspects of the moon or administered when the stars were favourable, but not a few were based on sound common sense and did their work well enough if the disease was not serious. Certainly they were no worse than some of the remedies prescribed by the doctors of the time, and many of them are still used successfully in country districts to-day.

In these household books also appeared receipts for special dishes and for the aromatic waters, scents, and sweetbags, which were then so popular. Every educated girl had some knowledge of distilling and many could prepare elaborate essences and perfumes as well as the more ordinary rose and lavender waters so constantly used in scent-making and cookery. Flowers of all kinds were carefully gathered and distilled for complexion washes and pastes, or mixed with spices to make pastilles which were burnt on chafing-dishes to sweeten the air of the rooms. "Take sweet Majoram, Damask Roses, Lavender, Rosemary, Maudlin, Balm, Thyme, Walnut leaves, Pinks, all of a like quantity to fill your still," says one recipe in *A Queen's Delight*, and Sir Hugh Platt in *Delights for Ladies* begins another very magnificently with "Take a thousand Damask Roses. . . ." Gloves were often scented with angelica or musk, and new-folded linen sprinkled with a compound of sweet-smelling plants that had been "set in the Sunne a fortnight". Some aromatic waters took weeks to prepare, like that known as Spring Nosegay to which various flowers were added as they reached their full perfection, but few grudged the hours spent in the stillroom in what must had been the most fascinating of all their varied labours.

In some houses an hour was set aside each day for spiritual instruction when children and servants alike heard the Bible read or were taught their catechism, and family prayers in the morning and evening were usual. There were also guests to entertain and meals to provide for such poor travellers or journeymen as came unheralded to seek the unfailing hospitality of the house. In such a life there was obviously little leisure for outside activities, and women did not normally concern themselves very much with the affairs of the great world. Yet it would be a serious mistake to think of them as mere housekeepers with no ideas beyond the domestic round. Their letters show them to have been well-read and intelligent; their diaries are full of shrewd and witty comments on the scenes and people round them. Many had great business ability, and it was no uncommon thing for a husband to leave all his affairs in his wife's hands whenever more pressing matters called him from home. It was no light thing to be at once the companion and partner of an educated man, the mother of his children, the unhurried hostess of his guests, and the just and capable manager of a complicated household. Markham was perhaps not drawing an entirely imaginary picture when he wrote that a good housewife should be

> . . . of chaste thought, stout courage, patient, untired, watchful, diligent, witty, pleasant, constant in friendship, full of good neighbourhood, wise in discourse . . . secret in her affairs, comfortable in her counsels, and generally skilful in all the worthy knowledges which do belong to her vocation.[1]

Domestic service must then have been a much more interesting calling than it is to-day. Although there was so much to be done, the work was not unduly heavy since it was shared amongst so many, and the daily round was cheered by variety and congenial companionship. Wages were low, but they were supplemented by "vails" and very often by presents and bequests in wills. In Stuart times they

Plucking Fowls, *c.* 1590

[1] Gervase Markham, *The English Hus-wife*, 1615.

tended to rise, as did the general level of prices. Dr. Dee, in Elizabeth's reign, paid his maid Lettice four nobles a year, about £1 in our money; in the following century 30*s*. seems to have been the average wage for an ordinary maid and rather more for a woman able to direct the work of others. In 1593 the Shuttleworth bailiff was paid 33*s*. 4*d*., but a similar servant in Dorset was paid 80*s*. in 1635, while at Lyme Park the steward who received 20*s*. a quarter in 1607 was paid £2 10*s*. a quarter in 1661. Clothes and other necessities were usually provided; if the servant had to find his own he was entitled to more money. In a great house elaborate liveries were sometimes worn, but the most usual dress for a man-servant was a bright blue coat, knee breeches, and white stockings. The women wore short white or coloured gowns, with aprons and tippets, and this pleasant and sensible fashion, which allowed for individual tastes and was at the same time workmanlike, continued almost unchanged until the beginning of the nineteenth century.

There was not then the rigid distinction which sprang up later between kitchen and parlour. Servants were regarded as part of the family. Their interests were bound up with those of their employers and they were permitted a freedom of speech that would probably surprise the mistresses of this democratic age. When they erred they were cuffed and beaten, but so were the children, and there was no sense of degradation in such punishments as there would be to-day. "This night I whipped Jane for her foolishness," wrote Adam Eyre in his *Diary* on 9 October 1647, "as yesterday I had done for her slothfulness"; and then, passing from the contemplation of her faults to that of his own, he adds: "and hence I am induced to bewayle my sinfull life, for my failings in the presence of God Almighty are questionless greater than hers are to mee."[1] Jane probably bore no malice, and certainly no doubt of his right to chastise his servants ever crossed Adam Eyre's mind or that of any master or mistress of the time. This was an age when the rod played a prominent part in the training of children, and, in the average household, servants were but older children. As such they were cared for and often loved, and if they had to bear the disadvantages of that status, they also shared in many of its advantages.

Nor had the word any particular class significance. Anyone who served in a house or on an estate was a servant, from the turnspit in the kitchen up to the chaplain. The waiting gentlewoman was as well born as the mistress and was very often her cousin; the chaplain, steward, and secretary, were probably gentlemen by birth and education, but they were included in the list

[1] *The Diary of Adam Eyre* (Surtees Society).

of servants and did not resent the title. When Marmaduke Rawdon went to the Canary Islands he took with him "fower sarvants", of whom one was "Mr. Marmaduke Harrison, a Yorkshire gentleman with whom he was acquented in his youth." This Mr. Harrison was his steward; the other three mentioned were his cash-keeper, Thomas Gill, John Wade, of Dover, who went because he was a good accountant, and a trumpeter "whose dewtie it was to sound when his dinner and supper were brought up, att anie time when he was disposed to be merry and drink healths abord, also when he understood he was arisinge or goinge to bed, also whensoever he went ashore or came abord during that voyage."[1]

A nobleman's household might consist of two or three hundred servitors, inside and outside, beginning with such high officials as the Steward, Gentleman Usher, Gentleman of the Horse and Auditor of the Revenue, and passing through carefully graded degrees down to the humblest scullions and stable-boys. There was a Clerk of the Kitchen who took charge of all the provisions and superintended the work of the cooks who, in a great house, were usually men. Sir Peter Legh kept a jester for his own amusement in James I's reign and also a piper; his father before him had maintained an entire band of musicians and a troupe of players who gave dramatic performances when he entertained his friends. There was usually a chaplain who conducted services in the private chapel and sometimes acted as tutor to the children. The ancient custom of training gentlemen's sons as pages in a nobleman's house was not yet extinct; such lads waited upon their patron at table and were taught the ways of polite society, and later on were found some place or occupation suitable to their status through his influence. On the smaller manors, and in towns, the establishments were naturally less imposing, but even so, many more servants were normally employed than would be the case to-day in a house of the same size.

Since all were human there were sometimes difficulties then as now. Sir Henry Slingsby's cooks were apparently in the habit of disappearing for two or three days together; in his *Diary* he complains bitterly of five different men who behaved in this way. They also drank, though he strove to win them from this vice by persuasion and "never grew passionate with them or threatened them much". Maids were sometimes idle or left without sufficient reason. Now and then a servant considered herself too good to do menial work, like the woman of whom Pepys wrote to Sir Edward Montagu in 1657 who, on being told what her duties

[1] *Life of Marmaduke Rawdon* (Camden Society).

were, replied that "she never had been used to make fires, wash rooms or clothes, scour or do anything like that". There were a few rare instances of Catholic families being betrayed by their servants when a priest visited the house to celebrate Mass, and when Charles II was hidden at Moseley in 1651 Mr. Whitgreave dared not trust any of his staff but one Catholic cook, and sent all the rest away to work in the fields. But for the most part loyalty and long service were far more common than their opposites, and servants took a pride in their position as the essential helpers of the families they served.

The day began early, for daylight was then "saved" by simpler means than those made known to us by Mr. Willett. Breakfast was served between six and seven o'clock in the morning and consisted of meat, ale, and bread, with fish instead of meat on fish-days. It does not seem to have been eaten in every house, and probably it was a matter of personal idiosyncrasy rather than custom. Harrison says it had formerly been a usual meal but had declined in his lifetime so that when he wrote in 1577 "each one in maner (except here and there some young hungry stomach that cannot fast untill dinner-time) contenteth himself with dinner and supper only."[1] It seems, however, to have been taken more frequently than is usually supposed. Townsmen ate it fairly regularly, and Queen Elizabeth's accounts show that chicken, rabbits, mutton, veal and beef, with ale and wine, were served at Court in the early morning. Pepys had a breakfast party on New Year's Day 1661, when he entertained his friends to oysters, neats' tongues, anchovies, wine, and Northdown ale. In *The Haven of Health* (1584) Thomas Cogan advises students at Oxford to eat only eggs, milk, and butter, in the morning, and Peter Erondell in *The French Garden* (1605) speaks as though an early meal was quite usual, at least for children. The habit evidently varied from house to house, and was perhaps less common in Stuart times than it had been in the early years of the Tudors. Towards the end of the seventeenth century a light meal of bread and coffee or chocolate was sometimes served about nine or ten o'clock in the morning, but this custom seems to have been confined to fashionable people in London whose hours of rising and dining were often much later than those of countrymen. Breakfast as a standard meal did not come into fashion until many years later when the steady moving forward of the dinner hour made it a necessity.

But if our forebears fasted in the early hours, they made up for it at dinner. This was the main meal of the day and was

[1] William Harrison, *op. cit.*

usually served about noon. Great quantities of meat and fish, tarts, pies, sweets, and cheese, were then eaten, with soups and pungent sauces, and salads which included such fascinating ingredients as borage flowers, bugloss, rosemary, and violet-buds. Our ancestors liked to see large joints of mutton, beef, pork, or venison, upon their tables, and to follow them with fish, capons, carbonadoes, and elaborate sweet dishes. Game was plentiful and varied; quail, teal, pheasants, snipe, larks, and pigeons, all appear on the menus of the time, and at Christmas peacocks and swans were eaten by the wealthy as well as the traditional boar's head. Turkey was still a new-comer and was less commonly served. In Tudor times an attempt was made to enforce periodic abstention from meat, not for religious or health reasons but to encourage shipbuilding and to overcome the difficulties caused by the high price of meat in towns. An Act of Parliament in 1563 ordered two fish-days in every week, with a penalty of three months' imprisonment or a £3 fine for those who ate meat on such days without a special licence. But with no religious sanction behind it this regulation savoured too much of domestic interference to be successful, and towards the end of the sixteenth century the Government was forced to let it lapse.

For sweets there were tarts of all sorts, custards, jellies, and fruit, both fresh and candied. There were also a great variety of boiled puddings, made of wheat or maslin flour and sweetened with honey or sugar. The Christmas pie which Misson specially commended in the seventeenth century was "a most learned Mixture" of neats' tongues, chicken, eggs, sugar, raisins, spices, and candied peel; it was the ancestor of our modern Christmas pudding and shared the honours of the festival with the older mince-pie. A favourite Tudor sweetmeat was sugar-sops, which was made of bread, sugar, and spices; another was marchpane, made from pounded almonds, pistachio nuts, sugar, and flour, mixed together and flavoured with essences. It was often moulded into elaborate shapes of animals or buildings, gilded and finely decorated, and was then served as the principal dish of the sweet course.

In simple houses the fare was less delicate but quite as substantial. A poor man's dinner consisted of beef or bacon, with ale, bread and cheese, and, in the country, green vegetables from his own garden. Soups also and thick broths formed a large part of his diet. In times of scarcity he was often forced to do without meat, but normally he was much better fed and had a higher standard of living than his contemporaries in other European countries. Farmers and yeomen fed generously, preferring

the solid to the fanciful. Fuller tells us that at their tables

> . . . you shall have as many joints as dishes; no meat disguised with strange sauces; no straggling joynt of a sheep in the midst of a pasture of grasse, beset with sallads on every side, but solid, substantial food. . . . Here you have that which in itself is good, made better by the store of it, and best by the welcome to it.[1]

Variety was added by the local products of sea or river which could be cheaply bought in an age when transport was difficult and preservatives other than salt almost unknown; and there was also the special dishes for which particular districts were famous, like the hotpots and oatcakes of Lancashire, the black puddings of the West Country, and the haslet, parkin and Yorkshire pudding of the three Ridings.

Meals were divided into courses, each of which consisted of a number of dishes varying from one or two to as many as sixteen or seventeen on special occasions. A crowded table was considered a mark of consequence, and all the dishes in each course were set out at once, the lavishness of the display presumably making up for the absence of any attempt to keep the food hot. The table was covered with a white cloth and garnished with ornamental standing-cups and silver, wooden, or pewter salts. Plates and dishes were generally of pewter or silver, though earthenware plates were used as early as 1542, and wooden trenchers were common in simple households until well into the seventeenth century. The rich drank from fine Venetian glasses and silver tankards, while poorer citizens contented themselves with the coarser English glass and pewter mugs.

Men wore their hats at table and removed them only when drinking a toast. In a great house meals were served with much ceremony, every servant having his appointed task in waiting, and every diner his allotted place, according to his degree, though the modern custom of seating men and women alternately at formal dinners seems to have been unknown. Before and after dinner a bowl of water for washing the hands was carried round by the waiters. This was a necessary rite, for much of the food was eaten with the fingers. Spoons and knives were used, and each diner was provided with a napkin, but forks did not become common until the very end of the seventeenth century. Before that time they were used only by extremely fastidious persons, or for special purposes, like the silver fork for green ginger mentioned in a will of 1463. What work could not be done by knife and spoon had to be done by the fingers, and the stains of meat, gravy, and fish, were washed away afterwards in the communal bowl.

[1] Thomas Fuller, *The Holy State and The Profane State*, 1642.

11 An Impromptu Dance, as recorded by a seventeenth-century Painter

12 A Tudor Kitchen (at Christ Church, Oxford)

From the plate in Ackermann's "Oxford"

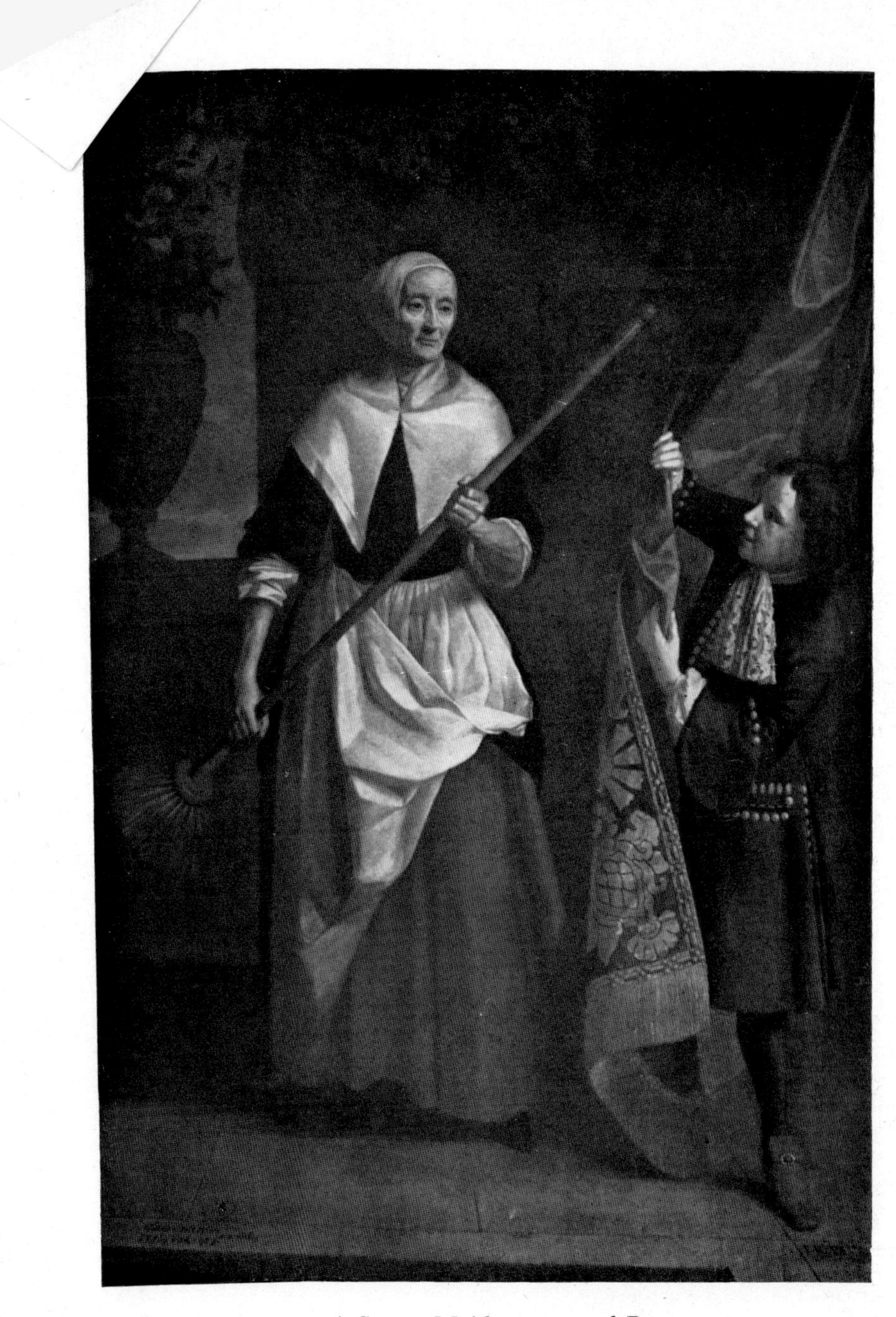

13 A Stuart Maidservant and Page

Reproduced from the painting by John Riley, by gracious permission of H.M. The King

This primitive custom seems to have been general everywhere except in Italy, for Thomas Coryat in his *Crudities* (1611) speaks of the Italian use of forks as something found only in that country. The conservative English were very slow to adopt this foreign fashion, and for a long time it was regarded as an affectation fit only for fops and ultra-refined persons. Coryat himself was nick-named Furcifer "only for using a fork at feeding but for no other cause", and what the ordinary Englishman felt about it is perhaps best expressed by Breton in *The Courtier and the Countryman* when he says

> As for us in the country, when we have washed our hands after no foul work, nor handling any unwholesome thing, we need no little forks to make hay with our mouths, to throw our meat into them.

Supper was a lighter meal, a modified version of dinner, served at varying hours between five and eight o'clock. Misson tells us that the English ate enormously at mid-day, but "their Supper is moderate; Gluttons at Noon and abstinent at Night."[1] Afternoon tea, of course, was unknown. Tea and coffee were introduced into England in the middle of the seventeenth century, and the latter quickly became a popular drink in the coffee-houses that sprang up everywhere in towns. One of the earliest of these houses seems to have been in Oxford, for Anthony Wood tells us that in 1650

> . . . Jacob, a Jew, opened a Coffey house at the Angel, in the parish of St. Peter in the East Oxon, and there it was by some who delighted in novelties, drank.[2]

The first London coffee-house was opened in 1652, in St. Michael's Alley. Thereafter such houses increased greatly in numbers, and became the favourite meeting-places of poets, writers and merchants, who gathered there to drink, read poems, hear the news, and discuss business deals. Tea at first cost £3 10*s*. a pound; in a few years the price dropped to a little over 20*s*., but even this sum put it beyond the reach of ordinary people, except as a luxury. It was made in the Chinese fashion, very weak and without milk, and served in shallow, handleless cups of fine porcelain. Chocolate came in about the same time and was at first more popular than tea. All these drinks, however, were luxuries sparingly partaken of in fashionable homes and hardly at all in others. If light refreshment between meals was needed, a glass of whey or fruit syrup, or a cup of sack sufficed, while

[1] M. Misson's *Memoirs*, translated by Mr. Ozell, 1719.
[2] Anthony Wood, *Athenae Oxoniensis*, 1681.

ale, and wine, continued to be the staple drinks at all the
lar meals.

In their leisure hours the country gentry hunted, fished, went hawking, and played a variety of games, some of which could be enjoyed at home on their own bowling-greens and tennis-courts. Indoors there were round games, cards, dice, and dominoes, and the most popular of all amusements, music and dancing. Every household could provide its own singers and its players upon the harpsichord, lute, virginals and viol, as every village in that musical age could produce its choir and team of bellringers. Pets were as popular then as they are now, and most families had their dogs and cats; a few had monkeys also, but these were expensive luxuries which might cost as much as £60 each. Dogs appear in many contemporary portraits, and one of the Earl of Southampton shows that he had his favourite cat with him even when he was a prisoner in the Tower in 1601. In the Lyme household accounts there are several homely entries concerning animals, such as twopence spent on one occasion upon "Katten meat", a shilling for a bell for the tame deer, and another shilling for two chains to hold the monkey, presumably when he became too mischievous to be allowed further liberty.

A String Trio, 1568

Women spent long hours in needlework which was then a fine art calling for much skill, patience, and good eyesight. Little girls began their education by making samplers on which they practised the delicate and intricate stitches that they would use later to beautify their homes, and grown women sometimes used them as a means of preserving a pattern seen and admired elsewhere. Coverlets and cushions, footstools, caskets and screens were all embroidered in lovely, conventional designs of birds, animals, flowers and fruit; tapestry pictures of Biblical or mythological

subjects were very popular in the first half of the seventeenth century, and minute pictures were sometimes made for the covers of specially treasured books. Dresses also, petticoats, gloves, and garters, were richly adorned with soft-coloured roses and carnations and the curling tendrils of vines. Puritan ladies sometimes embroidered texts upon their clothes, and Elizabethan samplers frequently included mottoes or verses in coloured silks. When upholstered furniture came into fashion whole sets of chairs were often embroidered in beautiful designs which took months, or even years, to finish. There were then no hot-iron transfers to simplify the work and no printed patterns; the needlewoman had to paint her own design upon the material or translate it directly into stitchery as she went along. And the exquisite work put into embroidery appeared also in plain sewing, with its almost invisible stitches and its delicate hemstitch and feather-work. No gentlewoman was considered truly educated who was not well trained in needlework, and there were few who did not devote many hours of their leisure to putting their skill to good account.

There were also books to read, guests to entertain, and letters to write to absent friends. Ink was often made at home of gum, copperas, and gall, but sealing-wax and paper had to be bought. The latter was expensive and was sparingly used, not only because of its cost but because postal charges were higher when there was more than one sheet in a letter. There were no envelopes and no stamps; when the sheets were full they were folded and sealed down with the address written on the outside. In Tudor times private letters depended almost entirely upon carriers whose slow-moving carts trundled at stated intervals between all the big towns. The Government postal service was then concerned with official correspondence only. In the seventeenth century, however, the Crown undertook the transport of private letters also, with the result that they travelled very much faster and cost more. Post-houses were established in every large town, and from these the mail was taken on to the villages by servants or the local carrier. The charges varied according to the mileage covered and the number of sheets used, and they were paid by the receiver, for whom a disagreeable letter was thus made doubly unpleasant by the fact that he had to pay for it. In 1660 an Act of Parliament permitted Members of both Houses to send their correspondence free of charge provided it was signed on the cover, and it quickly became usual for them to frank their friends' letters also, and to supply them in advance with signed covers. This kindly custom was open to

abuse, for packets of such covers were sometimes stolen and sold and occasionally a Member's signature was forged. But with high postal charges it was too easy a method of obliging friends and constituents to be given up, and the practice continued until 1839, when the privilege of franking was abolished altogether.

Chapter III
FARTHER AFIELD

LIFE in the country was diversified by a great variety of outdoor sports, in most of which gentle and simple alike could share. More than half the country was still open heath and moor where game was plentiful and human beings were not. Even cultivated lands were largely unfenced, for the old open-field system still lingered on in spite of new methods of farming and the consequent enclosure of much that had once been common land. In the south of England hedges were beginning to spring up round field and pasture, and by Charles II's time it was possible for a foreign visitor to remark that "one may sometimes travel half a day's journey between two hedges, or in an avenue of trees."[1] But in less highly developed regions there were vast tracks of unenclosed country over which hounds could run without hindrance, and great bird-haunted marshes that formed a fowler's paradise. Lakes and rivers teemed with fish; many householders had their own ponds stocked with tench and roach, and salmon still ran in the yet unpolluted reaches of the lower Thames. Fishing rights were sometimes owned by the lord of the manor alone and sometimes shared with his tenants; in many districts they were free to all or enjoyed, as at Newbury, by the burgesses of the town. There were, of course, a number of game laws which restricted the pleasures of the humble, but they were not very strictly observed, and it was usually possible for the countryman of whatever degree to find his recreations in the open air without undue interference from landlord or magistrate. It was not until 1671 that Parliament restricted the right of killing game to freeholders with a hundred pounds a year or more, and so deprived a host of smaller people not only of their pastimes but also of much good food that had formerly been theirs for the taking.

Hunting (17), hawking (14), fishing (15) and games, were the favourite amusements of the country gentry, and if the poor man was debarred from some of these by law or his own poverty, he could still enjoy a day's sport coursing hares and rabbits, or stalking wild birds behind a dummy horse of wood or canvas. Roger Ascham considered that every man's training should

[1] M. Jorevin, *Description of England and Ireland in the Seventeenth Century. The Antiquarian Repertory*, 1809.

include the "noble exercises" of riding, tilting, shooting, running, leaping, games, "and all pastimes generally, which be joyned with labor, used in open places, and on the day light, conteining either some fitte exercise for warre, or some pleasant pastime for peace."[1] These were the "lawful" recreations which educationists encouraged, as opposed to those "unlawfull" amusements, such as cards and dice, which led men to gambling and profligacy and were forbidden to students, servants, and craftsmen, except at Christmas, when most regulations were relaxed.

Gamblers at an Inn, 1502

Hawking (14) was essentially an aristocratic sport, for to own a falcon was a sign of gentility, and to train it an art about which many books were written. It was extremely popular throughout the sixteenth and early seventeenth centuries and only gradually declined as firearms improved and shooting became the more fashionable amusement. Hunting was everybody's pastime, from the great noblemen with their stag-hunts to the small squires and yeomen who often kept their own packs of hounds for hare-hunting, or the London shopkeepers who banded together to hunt in Epping Forest. "I think it not amiss," wrote Markham in his *Country Contentments*, "to begin and give that recreation precedency of place which, in mine opinion . . . doth many degrees go before and precede all other, as being most royal for

[1] Roger Ascham, *The Scolemaster*, 1570.

the stateliness thereof, most artificiall for the wisdom and cunning thereof, and most manly and warlike for the use and endurance thereof." Endurance certainly was needed, for the hunt was often a wild chase over rough country in which the small packs of hounds then used followed whatever scent they would, and every conceivable method was employed by the huntsmen. Hare-hunting was the most popular form of the sport, but badgers, deer, and otter, were all enthusiastically pursued and occasionally foxes also, though these did not become a usual quarry until much later.

Deer were hunted (17) in the parks and chases of the greater landowners, over land which was often enclosed in Tudor times for the purpose. This was a practice which called forth bitter but unavailing protests from the champions of the poor whose common lands and grazing grounds were taken to swell the estates of newly risen men. Harrison roundly accuses his contemporaries of destroying whole parishes for their pleasures and devouring poor men's fields; "if it be not a curse of the Lord," he says, "to have our country converted in such sort, from the furniture of mankind into the walks and shrouds of wild beasts, I know not what is any." But all such cries fell upon deaf ears in an age when wealth was rapidly changing hands and hunting was a universal passion. Agricultural methods were altering everywhere; the old mediaeval strips were being converted into single fields, arable lands were being enclosed for pasture, and waste lands turned to farming uses. All this brought about much individual hardship, especially when ancient commons were enclosed, but it greatly enriched the countryside as a whole and caused a far higher standard of production. The movement was already well established when Henry VIII came to the throne; its progress thereafter was slow but it was inevitable, and it had as many friends as enemies. Amid all these changes the richer landowners saw no reason why they should not do for their amusement what they had already done in the name of better tillage, particularly as the proportion of land taken for deer-parks was very small in comparison with that enclosed for more utilitarian purposes. Rightly or wrongly, the builders of every considerable Tudor mansion considered a park of some kind a necessary mark of consequence, and such ground, once taken, never reverted again to its original state of common land or open heath and forest.

Under the Tudor monarchs archery (16) was as much a duty as a sport, for every man was required by law to be an adequate archer and to see that his sons could handle bow and arrow from

the time they were seven years old. The longbow was still an important weapon in war; in the next century it was to be displaced by fire-arms, but throughout the Tudor period it was essential to the safety of the country, and large numbers of bow-staves were annually imported. In 1588 the levies raised to repel the Armada were composed of archers and gunmen in almost equal proportions; most Londoners had fire-arms but the majority of countrymen were still armed with bows and arrows. By an Act of Parliament passed in 1541 "the Fathers, Governors and Rulers of such as be of tender years" were obliged to train their charges in markmanship and were fined if they neglected to do so. The same penalty applied to all young men over seventeen years of age who failed to provide themselves with a bow and four arrows. Most parishes had their butts and marks which were erected at the public expense on some convenient open space, and everything possible was done by the authorities to encourage proficiency in shooting. Young men in villages sometimes formed themselves into archery companies, like that known as Prince Arthur's Knights which so pleased Henry VIII when he visited Mile End, or that other band of green-clad bowmen whom he met in the woods when he went a-maying with Queen Catherine. Displays, contests, and pageants, were frequently held and valuable prizes were sometimes offered by public-spirited citizens for the best performance. Even women occasionally followed Queen Elizabeth's example and became proficient marksmen. Yet in spite of legal pressure and much genuine enthusiasm, archery was already a dying art. Even in Tudor times the compulsory practices were often evaded and when, in the seventeenth century, the longbow finally gave place to the gun in war, the popularity which archery had once enjoyed was rapidly transferred to newer and more interesting forms of sport.

Games of skill and strength were very numerous. The gentry played bowls and tennis, though not the lawn tennis that we know. Theirs was a more strenuous game played on an enclosed court with stringed rackets and leather balls stuffed with hair. Bowls was played in private alleys, such as Boorde considered necessary in every great man's garden, or on public bowling-greens in towns and villages. It was on the public green in York that William Nevinson, the highwayman, asked the Lord Mayor what time it was and so established his alibi after his famous ride from Gad's Hill in 1671. Ninepins was a very popular game which could be played almost anywhere, and so were tipcat and stoolball. Village lads played a rough form of football, without proper rules or definite teams, which still survives in the Shrove

Tuesday games played in the streets of Atherstone, Chester-le-Street, Ashbourne and Corfe Castle. It needed great strength and endurance and a complete indifference to mud and hard knocks. Stubbes declares that it "may rather be called a freendly kinde of fight than a play or recreation; a bloody and murthering practice than a felowly sporte or pastime."[1] At Whitsuntide the famous Cotswold Games attracted large crowds who came to try their skill at wrestling, cudgel-playing, leaping, and tossing the hammer, and at every village festival there were races and dancing and, until the Civil War, riding at the quintain. Coursing matches were common, and in their due season there were hurling-matches, Morris-dancing, and skating. The skates used were originally of bone; it was not until the end of the seventeenth century that the iron skate was introduced from Holland and the sport, which had not before been clearly distinguished from ordinary sliding on the ice, received its modern name.

Skating, *c.* 1680

At Christmas the Mummers went round to every house, and on all the chief dates of the agricultural year there were traditional celebrations in which everyone took part. On Plough Monday in the north of England the sword-dancers performed their ancient dance and the Plough Stots toured the village asking for alms which had once been spent on keeping the Plough Light in the church and now went to provide ale for the ploughmen. At Midsummer the bonfires blazed on the hill-tops and houses were decorated with lights and greenery; at Hallowe'en, also, the villagers danced round their communal fire, a rite which was transferred after 1605 to 5 November to commemorate the Gunpowder Plot. May-day was still one of the high-lights of the year, with its Morris-dances, hobby-horses and Robin Hood plays. "The same day was a good May game at Westminster," wrote Henry Machyn in his *Diary* for 1555, ". . . with giants, morris pikes, guns and drums and devils and three morris dances and bagpipes and viols and many disguised, and the lord and lady of the May rode gorgeously with minstrels divers playing."[2]

These ancient ceremonies were frowned upon by the sterner Puritans who saw them only as occasions for rowdiness and vice.

[1] P. Stubbes, *The Anatomie of Abuses*, 1583.
[2] *The Diary of Henry Machyn* (Camden Society).

To Stubbes the Maypole was nothing but an idol and the gathering of May-boughs a cause of immorality amongst the young. Latimer gave vent in one of his sermons to his passionate indignation at finding a village church closed when he went there unexpectedly to preach and was told that the people were all out gathering boughs for Robin Hood's Bower. In 1584 the Visitor to St. Mary's, Shrewsbury, inquired "whether there have been any lords of mysrule, or somer lords or ladies, or any disguised persons, as morice dancers, maskers, or mum'ers, or such lyke, within the parische",[1] and a few years later he succeeded in putting down the Shearmen's Festival which marked the close of sheep-shearing. During the Commonwealth all such ceremonies were sternly repressed, though not always with complete success, but they sprang up anew after the Restoration. Their real decline only began in the late eighteenth century when deepening class distinctions caused many landlords to lose touch with their people, and to abolish whenever they could the old communal rejoicings in which their ancestors had delighted as heartily as their workmen and tenants.

Church-ales were held at Whitsun and sometimes at other seasons also to raise money for the parish. Aubrey tells us that in his grandfather's time there were no rates levied at Kingston St. Michael, for the church-ales provided all the necessary funds. This ancestor of the parish whist-drive was organized by the churchwardens and included feasting, games, sports, and Morris-dancing, under the direction of an elected King and Queen. At the Wakes the decorated rush-cart trundled round the district with its load of rushes for the church-floor, preceded by musicians and dancers, and after the procession there were amusements of all sorts, and a miniature fair with booths and stalls which were sometimes erected in the churchyard itself.

There was also bear- and bull-baiting. This brutal sport was popular with all classes. In 1526 a circus holding a thousand people was erected on Bankside, and another was built for fights between bulls and mastiffs in 1570. Every considerable parish had its own bear and bear-warden and looked to them for revenue; when the town bear died at Congleton just before the Wakes in 1662, the churchwardens regarded the event as a disaster and took some of the money set aside for a new Bible to buy a new animal. So, at least, says a persistent tradition from which sprang a derisive couplet still well known in Cheshire.[2]

[1] H. Owen and J. Blakeway, *History of Shrewsbury*, 1825.

[2] Congleton rare, Congleton rare,
Sold the Church Bible to buy a new bear.

14 Hawking

15 Fishing

From contemporary engravings

SEVENTEENTH-CENTURY SPORTS

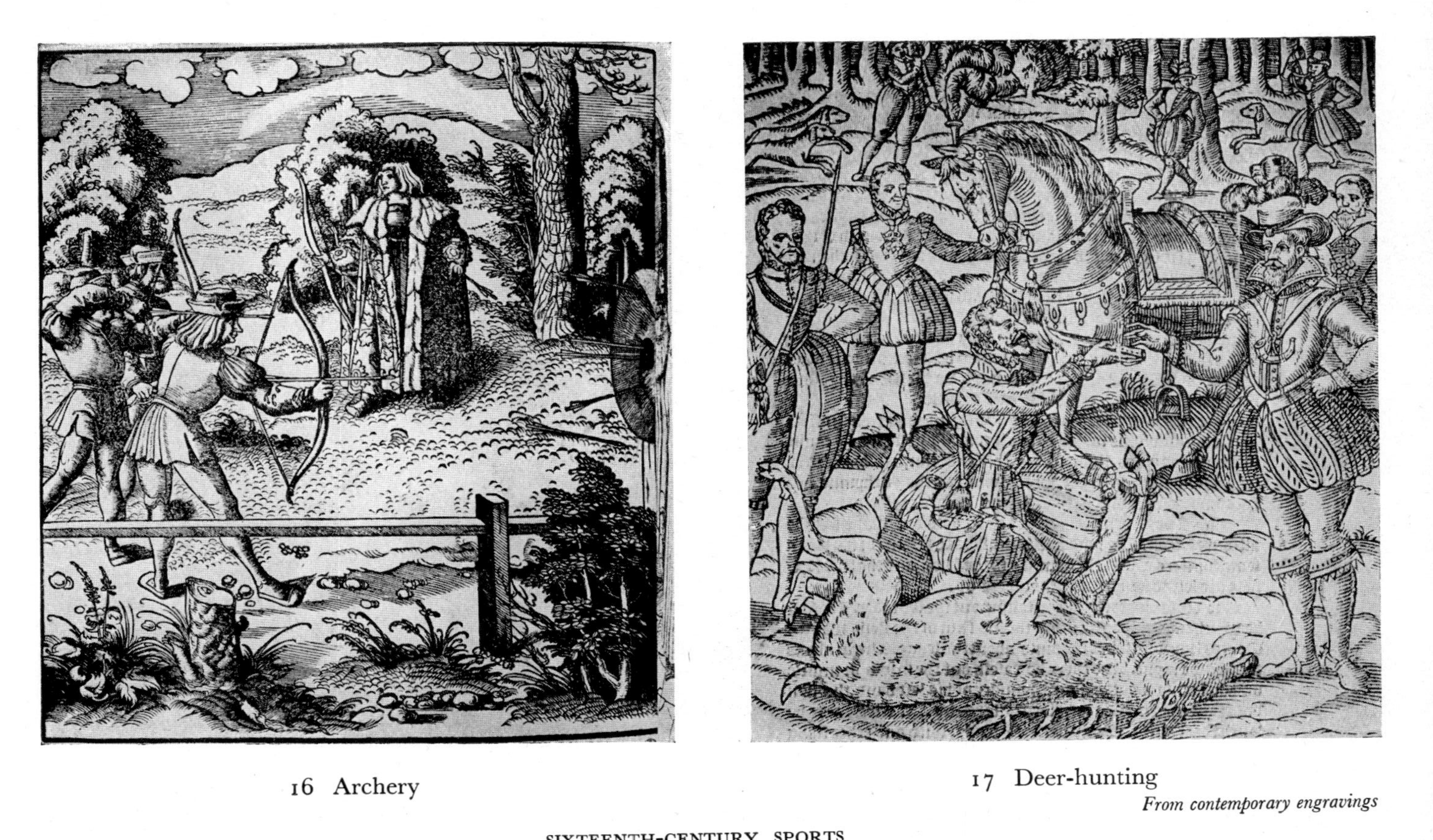

16 Archery

17 Deer-hunting

From contemporary engravings

SIXTEENTH-CENTURY SPORTS

Nantwich had no less than four bears in 1583 which were turned loose into the streets for safety during the great fire of that year, thereby adding considerably to the terrors of those who were fighting the flames. The bear-garden on Bankside was suppressed by Parliament in 1642, but the village baits were still held at Wakes and festivals; sometimes such contests were arranged on private grounds to mark a special occasion, like the bull-bait organized by Nicholas Blundell in 1712 when he opened his new marl-pit at Little Crosby.

Cockfighting was another amusement popular alike in London and the country. "Cocks of the game are yet cherished by divers men for their pleasures," wrote Stow in 1584, "much money being laid on their heads when they fight in pits, whereof some be costly made for the purpose."[1] Henry VIII built the first London cockpit near Birdcage Walk, and many others afterwards sprang up in the capital. In the country, trained birds were carried from one great house to another, or from inn to inn where "cockings" were frequently held in the yards. In 1654 the sport was forbidden by law, but it continued to flourish in spite of regulations for nearly three hundred years, and even after 1849, when a further Act prohibiting it was passed, it still went on secretly for a number of years.

Travelling (7) over the ill-kept roads of the time was no light matter. In summer the traveller was beclouded with dust and pestered with gnats from the undrained marshes; in winter he struggled through seas of mud and faced a variety of perils, from floods and snowstorms to the unwelcome attentions of highwaymen. Secondary roads were then little more than cart-tracks and even the main roads were often full of pot-holes and quagmires in which a wheeled vehicle easily became bogged. To lose oneself in unfamiliar surroundings was no uncommon disaster, for there were hardly any signposts and milestones were not always reliable. Even at the very end of the seventeenth century, when there were regular coach services between London and the larger towns, Celia Fiennes was surprised to observe that in Lancashire

> . . . at all Cross wayes there are posts with hands pointing to each road with ye names of ye great towns or market towns that it Leads to, which does make up for ye length of ye miles that strangers may not Loose their Road and have it to goe back againe.[2]

It was often necessary to employ a guide in an unknown district, when such could be obtained. Those who rode post had

[1] J. Stow, *Survey of London.* [2] Celia Fiennes, *op. cit.*

the benefit of professional guides, but others were forced to rely upon the not always willing co-operation of local people or the superior knowledge of some chance-met stranger. When Adam Martindale travelled from Chester to Burton-on-Trent in 1673, he trusted himself to the guidance of a young man encountered at Uttoxeter who offered to take him over the flooded district round Dove Bridge. Both passed over safely, but Martindale was somewhat horrified to hear later that his companion had never been that way before. John Chamberlain also was lost by his guide on Newmarket Heath and was forced to wander about with him for several hours on a wild night before the right road was found again. Country people were often unwilling to face the rigours of bad weather and worse roads in spite of the extra money it brought them; and when they did so, they could not always be relied upon to know more than two or three miles of the way, since simple folk did not travel much, and some never stirred from the immediate surroundings of their own villages.

Bridges were few and many rivers had to be forded, a proceeding that was often dangerous when the floods were out. When George Wandesford was riding to Richmond in 1651, he attempted to ford the River Swale and was swept to his death by a flood which "came sudainly and mightely" and carried him "into a poole near Catterick Bridge, above a mile from the place where he was drowned."[1] Frequently the traveller was forced to make a wide detour to avoid swollen streams, or trust himself to ferries when the fords were impassable. Ferries which carried horses, men and cattle together were the only means of crossing the wider rivers and estuaries, and useful as they were, they were extremely uncomfortable and not always safe. "A very hazardous passage by reason of 3 tydes meeting," says Celia Fiennes of one in the West Country, and after experiencing the rigours of a four-hour crossing in an open boat with fifteen horses, ten or twelve cows and "about seventeen or eighteen Passengers, call'd Christians",[2] Defoe preferred to go round by York rather than face the Hull to Barton passage a second time.

To these various discomforts was added the constant danger from footpads and highwaymen who abounded in lonely districts and constituted a very real menace to those who travelled alone. Discharged soldiers, vagrants, professional thieves, and men dispossessed and ruined by the upheavals of two troubled centuries all helped to swell the number of those who made a living by highway robbery. Young gentlemen sometimes took to the road

[1] *Autobiography of Alice Thornton* (Surtees Society).
[2] D. Defoe, *A Tour of Great Britain*, 1724.

for the sake of adventure, or to ease a temporary financial difficulty, and afterwards returned to normal life without necessarily forfeiting the regard of their friends. Travellers were forced to go heavily armed and whenever possible in companies, but they were usually a poor match for the organized bands that infested open heaths and moorlands, or the solitary, well-armed and well-mounted highwayman who knew every yard of his chosen territory.

Moreover, in spite of bitter complaints from the despoiled, the general attitude towards these marauders was curiously tolerant. It is certain that they could not have flourished as they did if they had not enjoyed the sympathy and sometimes the active help of many otherwise law-abiding citizens. In popular imagination they appeared as romantic figures who led a life of danger and died bravely in the end. Legends of their courtesy and courage, their chivalrous treatment of women, and their generosity to the poor circulated everywhere, though the Quarter Sessions Records could provide much grim evidence to the contrary. Sir Ralph Verney, whose personal integrity could not be questioned, numbered two highwaymen amongst his cousins, and not only used his influence for them when they were arrested, but received them in his house when they were free. Inn-keepers sometimes risked prosecution to help them with information, or concealed them from the watch in their lofts and cellars. The Yorkshire drovers are said to have made an arrangement with William Nevinson whereby they paid him a quarterly tribute and helped him when they could, while he in return protected them from all other thieves. Fynes Moryson declared that there were more road-thieves in England than in any other country but that "having taken purses by the high way, they seldome or never kill those they rob."[1] This was not, of course, entirely true, for clashes did occur in which sometimes the victim and sometimes the highwayman was killed or wounded, but it was perhaps true enough to account in part for the leniency with which their activities were viewed. "'Tis a great pity that such men should be hanged," said John Verney on one occasion, and thereby expressed the general sympathy with those whose almost certain fate was to end upon the gallows.

With all these difficulties to be faced, it is not surprising that journeys were limited so far as possible to spring and summer and were only undertaken in the darker season when they could not be avoided. The winter traveller who struggled through the deep mud, crossed unbridged rivers by ford and ferry, lost

[1] Fynes Moryson, *An Itinerary*, 1617.

himself on a barren heath, stood about in bitter winds while his servants righted a vehicle overturned in a pot-hole, and kept his arms always handy against thieves, had to be at once hardy in health and reasonably courageous. Yet all these inconveniences were not enough to stop the travelling Englishman when trade, duty, or pleasure, called him out. Then as now, judges went on circuit, students came up to their universities from all parts of the kingdom, and ambitious young men left their homes to seek their fortunes in London. Justices of the Peace, upon whom so much of the peaceful administration of the country depended, rode to their Quarter Sessions at regular intervals, traders flocked to market-towns and fairs, and goods travelled slowly but surely by carriers' carts or packhorse trains. Celia Fiennes rode all over England for her health, and throughout the seventeenth century the medicinal springs at such places as Knaresborough, Harrogate, Epsom, and Bath, drew many genuine patients and still more pleasure-seekers. In Charles II's reign horse-racing became a fashionable pastime under the active patronage of the King, and crowds flocked to Newmarket or Chester and even to little village race-meetings that had formerly had only a local interest.

There was a constant coming and going at the inns, for whose comfort and cheapness England then enjoyed a great reputation. "The world affords not such Inns as England hath," wrote Fynes Moryson in his *Itinerary*, "either for good and cheap entertainment, or for humble attendance on passengers." The traveller, he said, was always sure of excellent food and cheerful service at a moderate rate. He could order his meat to be dressed as he liked it best and, "while he eats, if he have company especially, he shall be offered music which he may freely take or refuse, and if he be solitary, the Musicians will give him good day with music in the morning." Harrison also remarks upon the good inns of his time, some of which, he tells us, could house two or three hundred people, provide them with a varied diet at short notice, and give to every visitor clean sheets "wherein no man hath been lodged since they came from the laundress, or out of the water wherein they were last washed."

Riding was the commonest method of travel, and it remained the fastest, if not the most comfortable, even when coaches had become well established. Those who were pressed for time hired post-horses which they rode for a stage and then exchanged for fresh animals at one of the inns along the road. Twopence a mile was the usual charge, rising in 1609 to threepence, with fourpence or sixpence for the guide. The more leisurely travellers used their own animals or hired a single horse for the entire journey. The

poor who could not afford horses or coach-fares went on foot or in carriers' carts, some of which carried passengers as well as goods. Invalids sometimes travelled in horse-litters, or in the chairs on slings which appeared towards the end of the sixteenth century. These were carried by porters and, though slow, were more comfortable for the sick than the early coaches. Quite long journeys were occasionally undertaken in them. In 1603 when James I came south with his followers, the French Ambassador's wife travelled all the way from Edinburgh to London in a chair, eight men taking it in turns to carry her in relays of four.

Private coaches began to be used in Elizabeth's reign. These were at first rather uncomfortable vehicles, with open sides and, of course, no springs. The great square bodies were supported by leather straps attached to upright posts rising from the axle-trees. Some slight protection from the weather was afforded by leather flaps or curtains, and these were replaced later by rough doors; in Charles II's reign glass windows were introduced, which could be pulled up and down. The jolting over bad roads was very considerable, and some unfortunate passengers were reduced to sickness by the motion. In 1626 Edward Knapp applied for a licence for an invention designed to improve coaches by the introduction of steel springs and iron axle-trees, but many years were to pass before springs came into general use.

In spite of early discomforts, however, the coach rapidly became popular and with it a smaller four-wheeled carriage for town use known as the calash. Together they crowded the narrow streets of the capital, causing innumerable traffic jams and much abusive argument between the footmen who preceded them and the independent drivers of drays and carts who were usually determined to stand upon their rights against all comers. To the old-fashioned they appeared effeminate, fit only for women and invalids; the noise of their iron wheels rattling over cobbled streets offended the lovers of quiet, and they were rightly accused of tearing up country roads and causing inextricable confusion in towns. John Evelyn, like many older men, looked back longingly to "those happy days" when

> . . . Surefoot, the grave and steady mare, carried the good Knight and his courteous Lady behind him to Church and to visit the neighbourhood without so many Hell-carts, rattling Coaches and a Crewe of damme Lacqueys, which a grave Livery Servant or two supplyed who rid before and made way for his Worship.[1]

But those times were gone for good when he wrote. The coach was

[1] J. Evelyn, *Mundus Muliebris.*

coaches — P.T.O.

too convenient a means of transport for any complaints to check its progress, and its use rapidly spread from the upper classes to all who could possibly afford the necessary outlay. Constant experiment made it lighter and more comfortable as the years passed; by the middle of the seventeenth century coaches of all sizes were available, and very gay they must have looked with their bright-coloured bodies and adornments of red velvet or gold lace. Pepys records with great pride how on May-day 1669 he and his wife

> went alone through the town with our new liveries of serge and the horses' manes and tails tied with red ribbons, and the standards gilt with varnish, and all clean, and green reines, that people did mightily look upon us; and the truth is, I did not see any coach more pretty, though more gay, than our's, all the day.[1]

After the private vehicle came the public. Stage coaches are mentioned in *The Carriers Cosmography* as early as 1637, when two coaches ran every week between Aldersgate and St. Albans, and it is possible that the service began even earlier. By 1658 coaches were running from London to Salisbury, Plymouth, Wakefield, and Durham, the charges varying from 20*s*. for the journey to Salisbury to 55*s*. to Durham. The proprietors did not always guarantee the time taken to reach the farther towns, perhaps wisely, for many mishaps might be met with on the roads. The Salisbury journey was advertised to take two days and that to Exeter four. In 1669 Anthony Wood left All Souls College, Oxford, at six in the morning and reached the Saracen's Head in London at seven at night; the fare was then 12*s*. and was later reduced to 10*s*. The opponents of stage-coaches had much to say about the discomforts and dangers of such journeys, and the laziness of those who preferred to sit all through the day instead of riding as a man should. In a pamphlet published in 1672 an embittered writer asks what advantage it is

> to be called out of their Beds into these Coaches an hour before day in the morning, to be hurried in them from place to place, till one hour, two or three within night; insomuch that, after sitting all day in the summer-time stifled with heat and choaked with the dust; or in the Wintertime, starving and freezing with cold, or choaked with filthy Fogs, they are often brought into their Inns by Torch-light, when it is too late to sit up to get a Supper; and next morning they are forced into the coach so early, that they can get no breakfast?[2]

But this diatribe had no more effect than most reactionary

[1] *Pepys's Diary.*
[2] *A copy of a Printed Letter from J. C. to a Postmaster in the Country, with directions for the management of his design for putting down stage coaches.* 1672.

complaints, and by the end of the century most large towns had their regular services to London which were well patronized in spite of all the discomforts catalogued above.

Once in the capital those who had no carriages of their own had the choice of river-boats or the hackney-cabs which first appeared on the streets early in the seventeenth century. The London Watermen were an old-established corporation, famous for their arrogance and their bad manners, which were not improved by the hotly resented competition of the new hackney-cabs. The Thames was then London's greatest highway, along which passed innumerable craft designed for trade or pleasure, from merchant wherries and boats plying for hire to magnificent royal barges and the scarcely less splendid vessels of the nobility. Hardy travellers enjoyed the excitement of "shooting the Bridge", whose nineteen narrow arches, with strong cataracts rushing between them, could only be passed in safety at certain phases of the tide. More nervous people found it convenient to disembark above London Bridge and rejoin their craft a little lower down.

On fine days, to go by river was a very pleasant method of getting about and much quicker than trying to pass through the congested streets, but it had its disadvantages in bad weather. But wet or fine there was always something to see there: the constant, varied traffic of boats passing between the houses that crowded down to the waterside as yet innocent of embankments; the lovely bridge with its overhanging dwellings; boys swimming in the water, and sometimes a race between two daring pleasure-boats; now and then a fine water pageant, like that which accompanied the newly elected Lord Mayor to Westminster on 29 October each year. Farther up the river were the pleasant pastures and gardens of rural villages like Chelsea and Putney, and here in the summer came picnic parties seeking a breath of country air. If the water near the houses did not always smell very pleasantly, noses were more tolerant then than they are now, and only occasionally was there some ominous sight to see, like the dead man floating four days in the river who once so troubled Pepys. For the average Londoner the Thames was at once essential highway and playground, and Roger North's description of one day spent upon it might have been echoed by many other citizens. "For the day proved cool," he says, "the gale brisk, air clear, and no inconvenience to molest us, nor want to trouble our thoughts, neither business to importune, nor formalities to tease us; so that we came nearer to perfection of life there than I was ever sensible of otherwise."[1]

[1] R. North, *The Lives of the Norths*, ed. A. Jessop, 1890.

Chapter IV

HORN-BOOK AND GOWN

LARGE families were common in Tudor and Stuart times. The crown of every marriage was a full nursery; to be childless was a grievous misfortune, and to have only one or two children often meant being left with none at all, for infectious diseases then took terrible toll of young life, and even those who escaped this scourge sometimes succumbed to the hard conditions and poor medical knowledge of the age. But if far too many babies died in infancy, the rest were the better loved because of it. The utmost care and devotion were lavished upon them and though discipline was severe, it was prompted by a genuine concern for the welfare of the children. "I wish you could see me," wrote Endymion Porter's mother when his children were staying with her, "sitting at the table with my little chickens, one on either side; in all my life I have not had such an occupation to my content, to see them in bed at night and get them up in the morning." These same children were constantly in their father's thoughts when he was away from them. "Kiss my little partridges for me," he wrote to his wife on one occasion, and on another, "Pray tell me how my little boys do and whether Charles will be black or fair."[1] Poor Mary Verney, struggling alone and in poor health with innumerable difficulties at Claydon, could still find time to send her husband an account of their little delicate boy who sang so prettily. Even the Puritan conception of children as brands to be plucked from the burning could not prevent occasional tender references to them, though one cry from a Presbyterian minister's heart shows that parenthood did not always bring with it the gift of understanding the very young. "What a deal of patience is requisite," wrote Henry Newcome in his *Diary*, "to beare any converse with our little children. How peevish and foolish are they!" And characteristically he adds, "and what fits doth our heavenly Father beare with us in."[2]

When the baby was coming it was customary for the young wife to wear an eagle-stone or some other accredited charm to help her to an easy delivery. Written charms were often preserved in families and lent round to friends as they were required.

[1] *Letters of Mr. Endymion Porter, Gentlemen of the Bedchamber to King Charles I*, ed. Dorothea Townshend, 1897.

[2] *The Diary of Henry Newcome*, 1661–3 (Chetham Society).

18 A Tudor Lady and her Children

From a drawing by Holbein

19 The Children of Charles I (1635)

Reproduced from a painting by Sir A. Van Dyke, by gracious permission of H.M. The King

20 The end of a Stag Hunt (1603): the Prince of Wales and the Earl of Essex

Reproduced from a painting attributed to Marc Gheeraerts, by gracious permission of H.M. The King

Eagle-stones, brought from abroad, were worn in silk bags round the neck until two or three weeks before the birth of the child. The midwife was chosen with as much care for personal character as for medical skill for she, more than anyone, had the power to injure the mother or the baby by witchcraft. In Elizabeth's reign she was required to take an oath that she would not permit the substitution of any other child for the one just born, and that she would not use "any kind of sorcery or incantation in the time of the travail of any woman."[1] Charms of a simple kind she certainly used, for everyone did so, and midwives were usually well versed in the traditional lore of the neighbourhood. To loosen all knots when labour began, to provide some ancient garment for the child's first wrapping, to carry it upstairs before it went down—these were the commonplaces of her profession, and no midwife worth her salt would have dreamt of neglecting them. In extreme cases she might send the father running to the church with a demand that the bells be rung to ease a difficult labour, or, if the family was of too little consequence to make such a request, she might come provided with an old piece of rope begged from the bellringers which she tied round the mother's waist during the worst of her pains.

If the mother could not nurse her own child, a wet nurse was employed. Artificial feeding was then very rare. Feeding-bottles were unknown, but a cow's horn was sometimes made to serve the purpose, or, in wealthier households, a silver papboat. The wet nurse also had to be very carefully chosen, for most people believed that the baby absorbed her moral qualities as it took the milk. If she was a drunkard or a fool, so would her charge be, and more serious defects had equally serious results. This was a belief which persisted for a very long time, and many late Georgian or early Victorian parents would have agreed with Thomas Phayre who declared in 1550 that no wet nurse should be a "dronkard, vyscyous nor sluttysche, for such corrupthethe the nature of the Chylde."[2]

Christening took place within a few days of birth and was an occasion of rejoicing, when presents were made to the mother and the baby, the midwife and nurse were rewarded with money gifts, and a large number of guests were regaled with wine, biscuits, and christening cake. The mother's room was often specially decorated with new hangings and ornaments for her lying-in, so that she might receive the godparents and her more intimate friends on the christening day and fittingly accept their

[1] Strype's *Annals of the Reformation*, 1709.
[2] Thomas Phayre, *The Regiment of life*, 1550.

presents and congratulations. In church the baby was presented at the font in a fine linen shirt with embroidered cuffs and bands, and was afterwards wrapped in a white cloth known as the Chrism cloth, as a sign that he was now a Christian. If he died within a month of his baptism this cloth was used as his shroud. The godparents usually gave him Apostle spoons, a full set if they were well-to-do, or one or two if they were not. Caudle-cups, porringers, bowls, and corals were also fashionable gifts. In poorer households money gifts were often made to the mother to help with the inevitable expenses, and the guests brought their own contributions to the feast, as they did at weddings. Aubrey tells us that in Oxfordshire every woman brought a cake and gave one to the minister at the church porch, and sometimes a special cake, called a rocking-cake, was baked for the father.

Cradles were then solid pieces of furniture, made of oak, with wide carved rockers and heavy trimmings of velvet and fringe. They were well filled with blankets and feather pillows and were usually placed close to the fire, for our ancestors had no doubt that warmth was a far better thing for the young than fresh air. Rattles were provided for the child's amusement and there were also corals with bells. These last were important, for not only did they help the baby to cut his teeth, but all nurses and most mothers believed that they protected him from witches and the falling sickness. Many believed that the red stone changed colour and grew pale when its wearer was ill. "The coral preserveth such as bear it from fascination or bewitching," wrote Reginald Scot in *The Discovery of Witchcraft* "and in this respect they are hanged about children's necks. But from whence that superstition is derived, or who invented the lye, I know not, but I see how ready the people are to give credit thereunto by the multitude of corrals that are employed."

The petting and cossetting of nursery days did not last long. In an age of early marriages there was no time for prolonged babyhood, and strong as was the affection of most parents, it was not shown by spoiling and indulgence. The child had to be trained for adult life as quickly as possible and a strict discipline, verging upon severity, was believed to be the best means to that end. A parent's word was law and filial piety the chief of infant virtues. Any lapse from prompt obedience or respectful bearing was met with swift punishment, and there were no fancy ideas about self-expression or the danger of inhibitions. Children addressed their parents as Sir and Madam and stood bareheaded in their presence; on special occasions they knelt before them to ask their blessing. Education began very early and was

from the beginning a strenuous undertaking well seasoned with punishments. The dull or slow-witted child particularly suffered severely, for little allowance seems to have been made for his difficulties, and his poor progress was more often ascribed to original sin than to inability to absorb the solid mental fare provided. Girls and boys alike were frequently beaten for childish faults, and tutors were not only permitted but expected to underline their instruction by a liberal use of the rod.

Repeating the Lesson, *c.* 1650

Most teachers regarded flogging as a necessary part of their curriculum, though there were a few more enlightened men who were beginning to feel that kindness and encouragement were better than punishment. One such was Roger Ascham, the learned tutor of Princess Elizabeth, whose system of education was based upon reason rather than repression. Another was Sir Thomas Elyot who, in the reign of Henry VIII, urged the claims of gentleness and common sense in teaching. In the following century Henry Peacham in his *Compleat Gentleman* declared that "correction without instruction is plain Tyrannie", and strongly criticized the type of master who "in winter would ordinarily on a cold morning whip his boyes over for no other purpose but to heat himself." There must also have been some parents who understood the difficulties of childhood and realized that what was perhaps permissible with a healthy, insensitive boy might be definitely harmful to the less hardy. One great-grandmother at

least did so and took upon herself to write to Ralph Verney, urging him to be more tender with his nervous and delicate little Edmund, then only three years old. "Let me beg of you and his mother," she wrote, "that nobody whip him but Mr. Parrye; if you doe goe a violent waye with him, you will be the furst that will rue it, for I verily beleve he will reseve ingery by it."[1] But such admonitions as these fell mostly upon deaf ears, as indeed they did in this case, and parents and schoolmasters alike continued to hold that those who spared the rod would inevitably spoil the child, and so fail in the most solemn duty laid upon them by Divine Providence.

Education began at a very tender age. Regular lessons were usually started at four years old, but two was not considered too young to embark upon one's letters. John Evelyn records that his little son could read English, Latin, and French, when he was only two and a half; by the time he was five he knew more Latin than most modern boys of ten or twelve, was acquainted with Euclid and the historical parts of the Bible, and "had a strong passion for Greek". He died then, poor child, so we shall never know whether his astonishing precocity would have continued into adult life or have faded into dullness, as so often happens with infant prodigies.

Young Lucy Apsley, who was later to marry Colonel Hutchinson, the regicide, could not only read perfectly when she was four years old, but could remember and repeat the sermons that she heard. Both these children, it is true, were exceptionally brilliant, but there was nothing unusual in setting babies to work at an age when they should still have been playing in their nurseries. From her own account we gather that Lucy was an insufferable little prig throughout her childhood. She tells us that she despised children's games and, when forced to entertain guests of her own age, "tired them with more grave instructions than their mothers", and pulled their dolls to pieces so that "they were glad when I entertained myself with other company."[2] As soon as she was weaned she had a French nurse so that she might learn English and French together, and by the time she was seven she had eight tutors to teach her languages, music, dancing, writing, and needlework. In Latin she outstripped her brothers, and every moment of her spare time was spent with a book, to the distress of her mother who thought that so much reading was bad for her health. It is consoling to note that she was not quite perfect; she scamped her music practice whenever she could, "and for my needle," she says, "I absolutely hated it."

[1] *Verney Memoirs*, ed. 1904. [2] Lucy Hutchinson, *Memoirs of Colonel Hutchinson*, ed. 1895.

Another and more human child, who had a tutor before he was breeched, distressed his anxious father because he preferred play to study. This was little Thomas Slingsby who could "tell the Latin words for the parts of his body and of his cloaths" when he was only three years old; but not satisfied with this, Sir Henry Slingsby wrote in his *Diary* when the boy was not yet five:

> I find him duller this year than last which would discourage one but that I think the cause to be his too much minding Play which takes his mind from his books; therefore they do ill that do foment and cherish that humour in a child and by inventing new sports increase his desire to play which causeth a great aversion to their book; and their mind being at first season'd with vanity will not easily loose the relish of it.[1]

First lessons were often given by the mother or nurse from the Horn-book, that cheap and simple primer made from a piece of wood shaped like a battledore upon which a printed page containing the alphabet, some numerals, and the Lord's Prayer, was pasted. Over this page was a sheet of transparent horn to keep it clean, and the whole was bound with brass and occasionally backed with leather. With it went a quill or straw called the fescue, with which the teacher pointed to the particular letter then being learnt. Children called their Horn-book the Criss Cross Row because there was a cross at the beginning and the end of the alphabet. These primitive schoolbooks could be bought from pedlars and usually cost about threepence, though the leather-backed ones were doubtless more expensive. They were light and easy for childish fingers to hold and had the added advantage that they were not easily destroyed. No doubt they were often used at play-time as the battledores they resembled, and perhaps now and then during lessons as a handy weapon for an exasperated teacher.

The Horn-book, *c.* 1600

Serious study began when the child passed into the hands of a

[1] *The Diary of Sir Henry Slingsby*, ed. Rev. D. Parsons, 1836.

tutor who usually taught both the sons and daughters of the family. Girls then received as sound an education as their brothers, at least amongst the well-to-do; it was not until considerably later that the idea gained ground that learning was unsuitable, or at least unnecessary, for a woman. Milton's daughters were able to read aloud to their blind father in Hebrew, Greek, Latin, Italian, Spanish, and French, and though we know that they performed the task unwillingly, they did it efficiently. Lady Jane Grey read Greek for the sheer pleasure of it, and Queen Elizabeth could make impromptu speeches in Latin, French, and Italian, whenever the occasion called for it. It was then quite usual for educated women to speak several languages and to read learned theological and historical works; nearly all had some acquaintance with music and many were capable musicians. Girls were generally educated at home by their brothers' tutor, or by masters who worked under the supervision of mother or governess. A few went to girls' schools, though these were rare establishments, and Catholic children of both sexes were sometimes sent to foreign countries where they could be brought up in their own religion beyond the reach of English anti-Catholic laws.

Many boys, after being grounded at home, went to the local Grammar School, or to one of the bigger schools like Eton, Winchester, or Westminster. "There are a great number of Grammar Schooles throughout the realme," wrote Harrison in 1577, "and those very liberally endowed, for the better reliefe of poore scholars, so that there are not many corporate townes now under the Queen's dominion that have not one grammar school at the least with a sufficient living for the master and usher appointed to the same."[1] Some years before the position had not been so good. Education suffered a serious, though unintentional, setback in the early days of the Reformation. When the chantries and collegiate churches were suppressed, the schools they had maintained were given a fixed sum of money in lieu of the lands that had been lost. This was often inadequate to begin with, and when the value of money fell, as it did soon afterwards, many schools declined rapidly or perished altogether. Thomas Lever's complaint that Sedbergh School was "now solde, decayed and lost" might have been made of many others whose endowments had disappeared in the general upheaval. Edward VI has usually received much credit for fostering education, but in fact most of the schools established in his reign had existed long before his time and were simply restarted by him on a new basis. In

[1] W. Harrison, *op. cit.*

Elizabeth's reign, however, many new schools were founded, amongst them Rugby, Uppingham, Merchant Taylors, and Harrow. The last was a gift made to his native village by John Lyon, a wealthy childless yeoman who in 1590 endowed a small school with one master and one usher. He intended it simply for the intelligent boys of his own locality who might be sufficiently ambitious to avail themselves of his charity; its future as one of the most famous English public schools was something of which he certainly never dreamed and perhaps might not altogether have approved.

The education given was chiefly classical, Latin, logic, rhetoric, some mathematics, and Greek, being the main subjects taught. At Harrow, archery practice was required by the founder's regulations and each boy had to provide his own bowshaft and strings. He also had to bring his own books, pens, ink and paper, and candles for the winter term. The boys were expected to know how to read and write before they came, and in many schools there was a regulation providing for their removal should they prove too dull to profit by the teaching given. At St. Paul's School parents were warned that "If your childe after reasonable season prouved be founde here unapte, and unable to learninge, then ye warned thereof shall take him awaye that he occupye not here roume in vain."[1] At Harrow a year's grace was given, after which the "unapt" scholar had to seek his education elsewhere from some more easily satisfied master.

More important even than Latin and Greek was religion. The catechism was carefully taught and examinations in it held once a week or oftener. In the boarding-schools there were prayers in chapel every morning and evening, and regular Sunday services which all were obliged to attend; at Winchester a chapter of the Bible was read aloud in every room after the children were in bed. There were also sermons, of which the boys were expected to render an account afterwards in writing. Sermons then played a large part in every child's training, both at home and at school, and some sort of shorthand seems to have been learnt for the purpose of taking notes. Ralph Verney, whose views on feminine education were somewhat narrow for his time, expressly desired that his goddaughter should learn neither Latin nor shorthand. The first he regarded as a vice in women, and the second he disliked because "the pride of taking sermon noates hath made multitudes of woemen most unfortunate."[2]

Lessons began early in the morning and continued until dinner-time, beginning again in the afternoon. At Westminster,

[1] Dean Colet, *Aeditio*, 1537.

[2] *Verney Memoirs.*

towards the end of Elizabeth's reign, the Dean used to send for the older boys at night and keep them till eleven o'clock, teaching them Greek and Hebrew. John Brinsley in *Ludus Literarius*, published in 1612, says the children of this school were allowed a quarter of an hour for recreation or breakfast at nine o'clock in the morning and a further fifteen minutes at three o'clock in the afternoon. This he considers a wise arrangement, but he hastens to add that "very great care is to be had in moderating their recreation. For schools, generally, do not take more hindrance by any one thing than by over-often leave to play." To modern eyes the danger does not appear very acute, for the hours he advises are from six o'clock in the morning until half-past five at night, with two hours off in the middle of the day for dinner. One half-holiday a week was allowed, usually on a Thursday, with an occasional extra afternoon on a holy day, or to mark some special event.

A love of learning was not confined to the gentry. Many yeomen's sons attended the local Grammar School, or were coached by the parish priest before going on to the University. This often represented a genuine sacrifice on the part of the father, for clever boys frequently passed into the ministry, or took up some other calling which drew them away from the farm. Their sisters had not quite the same opportunities, for most of the free schools were closed to them, but many could read and write, and money was often left by their parents for their education "according to their degree and calling". What exactly was meant by this is not clear, but since in some wills the purchase of books is expressly mentioned, it seems as though reading was thought a necessary accomplishment in addition to needlework and a knowledge of domestic matters.

Less wealthy farmers contented themselves with sending their children for a year or two to the local dame school. Such schools were often taught by a woman, or by some master who had elected to settle in the village and open a school there. It was not considered a disgrace in simple circles to be unable to read and write, but most men above the rank of labourer desired their children to have some education, if only to be able to read the Bible and understand such necessary documents as a written indenture or a will. So much learning the village school could provide, and for the unambitious it was enough. Breton was probably expressing a view widely held in rural communities when he made his countryman say

> . . . this is all we go to school for; to read common Prayers at church and set downe common prises at Markets; write a letter and make

a Bond; set downe the day of our Births, our Marriage day, and make our Wills when we are sicke for disposing of our goods when we are dead; these are the chief things that we meddle with.[1]

Those who had not even this little knowledge depended upon the local clergyman or schoolmaster to help them in any difficulty that might arise, and these, says Breton, "for our plaine matters will serve our turnes well enough."

Boys who were destined for the universities matriculated at twelve or thirteen in Tudor times, at sixteen in the later part of the seventeenth century. A few waited until they were two or three years older but this was not usual. Francis Legh was eighteen when he went to Oxford in 1608, but his brother Thomas, who went with him, was only fourteen. Peacham deplored the custom of sending young lads into a new, strange world, away from the supervision of father or schoolmaster, but his ideas on education generally were in advance of his time, and there were but few who agreed with him. "Many fathers," he says, "take them from school too early, as birds out of the nest before they be flidge", and he goes on to complain that "these young things have no more care than to expect the carrier, and where to sup Fridaies or fasting nights; no further thought of Study than to trim up their Studies with pictures, and place the fairest Bookes in openest view, which, poore lads, they scarce ever open or understand."[2] Custom, however, and the uncertainties of two difficult centuries, made men of striplings and women of little girls, and most parents considered that a boy who might have the cares of matrimony upon him at sixteen was quite old enough to begin the last stage of his education at an age when to-day he would still be in the lower forms of his public school.

Moreover, undergraduates lived under a very strict rule. After the confusion and disorder of the first years of the Reformation, when for a time it seemed as though they might perish with the monasteries, and the seesaw changes of Edward's and Mary's reigns, the universities took on a new lease of life under Elizabeth. Commissioners were appointed to procure such reforms as were necessary; a firmer discipline and a more orderly system of matriculation were introduced, and the number of students which, for various reasons, had somewhat declined in the previous reigns, increased steadily as the position improved. The choice of a college was often dictated by the student's birthplace, men

[1] N. Breton, *The Courtier and the Countryman*, 1618.
[2] H. Peacham, *The Compleat Gentleman*. 1622.

from a particular county preferring to go to a college where they would meet others from the same districts and hear the familiar local accents and phrases that were then used by gentle and simple alike. At Oxford, Cheshire students usually went to Brasenose, those from Buckinghamshire to Magdalen, and Westmorland lads to the Queen's; in 1571 Jesus College was founded by Hugh Price mainly for the benefit of Welsh students.

Undergraduates were expected to keep their terms without interruption and to work hard throughout their time of residence. Peacham feared that they would be "caught up like young lapwings by the sweetness of Libertye and varietie of Company", but to modern eyes the liberty allowed would not have been very conspicuous. Students were forbidden to go to taverns or fairs, to play cards or dice except in the twelve days of Christmas, to keep dogs or hawks, or to wear their hair long. They were strictly confined to their colleges for most of the time, and could not go about the town unless they were accompanied by their tutor or an M.A. They had to be indoors at nine o'clock at night and, in many cases, slept under their tutor's eye in truckle beds in his room. Those who broke the rules were punished by fines, impositions, or a beating; in extreme cases they might be expelled, but rustication was not usual because of the difficulties of travel.

Work went on from five o'clock in the morning, when the Chapel Bell was rung, until five or six at night when, after evening chapel, the students went to supper. The intervening hours were spent in attending lectures, taking part in disputations, and studying with their tutors. In many colleges the small rooms now used as bedrooms were studies, the present sitting-rooms being the "great chambers" in which tutors and students slept together. The instruction given was, like that of the schools, mainly classical, but theology, philosophy, cosmography, and mathematics, were all important subjects. Cosmography included astronomy and geography, which do not appear to have been taught at home or in the schools. "I have not initiated you into the science of Geography," wrote Mr. Crowther to Ralph Verney, then aged seventeen and still at Oxford. In another letter he sends him a genealogy of kings, presumably to help him in his history studies, and urges him to spend three or four hours every day on logic and divinity. Third-year students at Oxford were required to read Moral Philosophy and Greek and Bachelors reading for their M.A. had to study metaphysics, geometry, Greek, and ancient history. The Elizabethan Statutes for both Universities also provided for lectures in Medicine, Civil Law, Dialectic, and Rhetoric.

In their leisure hours undergraduates were allowed to ride, if they had horses, to swim, wrestle, tilt, and go hawking, but bathing, for some reason, was forbidden, and ball games were not encouraged, though tennis seems to have been permitted. Tutors had sets of pupils known as "companies", and over these they presided with all the watchful care of a father. It was usual for them to keep their charges' money and pay all their expenses. "Your older sonne thinks he should keepe his own money," wrote Richard Taylor to Sir Peter Legh in 1612, "wch I hold highly inconvenient, for experience hath taught me that some young gentlemen can hardly be kept in anie order, let them but have an angel or two in their purse."[1] Francis Legh was then twenty-two years old and might reasonably be thought capable of managing his own affairs, but evidently it was not customary, for Taylor goes on to say that "it would breed me a great trouble with the rest of my scholars & bring such an ataxie and disorder among them that I could not easily remove."

Thirty pounds a year was the sum allowed by Sir Peter Legh for the maintenance of each of his sons in the early years of James I's reign. Their tutor considered this inadequate, but in spite of constant applications he was not able to extract more from the careful baronet. Out of it he had to pay for their board and lodging, their clothes, and such pocket-money as their father saw fit to allow them. In one letter he refers also to £15 paid "for discharging their admission and makeing their gowns at the first", and later to £26 for "charge of proceedings and some formalities for your younger sonne." In all he spent £139 5*s.* 2*d.* on the two boys during their first two years of residence. A little later in the century Sir Edmund Verney undertook to allow his son £40 a year and to pay for his gown. He wrote also to inquire about the tutor's fees, and young Edmund answered that he had "asked Mr. Sessions what it were fit for me to give my Tutor. He told me Mr. Jones gives him £1 5*s.* the quarter, and that he would advise me to give him the lyke."[2] Certainly the tutors earned whatever money they received, for, in addition to looking after the physical and moral welfare of their charges, they must have spent much time in accountancy and in writing reports and letters to the parents.

Nevertheless, in spite of rules almost monastic in their severity, undergraduates managed then, as now, to indulge in occasional wild pranks and to enjoy themselves very heartily. If their amusements were often more boisterous than wise, that was only to be expected of such young lads in an age that was far more

[1] Lady Newton, *The House of Lyme.* [2] *Verney Letters*, ed. 1930.

rough than our own. Even the Seniors sometimes fell from grace, for we read of a Lincoln Fellow confined to the Bocardo for debt in 1550, and a sad fight between two graduates in 1685, when one bit off a piece of the other's nose. There were constant complaints of the students' idleness, their hard drinking, their addiction to pleasures of all kinds rather than study. "Is this the antient Discipline of that Universitye for Schollers," wrote the Oxford Chancellor, Lord Leicester, in 1582, ". . . to learne indeed nothing ells but to jelt in the streets and to tipple in Tavernes?" The Puritan Sir Simmonds D'Ewes, himself a student of St. John's, Cambridge, in 1620, complained of the number of stage plays in which his fellows took part, and declared that he wearied of his College because of the rioting, drinking and swearing that went on there. Anthony Wood blamed King James's visit in 1605 for an increase of drinking at Oxford, for, he says, "in the days of Queen Elizabeth it was little or nothing practised (sack being then taken rather for a cordial than a usual liquor, sold also for that purpose in apothecaries' shops) and a heinous crime it was to be overtaken with drink or smoake tobacco."[1] Lord Leicester, probably, would not have agreed with him. Oxford, indeed (and no doubt Cambridge also) seems never to have been quite what it was. After 1650 the coffee-houses were blamed for the decay of study, and it is interesting to note that in 1935 a retiring scout of Wadham College declared that "the place has never been the same since we have had women and coffee shops."

The Renaissance and its accompanying zeal for learning brought a great increase in the number of wealthy students at both universities. Harrison complains that the colleges had been "erected by their founders at the first for poore men's sons, whose parents were not able to bring them unto learninge; but now they have the least benefit of them, by reason the rich do so encroach upon them."[2] Poor scholars there still were in plenty, but there were also Gentlemen Commoners and ordinary Commoners at Oxford, Fellow Commoners and Pensioners at Cambridge, and Noblemen in both places. Gentlemen and Fellow Commoners were allowed special privileges, such as the right to be addressed as "Mr." and to have their own table; in Charles II's reign they were given a distinctive badge which was denied to ordinary undergraduates and Bachelors. Noblemen had even greater privileges and were allowed to wear coloured gowns, forbidden to all other students, and a gold hat-band.

[1] Anthony Wood, *The Life and Times of Anthony Wood.*
[2] W. Harrison, *op. cit.*

There were also Servitors and Sizars who paid for their education by service instead of fees, a system which had its advantages since it permitted poor boys who were not eligible for free places to take their degrees and not infrequently to become Fellows.

These distinctions, so alien to the ideas of our own day, suited the notions of the time. Just as in the grammar schools the sons of squires sat side by side with the sons of their fathers' farming tenants, so in the university nearly all the divisions of contemporary society were represented. Nobleman and Servitor, Commoner and Scholar, received exactly the same education, and there was no loss of social status in being a poor scholar, or paying one's way by menial work. It would, indeed, have been unsafe to look down upon the free scholars on the grounds of poverty for, if contemporary complaints are to be believed, many of them were not poor men at all. Harrison declares that

> in some grammar schooles likewise, which send scholars to these universities, it is lamentable to see what bribery is used; for, ere the scholar can be preferred, such bribage is made that poor men's children are commonly shut out, and the richer sort received (who in times past thought it dishonour to live as it were upon almes).[1]

How much truth there was behind this accusation it is difficult to say. Probably, like many of Harrison's complaints, it was somewhat exaggerated, but there seems to have been a growing tendency for people of middle status to crowd in upon places originally designed for the really poor. In 1549 a Royal Commission found it necessary to enforce the poverty clauses at All Souls, Oxford, with a stern reminder that all colleges had been built for the children of the poor. In the latter part of the seventeenth century an evil custom crept in of granting degrees more easily to men of rank than to poor scholars. In 1671 Anthony Wood wrote bitterly that "Poor folks' sons study hard, and with much ado obtain their degrees in Arts and a fellowship, but now nobelmen's sons are created *Artium Magistri* for nothing, get fellowships and canonries for nothing, and deprive others more deserving of their bread."[2] But on the whole the system worked well enough. It provided opportunities of learning for all conditions of men and made each university a real mirror of the national life. It allowed all classes to mix freely at an impressionable age, and gave the poor man a chance of advancement not to be found in any other sphere. It was not until the nineteenth century that Noblemen, Gentlemen Commoners and Servitors

[1] W. Harrison, *op. cit.*

[2] Anthony Wood, *The Life and Times of Anthony Wood*, coll. A. Clark, 1904.

finally vanished from the scene. By then they had become an anachronism, but even so the change was not brought about without some opposition. There were many who, like Mr. Gladstone, deplored their passing, not only from a natural love of old ways, but also because they sincerely believed the ancient divisions provided a very valuable lesson in the structure of society, and were not without their uses in the formation of character.

Chapter V

MARRIAGE

A TUDOR or Stuart marriage was a matter of family policy rather than romance. The modern belief in freedom of choice and the necessity of romantic love as a basis of married happiness would have been quite incomprehensible to the parents of that age, and even the young people seem to have had some doubts upon the matter. Dorothy Osborne, who remained faithful against much opposition to the man she loved, and married him in the end, could yet write in all seriousness that

> to marry for love were no reproachful thing if we did not see that of the thousand couples that do it, hardly one can be brought for an example that it may be done, and not repented of afterwards. Is there anything thought so indiscreet, or that makes one more contemptible?[1]

She was herself to provide one of these rare examples when, after her father's death, she married Sir William Temple and was completely happy with him, but there is no doubt that in this letter she was expressing the general opinion of her time.

Love as a serious consideration in match-making did not come into fashion until the end of the eighteenth century, or a little later. Before then it was a matter for the poets; marriage, on the other hand, was the concern of the parents, and love between those most intimately affected was looked for after, not before the wedding. Amongst the poor a greater freedom of choice was possible, for there was no property to be considered. The young people could follow their fancy unhampered by family ambition or prestige, though even here it is probable that matter-of-fact qualities like steadiness in the man and housewifely ability in the woman counted quite as much as more superficial attractions. Such liberty was not for the gently-born. It was the father's duty to choose a suitable partner for his son or daughter, and to do it in such a way that he settled the child well in life and at the same time enhanced the wealth and dignity of the family. This was one of the great responsibilities of parenthood, and to neglect it would have seemed as reprehensible as failing to clothe or educate a child.

Finance and the proper disposal of property were the chief

[1] *Letters of Dorothy Osborne* ed. G. A. Parry, 1914.

considerations; if the betrothed couple were fond of each other, that was an added advantage, but it was not a matter of primary importance. Very often, indeed, they were too young to have any strong views on the subject. The law permitted the marriage of girls at twelve years of age and of boys at fourteen. By custom both were usually older when the actual ceremony took place, but fifteen was not an uncommon age for the bride and sixteen or thereabouts for the groom. A woman still unmarried at twenty-one was an exception, and such delay was usually due to the poverty of her parents or to some unusual circumstance in her own or her father's life.

Plans for an alliance between great families might be made soon after the birth of a child, and betrothals at a very early age were not unusual. Robert Barre, of Backford, was pledged to Elizabeth Rogerson in 1538 when he was only three years old, and it is perhaps not surprising that he had to be "lured for an apple bie his uncle to goe to the church." Little Mary Villiers, one of Charles I's wards, was barely out of the nursery when she was contracted to the Earl of Montgomery; she was only nine when, after the Earl's death, Endymion Porter saw her climbing trees in her widow's weeds and pretending to be a bird. In 1639 Mary Blacknall was married to Ralph Verney when she was only thirteen and her bridegroom not quite sixteen. Fifty-six years later the young Duke of Bedford, then aged fourteen-and-a-half, escaped from his doubtless tedious wedding banquet to play in the garden with his thirteen-year-old bride, Elizabeth Howland. Some hours later, when the missing children were being anxiously sought for by the guests, he was seen returning alone to the house, while the newly made Duchess, having in the course of play torn the beautiful lace of her gown to ribbons, was hiding from the anticipated scolding in a barn. After such early marriages as these, the girl usually returned to her mother and the boy to his studies until they were old enough to live together as man and wife.

Although both sons and daughters were expected to accept the arrangements made for them, it was not customary to force a boy or girl to marry anyone who was absolutely distasteful. Sons were nearly always given the right of refusal, if they were old enough to exercise it, and a loved daughter was only rarely constrained to marriage she actively disliked. The father's powers were wide, but public opinion no less than natural affection forbade their too arbitrary use. "I crye out upon forcement in Marriage, as the extreamest bondage that is," wrote George Whetstone[1] in 1582, and Thomas Fuller in *The Holy State* advised

[1] George Whetstone, *An Heptameron*, 1582.

strongly against it because " 'tis to be feared that they that marry where they do not love will love where they do not marry." Dorothy Osborne had to wait until her Royalist father's death before she could marry her William, who was of the opposite political camp, but she was not compelled to accept any other suitor. Even Mary Blacknall's uncles stipulated that she should not be forced into marriage against her will, but should be allowed to consent or refuse when she was old enough to do so. Thirteen may not appear to us a sufficient age for such a decision, but childhood was shorter then, and the Court of Wards which was finally responsible for the little orphan evidently saw no objection to the arrangement. In this case the guardians were justified by the issue, for hers was one of those marriages which, though entirely mercenary in conception, yet turned out an unqualified success. Family affection was a strong bond, and few parents, however stern or ambitious, were prepared to condemn their children to an obviously unhappy life, though many were willing to go to great lengths to prevent what they considered unsuitable matches.

Then as now, a determined young person was often able to wear down the resistance of older relatives. In 1634 William, Lord Russell, the Earl of Bedford's heir, announced that he wished to marry Anne Carr, and that he would have her or no one. He was then twenty-one and she nineteen; they had known each other as children and were very deeply in love. The Earl refused even to consider such an alliance, and perhaps in this instance his reluctance is understandable. Anne's mother was the notorious Countess of Somerset, once Countess of Essex, who had freed herself from her first marriage with the help of Simon Forman, a noted conjurer and worker in magic. This man had supplied her with charms and philtres to render her husband impotent and so enabled her to bring a successful suit of nullity against him. After her second marriage she turned again to witchcraft, and this time the matter was more serious. She was accused of murdering Sir Thomas Overbury by poison, her accomplice being Anne Turner, another purveyor of charms. Both women were brought to trial and convicted in 1616, but the Countess was afterwards pardoned by James I. A more undesirable mother-in-law than this woman, a confessed murderess and a witch, it would be hard to find, especially in an age when all believed in witchcraft and some thought it hereditary, and it is not surprising that the Earl was determined to protect his heir from the possible consequences of such a marriage.

But if he was firm, so was his son. To all his father's remonstrances he turned a deaf ear, but even so, he did not attempt to marry without that father's consent. Three years were to elapse before he was finally permitted to have his way, and perhaps he would not have had it then if Charles I had not used his influence on behalf of the lovers. The Earl demanded a dowry of twelve thousand pounds, a great sum which he may have hoped the girl's father, impoverished by the expenses of his wife's trial, would not be able to pay. But it was promised and part of it paid, and on 11 July 1637, William and Anne were married in London. Except perhaps on the financial side (for the balance of the dowry does not seem to have been forthcoming) the Earl never had cause to repent the permission so hardly wrung from him. The marriage was a complete success, and in the course of time he became extremely fond of his once unwanted daughter-in-law.

Piers Legh, of Lyme, who fell in love with another Anne, was not so fortunate. She was the daughter of Sir John (afterwards Lord) Savile, of Pontefract, and was apparently well fitted by rank and character to marry into the Cheshire family. Unfortunately her dowry was small and her father's politics differed from those of Sir Peter Legh, who refused his consent to the marriage and obstinately adhered to that decision. After seven years of fruitless argument Piers, who was then thirty years old, lost patience and married the girl without his father's permission. Sir Peter never forgave him, and he does not appear ever to have seen his son again, though pride constrained him to make some provision for the support of the young couple. When Piers died in 1624, leaving three daughters and an infant son, the grandfather claimed the boy and brought him up at Lyme. His mother was only allowed to see him at stated intervals. Unlike Anne Carr, she never succeeded in winning her hostile father-in-law's affection and her visits to Lyme were not very frequent. In a pathetic little letter to Francis Legh she asks after "littell Peter" and begs his uncle to "send me word if he learne his Booke well, say his prayers dayly, please his grandfather, and carry himself to all as is fitting, which I shall be glad to heare of him—may God bless him."[1]

Suitable marriages for daughters were sometimes difficult to arrange if the father was not wealthy. A sufficient dowry was a necessity without which few well-bred girls could hope to marry, and in that age of large families it was not always easy to find it. The alternatives to marriage were not attractive. There was no career open to women above the rank of servants, and a portionless

[1] Lady Newton, *The House of Lyme.*

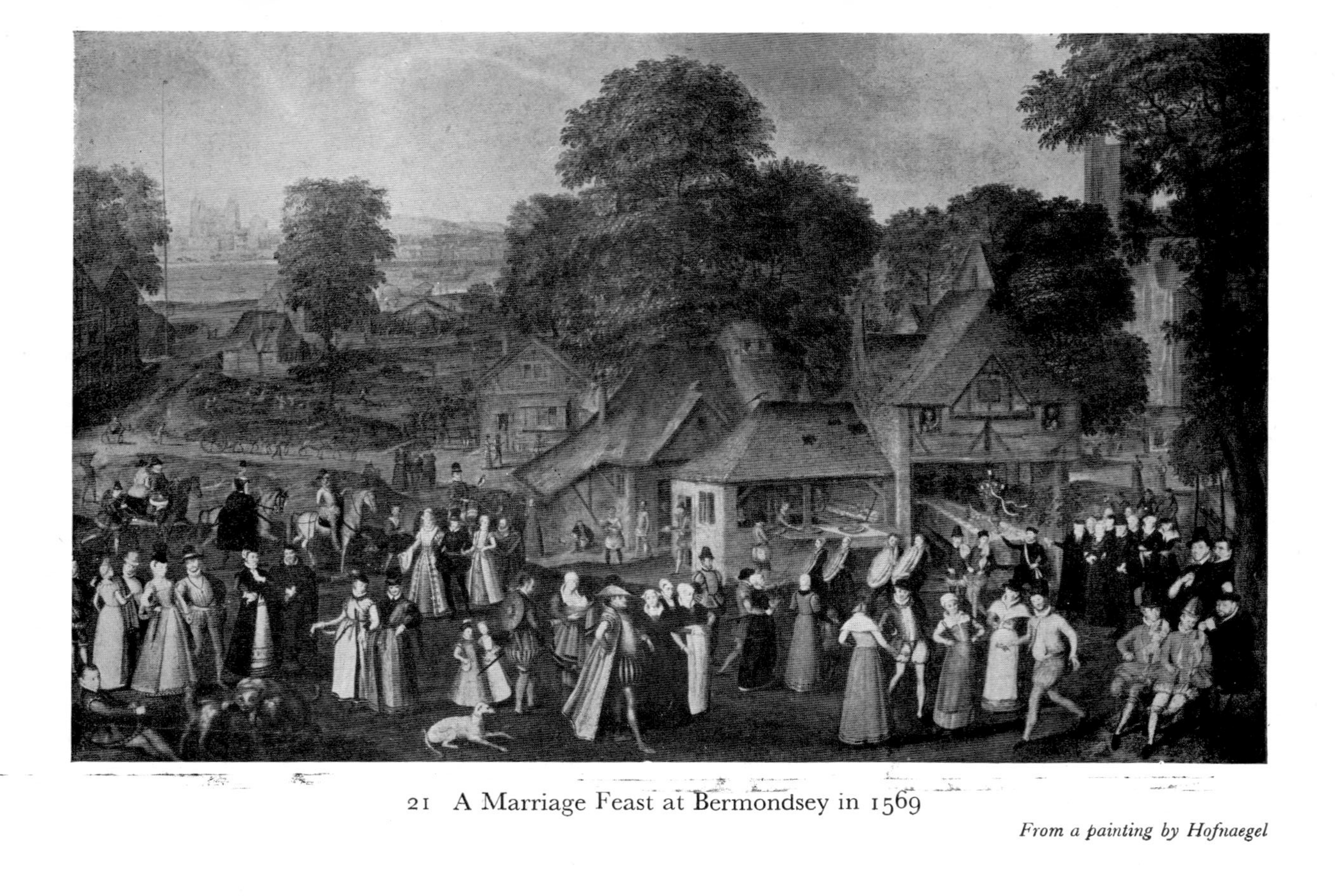

21 A Marriage Feast at Bermondsey in 1569

From a painting by Hofnaegel

22, 23 Ladies' Dresses of the early Seventeenth Century

From portraits by Hollar and Gheeraerts

24 A Boy of 1626

From a portrait by Geo. Geldorp

25 James I, aged eight (in 1574)

From a portrait by an unknown artist

girl had no prospects before her but a life of dependence at home, or a position as companion or "waiting gentlewoman" to some richer relative. Almost any marriage must have seemed better than this; the wife of even the most uninteresting husband had at least an assured position and was mistress in her own sphere, which was more than could be said for a spinster. It was doubtless this fact, quite as much as the teachings of their elders, which accounted for the cheerful acceptance of arranged marriages by girls who were very far from being uneducated nonentities or characterless dolls. Only as wives and mothers could they hope to use their undoubted capabilities and take their proper place in the life of their age.

The dowry system obtained amongst yeomen also, but here perhaps it was not quite such a burden. This was a period when many yeomen were rising rapidly in wealth and importance and yet kept for the most part to their natural simplicity of living, so that it was often easier for them to provide good portions for their daughters than it was for the poorer members of the class next above them. Such girls often married well, either men of their own rank and equal wealth, or one of the smaller squires who thus acquired a capable wife and at the same time strengthened his estates with her dowry. Class distinctions at that period were ungrudgingly recognized, but they were not so rigid as they had once been or as they were to be again. The younger sons of gentlemen were apprenticed to trade without loss of caste; the sons of yeomen frequently became lawyers or clergymen, made money as merchants, or passed imperceptibly into the ranks of the landed gentry by the acquisition of estates. Gentry and yeomanry were united by a common interest in the land, and in marriages between them the advantages were mutual.

Nor was it always the husband who came from the higher class. There were many instances in Tudor and Stuart times of squires' daughters marrying yeomen with the full consent of their families and complete satisfaction to themselves. Such matches often hastened the gradual rise in status of those yeomen who had the money to support a better position. His marriage to a gentleman's daughter was one of the claims put forward by Shakespeare's father when he applied for the right to bear arms. In Henry VIII's reign Richard Barker, of Hoo, whose father had been a simple maker of "treen dishes, ladelles and potledes", considered himself entitled to be styled a gentleman because he had married Sir Luke Walter's sister, and brought an action in the Court of Star Chamber against someone who had called him a yeoman. It was not until the eighteenth century that

social divisions became so clearly marked as to make such unions impossible and set up an almost impassable barrier between farm or counting-house and the manor. That Jane Austen's heroines should have been ashamed of their relatives who were in trade, and her Emma unable to call upon Harriet once she had married a farmer would have seemed merely funny to the average man of the earlier period, if indeed he had been able to grasp exactly where the difficulty lay.

The negotiations between two wealthy families were often extremely complicated and sometimes dragged on for months or even years before a satisfactory conclusion was reached. In the domestic sphere also vast preparations were needed. A large part of the bride's trousseau was made at home, though the more elaborate items would probably be bought in London or the nearest town. Her house-linen also was mainly of home manufacture, since most households spun their own flax and wool, and a well-filled bride-chest contained much napery made beforehand by the mother and her maids. In kitchen, stillroom, and brewhouse, the servants were busily employed for weeks before the wedding, preparing for the banquets which formed part of the celebrations. A marriage was then a gay and colourful affair in every class and lavish hospitality was the rule. The Reformation modified the religious rites to some extent, lessening the importance of the earlier betrothal and shifting the first part of the ceremony from the porch to the body of the church, but it was powerless to sweep away the ancient, jovial customs which had grown up round them. Even in the most sober families a wedding was an excuse for much rejoicing of a hearty and vigorous kind which often went on for several days and sometimes as long as a week or more.

In the sixteenth and early seventeenth centuries the bride wore her hair loose, with a circlet of myrtle or corn-ears, or a more elaborate crown such as that mentioned in the Churchwardens' Accounts for St. Margaret's, Westminster, when £3 10*s.* was paid in 1540 to "Alice Lewis, a goldsmith's wife of London, for a serclett to marry maydens in." Her dress was usually white or russet in colour. Stow tells us how Princess Elizabeth, James I's daughter, went to her marriage in 1613 "attired all in white, having her hair hanging down in faire and seemly tresses."[1] Knots of coloured ribbons were sewn on the bodice, skirt and sleeves of the wedding-dress and these the young men of the party pulled off after the ceremony to wear in their hats as bride-favours. Gloves and scarves were important items of dress for

[1] J. Stow, *Survey of London*, Strype's edition.

everyone. The guests all wore bright-coloured scarves, and fringed and gauntleted gloves were given by the bridegroom to his friends and sometimes to the officiating clergyman as well. The bride's gloves were usually very elaborate and were afterwards given to the bride-men who led her to the church. The ring used might be either a jewelled or enamelled hoop with a motto inscribed inside, or a gimmal ring consisting of two hoops which could be separated. At the formal betrothal one half was given to the girl and the other to the man, and the two parts were then united again on the marriage day to form a single wedding-ring. Plain gold rings, such as are worn to-day, began to come in about the middle of the seventeenth century when Puritan influences were at their height.

In country districts the path to the church was strewn with flowers and rushes, and along it the bride was led by two bachelors who acted as her bride-men. The groom was led in by the bridesmaids who carried gilded branches of rosemary, the flower of love and constancy. The Reformation swept away the lengthy nuptial Mass, but the sermon was retained, and also the ancient custom of drinking wine with sops in it at the end of the ceremony. The married pair and the witnesses all partook of this; sometimes a sprig of rosemary was dipped into it before they drank. The cups used were often kept in the church for the purpose. In an inventory made about 1547 at Wilsdon we read of "two masers that were appointed to remayne in the church for to drynk at bride-ales", and such bowls are still to be found in some English churches.

When the procession returned home there was a banquet and entertainments of various kinds (21). "Then all the Company went home to the Bridge House to dinner," wrote Stow of a London wedding in 1562, "where there was as good cheer as ever was known, with all manner of Musick and Dancing all the remainder of the day; and at night a goodly Supper; and then followed a Masque until midnight."[1] In the villages the young men rode races for the bride's garters, or for a cake which the winner carried on a wooden sword or spear. In some districts the bride and groom were expected to leap over the louping-stone in the churchyard, or found their homeward way barred by a flowery garland over which they had to jump or pay forfeit. Ancient charms were consulted to see if they would be happy, and who would be the next to marry; in the North of England a plate of cake was broken over the bride's head as soon as she reached her home and omens for her future were read from the

[1] J. Stow, *Survey of London.*

broken pieces. At least two hearty meals were provided on the wedding day, with as much subsequent entertainment as the parents could afford. The poor overcame the difficulty of expense by holding bride-ales at which the newly married girl sold ale for as much as her friends could afford to pay, and every guest brought a contribution to the feast, "each one bringing such a dish, or so many, as his wife and he do consult upon."[1]

At night the sack posset, made of wine, milk, eggs, sugar, and spices, was prepared and drunk by all present with much hilarity. "When bed-time is come," says Misson, "the bride-men pull off the bride's garters, which she had before unty'd, that they might hang down, and so prevent a curious hand from coming too neer her knee. This done, and the garters being fasten'd to the hats of the gallants, the bridesmaids carry the bride into the bride chamber, where they undress her and lay her in the bed."[2] Meanwhile the groom was taken to another room to be similarly served by his friends. When both were in bed the company poured into the room to wish them joy, to fling the stocking and practise other traditional rites until the time came to draw the curtains and leave the married pair in peace. "We saw Sir Richard and his fine Lady wedded," wrote Edmund Verney in 1675, "and flung the stocking and then left them to themselves, and so in this manner ended the celebration of this Marriage à la mode,"[3] though not for the guests, apparently, for he goes on to say that afterwards there was "Music, Feasting, Drinking, Revelling, Dancing and Kissing" until a very late hour. In the morning bride and groom were awakened by the local musicians who came at daybreak to play beneath their window. There was then no honeymoon, nor any idea that husband and wife might wish to spend a little time alone together. They had all the rest of their lives for that. Usually the first few weeks after the wedding were spent with the girl's family, but when she left her father's house at last it was to go directly to her new home and assume the responsibilities which must often have seemed rather terrifying to a wife not yet out of her teens.

During the Commonwealth the religious significance and the secular rejoicings of marriage were both heavily overlaid. The use of the Book of Common Prayer was forbidden, and church weddings were replaced by marriages before a civil magistrate. The banns were sometimes called in the parish church, but quite as often at the market cross. A marriage certificate of 1651 states that

[1] W. Harrison, *op. cit.* [2] M. Misson's *Travels in England.*
[3] *Verney Memoirs.*

Marmaduke Inman and Prudence Lowcock, both of the parish of Knaresborough, were this day married together in Ripon, having first been published three several market-days, in the market-place, at Knaresborough, according to an act of parliament, and no exceptions made. In the presence of Thomas Davie and Anthony Simpson.[1]

It cannot be supposed that such drastic changes were acceptable to any but the most fanatical followers of the Commonwealth government. Religion and custom were both affronted, and a naturally conservative people were not easily converted to weddings drained alike of all spiritual feeling and all human colour. They were, however, forced to submit, for the government refused to acknowledge any other form as legally binding. In her autobiography Anne Murray, an ardent Royalist, describes her own marriage to Sir James Halkett in 1656. She relates how "conforme to the order of those that were then in power, who allowed of noe mariage lawfull butt such as were maried by one of there Justices," she went to the house of Justice Elkonhead in Woolwich where

> . . . the Justice performed what was usuall for him at that time, wch was only holding ye Directory in his hand, asked Sir James if hee intended to marry mee, hee answered Yes; and asked if I intended to marry him, I said Yes. Then says hee, "I pronounce you man and wife." So calling for a glass of sacke, hee drunk and wished much hapinese to us; and wee left him, having given his clarke mony, who gave in parchment the day and witnese and attested by the Justice that hee had maried us. Butt if it had nott beene done more solemnly afterwards by a minister I should not have beleeved it lawfully done.[2]

There must have been many who felt as she did in an age when the average man and woman was deeply concerned with religion. In her case she overcame the difficulty by a second marriage quietly performed by a Church of England clergyman "in my brother Newton's closett", and so conformed both to the laws of the Church and of the government then in power.

But whether the marriage took place before a priest or a magistrate, it was for life. Separation was possible, though it was rarely sought; divorce required an Act of Parliament for each individual case, and its extreme difficulty and expense made it an impracticable remedy for all but the most exceptional troubles. Ordinary people never thought about it at all, and few contemplated any interruption in their married lives but the

[1] J. S. Fletcher, *Memorials of a Yorkshire Parish*, 1917.
[2] *The Autobiography of Lady Anne Halkett* (Camden Society).

final one of death. It was perhaps this fact as much as any other which made most marriages so successful, even when they had been arranged by parents for purely mercenary reasons, and had been entered upon without any previous love between bride and groom. Both regarded it as an enduring contract which could not be broken, and both were ready to build their shared lives upon a firm foundation of mutual fidelity and tolerance.

Some failures there were, of course, since husbands were not always as kind as they might have been, nor wives as loving. Money was sometimes a cause of quarrel, especially when the marriage settlements had not been drawn up with sufficient care. The husband had complete control over his wife's money unless her rights had been protected beforehand, and occasionally he misused it and failed to provide adequately for her needs. Ambition also might lead to the neglect of wives, especially in Elizabeth's time, when the masculine nature of the Court caused many women to be left alone for long periods while their husbands were in London, or following the Queen about the country on her progresses. Nor were temperamental or religious differences easier to bear, particularly in an age when the husband was the master of the house in a very literal sense. Milton's young third wife was made so miserable by her renowned but dour husband that she left him, and only returned when she heard that he was paying over-much attention to the handsome daughter of Dr. Davies. Lady Falkland paid for her conversion to Catholicism by permanent exile from her husband's house and a life of poverty. Even the kindly Elias Ashmole had his matrimonial difficulties, for his second wife, Lady Mainwaring, sought a separation from him in 1655. That she was twenty years older than he and had a grown son who resented the marriage may have had something to do with it, but whatever the true cause, her husband seems to have been very aggrieved by her action. In his *Diary* he writes

> The cause between me and my wife was heard when Mr. Serjeant Maynard observed to the court that there were 800 sheets of depositions on my wife's part and not one word proved against me of using her ill or ever giving her a bad or provoking word.[1]

Yet in spite of this unhappy affair he was quite ready to marry again, and as soon as death had released him from his dissatisfied and unsatisfactory partner, he lost no time in taking a third wife with whom he seems to have lived quite contentedly.

Such cases were the exception to a happier rule, and though

[1] *Diary and Letters of Elias Ashmole*, ed. R. T. Gunther, 1927.

there may have been more unsuccessful marriages than we know of, the surviving letters and diaries of the time show how deep was the affection and confidence that often existed between man and wife. For all the husband's legal dominance, a woman was usually the trusted partner in all his affairs, his agent when he was away, and sometimes, during the Civil War, the actual defender of his property against armed despoilers. Lord Derby's wife defended Lathom House for many months in his absence and endured the harrowing experience of seeing a cannon ball burst into the room where her children were taking a meal. During the Commonwealth, Mary Verney returned alone from France to represent her husband when there was a chance of freeing Claydon from sequestration and did not rejoin him until, in spite of many difficulties, she had succeeded in her delicate task. Some wives, like Lady Fanshawe, followed their husbands through all their adventures and endured innumerable hardships and dangers whilst doing so. And whether in peace or war, there runs through the majority of surviving memoirs and letters the bright thread of love and fidelity. "Dearest Hart," writes Endymion Porter to his Olivia, and again, "My only Love," and signs himself "your true friend and loving husband." If Lady Brilliana Harley begins her letters to Sir Robert with "My deare Sir", she goes on to say in one of them, "I much longe to heare from you, but more a thousand times to see you, which I presume you will not believe because you cannot possibly measure my love."[1] When Lady Fanshawe, after being parted from her husband for a time, was at last able to rejoin him, she recorded happily that "We went by Bristol very cheerfully towards my North star, that only had the power to fix me";[2] and after fifty years of married life William Blundell was able to write, from a long experience of shared troubles, "as for this little groaning wife of my own, I think she will never fail me."[3]

[1] *Letters of Lady Brilliana Harley*, Camden Soc.
[2] Lady Fanshawe, *Memoirs*, ed. Sir M. H. Nicholas, 1829.
[3] M. Blundell, *Cavalier*, 1933.

Chapter VI

SICKNESS AND DEATH

THE shadow of death was never very far away from any household in the sixteenth and seventeenth centuries. Medical science was only just beginning to free itself from its mediaeval swaddling-bands, and the average physician still followed the ancient rules laid down by Hippocrates and Galen. Antiseptics and anæsthetics were alike unknown. If an operation had to be performed, the patient suffered tortures while it lasted, and though it was frequently successful, he often died afterwards from shock or gangrene. Infectious diseases ravaged the country and were regarded as Acts of God, or the result of corruption in the air or some peculiar aptness to the disease in the individual sufferer. The humoral doctrine still held sway, and on it the current theories of diet and treatment were based. Men's bodies were supposed to consist of four humours or fluids which made them sanguine, phlegmatic, choleric, or melancholy, according as one or another predominated in their make-up. An excess of any humour caused illness, and it was the physician's chief concern to preserve a proper balance between the four. This he did by cupping and bleeding (27), by administering drugs and by regulating diet, for all foodstuffs were thought to consist of the same elements and to lessen or increase particular fluids according to their nature. Semi-magical remedies were still used by doctors as well as laymen, and even the most learned believed that the stars influenced men's lives in sickness and in health. Sanitation was little regarded. Most doctors realized that disease flourished more easily where there was dirt, but it was beyond their powers to convince the ordinary man that many of his troubles were caused by his own insanitary habits, and the foul streets and poor drainage which he so cheerfully tolerated.

In the latter half of the seventeenth century, it is true, new conceptions of disease and treatment were in the air. Charles II's reign was distinguished by a great wave of scientific interest, an interest fostered and encouraged by the King who shared it, and exemplified by the curious and varied inquiries of the newly formed Royal Society. Men of learning everywhere were discovering the wonders of the physical world around them and devoting themselves to the study of minerals, birds, and plants, the movements of stars and tides, and the possibilities of mechanical

26 The Apothecary's Shop

27 Cupping and Bleeding

From contemporary engravings

SEVENTEENTH-CENTURY DOCTORS

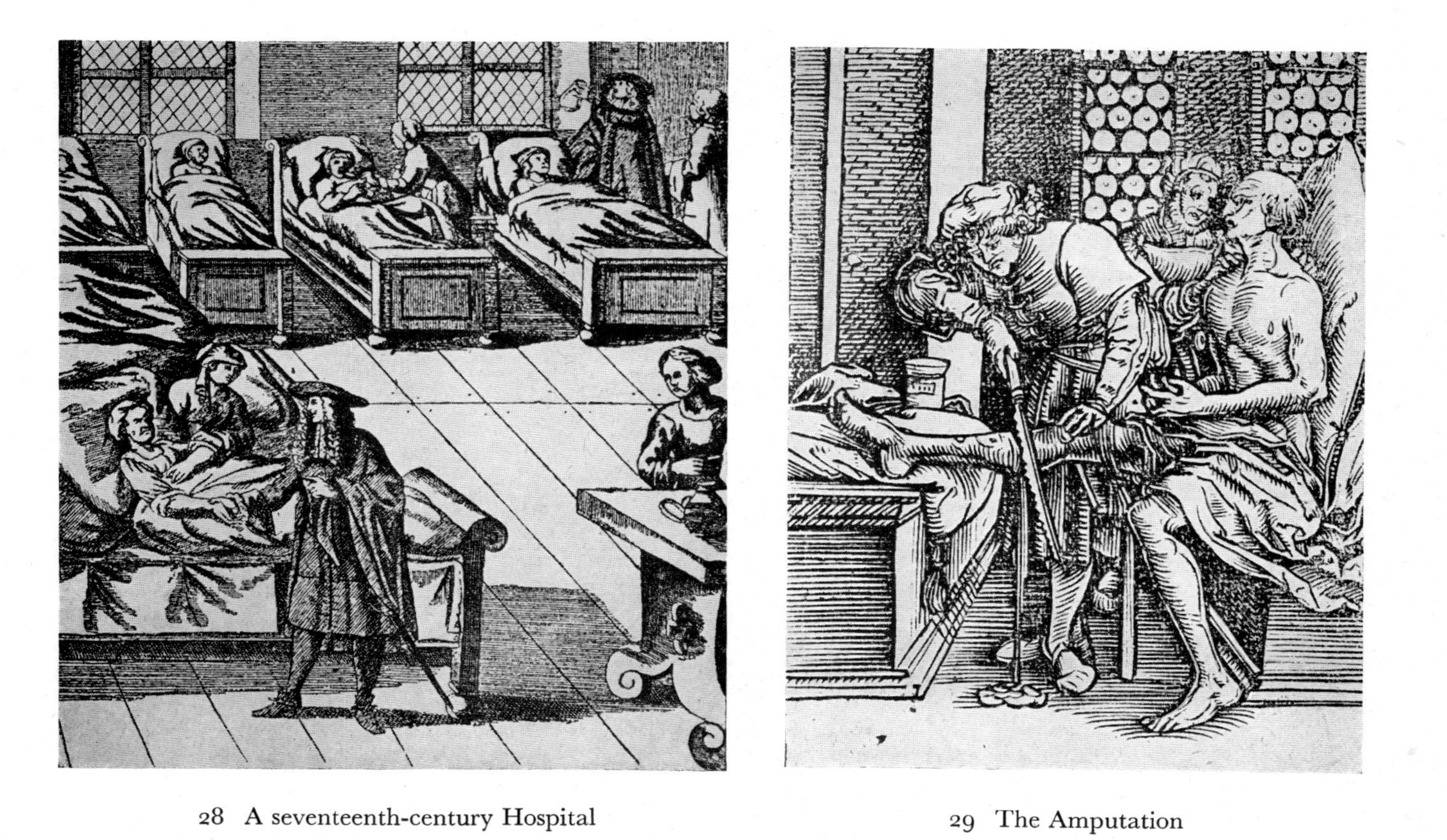

28 A seventeenth-century Hospital

29 The Amputation

invention. In this general search for truth medicine was not neglected. A group of progressive London doctors was struggling to shake off the trammels of ancient theories and to arrive at more certain ways of combating disease. Amongst them was Thomas Sydenham, who experimented with fevers and came to the revolutionary conclusion that much harm was done by over-nursing, and that the surest way of vanquishing Nature's ills was to follow in her footsteps. He decided to do nothing at all for his patients but to forbid them meat and fermented liquors, and he tells us that

> . . . and while I so watched the disease, it departed; slowly and safely—still it departed. From thence, therefore, I considered that this method should be applied to all other such cases as I might thenceforward have to treat; a fact of no small magnitude if we considered either the gravity of the symptom or the uniform success of the treatment.[1]

Such men, however, were exceptional even in his time, and still more so before it. Most doctors were quite content to use the well-worn remedies known to their predecessors and saw no reason to embark upon the dangerous seas of experiment and discovery. Such knowledge as they possessed was not sufficient to conquer the infectious fevers which constantly decimated the countryside. Plague and smallpox were rife, encouraged everywhere by dirt, ignorance, and the prevalence of fleas. Men were constantly reminded of the uncertainty of life by the news of friends and relatives struck down untimely, or by the more tragic sight of an empty cradle in their own homes. The death-rate amongst young children was appallingly high, and yearly child-bearing did little more than keep the population level. There were but few parents who never had to mourn a loved son or daughter, or more probably several. Only rarely could any woman hope to rear all her children, or herself survive to an advanced age in face of the general ignorance of such vital matters as diet, sanitation, and the causes of infection.

Cupping and bleeding were the standard remedies in almost every sort of disease. In an age of heavy eating and drinking, they were often useful enough, but they sometimes resulted in dangerously weakening the patient. Charles II's death was certainly hastened and perhaps caused by the drastic treatment he received from doctors only too anxious to save his life. Strong purges and emetics were also fashionable, and so was the rigid exclusion of fresh air from all sick rooms. A curious remedy for

[1] Thomas Sydenham, *Works*, I.

feverish illnesses was the application of a pigeon cut in half to the patient's feet; in some cases a bullock's melt or a sheep's lung was used instead. In 1603 Dr. Thomas Lodge used live pullets from which the tail feathers had been plucked to draw the venom from plague carbuncles. The birds were placed upon the sores until they became infected and died, and the treatment was repeated until the last bird escaped the contagion, after which it was believed that the patient would recover. This remedy was considered very efficacious during the epidemic of 1603, and sixty-two years later it was still the standard practice in the great plague of 1665.

The Dentist, 1568

Herbal infusions and decoctions were widely used both by official physicians and by housewives responsible for the health of their families. Every ailment was supposed to have a herb or herbs divinely appointed for its cure. Scurvy, which Dr. John Peachey described in 1696 as "the most reigning Disease in this Kingdom", was cured by the juice of scurvy-grass, or by fresh cuckoo-flower heads eaten as a cress. Houseleek juice mixed with cream was a first-aid remedy for burns or for the shingles; a conserve of cowslips, or palsy-worts, prevented madness and cured paralysis, conserve of violets eased a fever. Gerard recommended the roots of Royal Fern, boiled and taken in liquor, for wounds, and Nicholas Culpeper declared that the distilled water of may-flowers would draw out the most venomous thorn, "for the thorn giveth a remedy for his own pricking." John Hall, Shakespeare's son-in-law, who practised medicine in Warwicskhire from 1607 to 1635, treated his daughter for neuralgia with cloves, cinnamon, nutmegs, and pepper, infused in Acqua Vitae, and apparently cured her by this means. Another of his patients was relieved of a tertian ague by an emetic infusion mixed with syrup of violets. When Elias Ashmole "fell ill of a surfeit occasioned by drinking water after venison", he cured himself

by the simple process of holding a piece of briony root in his hand for a quarter of an hour. Infection was warded off by chewing rhubarb, lovage, or tobacco, or by the use of pomanders made of herbs and spices. Dr. Lodge also considered an Eastern hyacinth stone worn on the person to be useful for this purpose, and amulets of all kinds had a ready sale, though not all doctors approved their use.

The sick were nearly always nursed at home for the very good reason that hospitals (28) were rare and very bad. Few entered them who were not driven by dire poverty or the total lack of friends to tend them in their own houses. The treatment was extremely rough and ready, and those inmates who recovered probably did so more from the toughness of their own constitutions than from the nature of the help they received. The nurses were almost entirely ignorant and were not in fact required to have any real medical skill. It was sufficient if they could produce certificates of respectability and would conform to the not very exacting standards of cleanliness then obtaining. The patients were herded together, four or six in a bed, in wards which could rarely be properly cleansed because the size and arrangement of the beds made it almost impossible. There was no proper isolation of infectious cases, except for smallpox patients who were kept in separate wards, with their beds shrouded in red curtains, according to the ancient belief that red was a colour helpful to the sick. This was a custom followed in private houses as well as hospitals; fever patients were commonly dressed in red bed-gowns and surrounded by as many red objects as possible so that they might help their own recovery by looking at them.

Those suffering from bubonic or pneumonic plague were not admitted to ordinary hospitals but were either immured in their own houses or taken to the Pest-house, if one existed in their district. The City of London had such an institution in St. Giles', Cripplegate, built in 1594; it was totally inadequate for the needs of so large a town and remained the solitary plague hospital for Londoners from that year until the last epidemic in 1665. Another was built in 1642 in Tothill Fields for the citizens of Westminster, and later in the century three more came into being for people in the surrounding districts, one at Stepney, another at Marylebone, and a third in Soho Fields. Where there was no Pest-house, or when it was full, cabins were built on the outskirts of towns to accommodate the plague-stricken. The Congleton Corporation accounts for 1641 show that twopence a day was allowed there to people so confined, and fivepence daily to two wardens to supervise the cabins, and "one other for the streets,

to kill dogs."[1] Cats and dogs were believed to carry infection and were often destroyed in large numbers during an epidemic, with the lamentable result that the flea-bearing rat, the most serious danger, multiplied greatly in the absence of its natural enemies.

The plague was undoubtedly the most dangerous and the most justly dreaded of all the diseases which afflicted our ancestors. England was never entirely free from it from the time of the Black Death until after 1665. In isolated cases or virulent epidemics it constantly appeared in different parts of the country, particularly in towns and ports where overcrowding and insanitary habits made the residents specially susceptible to any sort of contagion. In Chester there were five serious outbreaks between 1507 and 1603, and another during the Civil War in which a quarter of the inhabitants died. London was hardly ever without some cases of plague throughout the Tudor period, and both the sixteenth and seventeenth centuries were marked by several violent epidemics. In 1603 thirty thousand people perished there; twenty-two years later came another and equally bad visitation, followed by a milder one in 1636. Thereafter the capital was comparatively free from this scourge until the last great outbreak in 1665, after which the disease rapidly declined and finally ceased to be a serious menace in any part of England.

The rapidity with which the plague carried off its victims was one of its most horrifying features. In some cases a few hours were all that was granted between the first signs of infection and death. Defoe tells us that in 1665 many fell dead in the streets who had not realized the plague was on them. Pepys records in his *Diary* how on 10 August 1665, he went home to make his will, "the town growing so unhealthy that a man cannot depend upon living two days." All who could fled from the stricken towns to the purer air of the country, but even there they were not always safe. James I's Court was forced to move constantly in 1603, for the plague followed them from place to place. In 1625 the little Cheshire township of Malpas suffered heavily as the result of infection supposed to have been brought from London by one of the villagers. The conditions in such small places were truly terrible, for few families were untouched, and hardly anyone remained to nurse the sick or bury the dead. The Malpas Parish Registers record how one man, Richard Bradley, feeling his end approaching, caused his nephew to dig a grave and line it with straw, and then, while he still had strength to reach it, laid down in it and so died. "This he did," says the compiler of the Register,

[1] J. Corry, *History of Macclesfield*, 1817.

"because he was a strong man and heavier than the said nephew and another wench could bury." In 1665 an even worse outbreak in Eyam almost depopulated the village, two hundred and fifty people dying out of a population of three hundred. In Dorset certain box hedges are still pointed out as the remains of many such planted in haste during the epidemics of the sixteenth and seventeenth centuries, in the belief that box kept away the contagion.

Antidotes to infection were many, but few were of much use except in so far as they gave courage to their users. Andrew Boorde wrote in 1542 that the surest method of escape was to leave the stricken town, but if that were impossible, sweet herbs should be burnt, a continual fire kept on the hearth, and all wine, cider, beer, and "gross meats", avoided. Henry VIII advised the use of sage, rue, elder and bramble leaves, stamped, and mixed with wine and ginger. "Take a spoonful of the same," says this receipt, "and you shall be safe for twenty-four days. Nine times taking of it is sufficient for a whole year by the Grace of God."[1] Rue was a popular preventive; it was laid along the window-sills to sweeten the air, and coaches were sometimes hung with it when their owners were forced to journey through plague-stricken streets. Dried ivy-berries, powdered and dissolved in vinegar, were considered useful, and in *The Charitable Physitian* (1639) Philbert Guibert recommended the use of scented candles made of wax, red roses, juniper, cloves, and other spices. But the most valued remedies were onions and unicorn's horn. The first were peeled and left for ten days in the house to absorb the infection from the air, or used as poultices for plague swellings; the second was mixed with angelica root and swallowed to expel venom and bring on perspiration. What exactly it was that passed as the horn of this mythical animal we do not know for certain, but large quantities were undoubtedly sold and used in complete faith that it was the genuine article.

No one then realized the connexion of rats and their fleas with the disease. Dogs found wandering in the streets were killed, but the rats which infested so many houses were ignored. Clothes were understood to carry contagion, and from time to time the authorities issued orders forbidding the sale of garments from infected houses until they had been well aired and left unused for three months. Straw and rushes also had to be burnt, and sometimes infected bedding was thrown into the river to prevent its further use by the survivors. In 1576 when plague broke out in Philip Antrobus' house at Northwich, all the household

[1] William Lovel, *The Duke's Desk,* newly revised, 1672.

linen was thus thrown away, an action which resulted in a claim for compensation sixteen years later. Both in Eyam and Congleton the outbreaks were attributed to boxes of clothes sent from tainted centres, and probably they were so caused if the garments harboured fleas. Though all stood in peril of it, it was the poor who suffered most from the plague, and this was mainly because their ramshackle houses provided a more congenial shelter for the black rat and its parasites than the stone or brick homes of the well-to-do.

Almost as deadly as the plague were the smallpox epidemics which from time to time overran the country. This disease was new in the early years of the sixteenth century, and seems then to have been comparatively mild and confined chiefly to children. In the following decades it steadily increased in virulence, and became so common that most people believed they were bound to catch it at some time or another. Thomas Sydenham considered its greater malignance in his day was due as much to the prevalent methods of nursing as to any other cause. The patient was confined in a heated room, with closed windows and drawn bed-curtains, and plied with cordials to make him sweat. Fresh air and cooling diets were Sydenham's own remedies, but they were only gradually adopted by his fellow-physicians, to most of whom air was anathema both then and for many years afterwards.

Because it was less dangerous in childhood, many parents deliberately put their children in the way of infection, believing they could hardly escape it altogether, and would do better to get it over early. In later life it was often fatal, and those who recovered frequently bore its ugly marks for the rest of their days. Pitted and ruined faces were all too common, and, for woman sufferers at least, the sharp fear of disfigurement must have been almost as keen as the fear of death. "My Lady Sunderland has them at Rufford," wrote Lady Savile in 1661, "which you may believe put that house in great disorder, and her Ladyship noe lesse, who will consider beauty to her latest day."[1] Poor Dorothy Osborne lost her looks in this way just before her marriage; it is pleasant to remember that it made no difference to the lover for whom she had waited so long, and he continued to adore her in spite of her marred face.

Another common trouble, more inconvenient than dangerous, was ague, for which many curious remedies were prescribed. "I took early in the morning a good dose of Elixir and hung three spiders about my neck," wrote Elias Ashmole in his *Diary*,

[1] Lady Newton, *The House of Lyme.*

"and they drove my ague away." Aubrey records that cinquefoil which had been gathered in certain aspects of the moon, powdered, and mixed with white wine, was believed by some to be efficacious. "With this receipt," he says, "one Bradley, a quaker at Kingston Wick upon Thames (near the bridge end) hath cured above a hundred."[1] Another healer in Bedfordshire used meadowsweet, with a little green wheat added. Doctors frequently prescribed violets in some form, or the distilled water of coltsfoot; and in the seventeenth century there was much argument amongst the learned as to whether Peruvian bark was, or was not, a proper remedy for this ailment.

Many children suffered from rickets, a disease first mentioned by name about 1620, though it probably existed in England before that date. Glisson in *De Rachitide* says it was more common among the well-to-do than the poor, and this may have been because the children of the poor drank more milk. In better-class circles milk was thought suitable only for infants and the very old, and a child was usually put on a diet of bread, soup and gruel as soon as it was weaned. Little John Verney seems to have suffered from rickets in 1647, for his mother writes to her husband

> For Jack his leggs are most miserable, crooked as ever I saw any child's, and yett thank god he goes very strongly and is very strayte in his body as any child can bee.[2]

Another Verney child was sent to Utrecht to be cured of "crookedness" by Dr. Skatt who specialized in such cases. His method was to strap the child in an iron and leather corselet from which he was released only once a week in order to change his shirt. A less drastic remedy known to country people in Norfolk was eating ravens' livers. Dr. Thomas Fuller speaks of a woman in the West of England who "hath happily healed many, by cauterizing the Vein behind the ear."[3] How far these remedies were efficacious we cannot tell, but certainly some died of the disease. The London Bills of Mortality mention fourteen deaths from this cause in 1634 and between four and five hundred annually in the three years from 1658 and 1660. It seems probable that John Evelyn's gifted little son died of it also, for the unhappy father tells us that he had the body opened and found the child was "liver-grown", a term which seems to have been used at one time for a rachitic condition.

When death approached, the pillow was drawn from under

[1] J. Aubrey, *Miscellanies*, 1696. [2] *Verney Memoirs.*
[3] Thomas Fuller, *Good Thoughts in Bad Times, Together with Good Thoughts in Worse Times*, 1649.

the dying man's head to ease his passing, for it was a general belief that no one could die who lay upon feathers. The passing bell was tolled "to admonish the living . . . of any that are dying, thereby to meditate of their own deaths, and to commend the other's weak condition to the mercy of God", as the Articles of Visitation for the Diocese of Worcester put it in 1662. During the Commonwealth this practice was regarded with suspicion, as savouring of popery, and in some parishes it was given up, but like church weddings, it was too firmly rooted in the traditional life of the country to be lost altogether, and it was restored with the monarchy. When all was over the corpse was decently laid out and wrapped in a white shroud of wool or linen. An Act of Parliament in 1666 ordered that all shrouds should be woollen and levied fines for any breach of this regulation, but some families clung to the finer material and cheerfully paid the fine rather than forgo the privilege of burying their dead in linen shifts.

The period of mourning was then very long and, to modern eyes, rather terrible in its unrelieved gloom. The principal rooms and the staircase were swathed in black hangings, and the beds dressed with black curtains, counterpane, and blankets. Some families possessed a special mourning bed and lent it round to their connexions whenever a death occurred in any related house. In it the head of the household slept and, when the best bed stood in the parlour or Great Chamber, sat upon it to receive the condolences of his friends. Black clothes devoid of any touch of white or colour were worn for a long time. Three years was not considered too long for a parent, and widows sometimes wore their heavy black veils for the rest of their lives unless they married again. The effect of so much material darkness upon minds already shadowed by grief must have been depressing in the extreme, but to curtail the period of mourning or omit any of the prescribed customs would have been considered disrespectful to the dead, and quite out of the question in any family of good standing.

Funerals were surrounded with as much pageantry as possible and were often very costly. Mourning suits, rings, scarves, and gloves, were given to friends and relatives, doles of money or gifts in kind distributed to the poor. At the funeral of Sir Walter Calverley's sister, sixty gentlemen received gloves and scarves and a further seventy people had gloves alone; seven hundred poor people received twopence each, a sum worth much more then than now. When Sir Peter Legh died in 1636 his corpse was carried thirty miles from his home to the family chapel in

Winwick Church, and followed by several hundred mourners from his own household and those of the neighbouring gentry. Martin Bucer, a well-known Cambridge divine, was attended to his grave in 1550 by three thousand people and had three sermons preached over his remains, "which three sermons," remarked Edward VI in his *Diary*, "made the People wonderfully to lament his Death." Children and unmarried girls were accompanied by bands of young people dressed in white, the coffin being covered by a white pall instead of the more usual black and sometimes, in the case of children, slung on white scarves carried by women. In a letter written in 1603 Sir William Waad refers to "the streets strawed with flowers when maids of any sort are buried . . . and for bachelors they wear rosemary, as if it were at marriages."[1] At such funerals a maiden's garland of real or imitation flowers upon a framework of linen or paper, with a white glove in the centre to denote innocence, was often hung over the place where the dead girl normally sat in church. Later it was removed to the west wall or hung in the chancel. Such garlands are still to be seen in some English churches, though most of those still surviving date only from the eighteenth century.

Black gowns were frequently provided for a number of poor people who took part in the procession and were paid for doing so. In 1592 £2 7*s*. 8*d*. was paid to the mourners at Mr. Shuttleworth's funeral, "and 10 score and 11 people were dyned at sixe-pence and five-pence the meall."[2] Sir Thomas Gresham in 1575 provided in his will for two hundred men and women to be clothed in material costing 6*s*. 8*d*. a yard; the total cost of his burial, with its paid mourners, musicians, banquet, and other rites, amounted to the immense sum of £800. Few indeed could go to such lengths but very considerable sums were usually spent at these times, and even the poor observed as many of the traditional rites as they could possibly afford, with the generous help of friends and neighbours who all contributed something towards the expenses.

Only the well-to-do were "chested", poorer people being usually buried in their shrouds alone. Coffins were covered with black palls adorned with yew and rosemary and carried on a bier by six or eight men. The procession was preceded by a band of musicians, and if the funeral was at night, by torch-bearers. The mourners carried branches of evergreens in their hands and dropped sprigs of yew and rosemary into the open grave, which was afterwards covered with flowers and garlands. Those who

[1] *Calendar of State Papers, Domestic,* Jas I, Vol. III.

[2] *The House and Farm Accounts of the Shuttleworths* (Chetham Society).

had worn armour during their lives often had special suits of funeral armour left upon their tombs. The situation of the grave itself was an important matter. The north side of the churchyard was avoided by all, for there lay suicides and unbaptized children. Many people desired to lie within the church, and the unboarded floors were constantly disturbed for this purpose. The consent of the churchwardens had to be obtained and a special fee paid for the privilege. To counteract any unpleasant odour arising from these shallow intramural graves it was usual to burn juniper and frankincense on special occasions, such as the greater festivals or the visit of any high dignitary; at other times, presumably, the scent of the rushes on the floor was considered a sufficient safeguard.

No funeral was complete without a meal of some kind which was served as soon as the procession returned from the church. The nature of the repast naturally varied with the finances of the family. In 1645 Thomas Leadbeater, a farmer of Cranage in Cheshire, desired his children to "bringe me home with bread, cheese and drinke." This was the simplest form of burial feast; in richer households a dinner of cold meats, biscuits, sweets, and wine, was usually offered. "Nothing was lacking," says Stow of one of these meals in 1566, and probably this was true of most, since a lavish table was at once a measure of regard for the dead man and a proof of the family's wealth. Fabyan, who died in 1513, ordered the provision of bread, cheese, and ale, for all comers at his burial, and the same with the addition of roast beef and mutton at his Month's Mind, the service anciently held a month after death. In 1544 Margaret Atkinson left directions in her will that the entire parish should be invited to a meal on the Sunday following her funeral, and that for it

> . . . there be provided two dozens of bread, a kilderkin of ale, two gammons of bacon, three shoulders of mutton and two couple of rabbits, desiring all the parish, as well rich as poor, to take part thereof; and a table to be set in the midst of the church, with every thing necessary thereto.[1]

In the seventeenth century such lavish bequests were less usual, but the poor were rarely forgotten, and few families were so ungenerous as to confine their hospitality to their friends alone. In a deeply religious age charity was felt to be the first of Christian virtues, excellent at all times, and never more suitably exercised than in commemorating the loved dead, or marking one's own exit from an uncertain world. And there was something more.

[1] J. Stow, *op. cit.*

In spite of occasional examples of avarice and injustice, in spite of enclosures carried through without regard to the distress they caused, and hardships that might have been avoided by a little thought in higher circles, there was then a very real community sense, especially in the villages, which made it seem quite natural to share the great occasions of life with all one's neighbours, rich and poor alike. Christenings, weddings, and funerals, were occasions for largesse freely given and as freely accepted, both in money and kind. And if more came than were expected, then what was available had to be stretched to go round a little farther. "There was £5 to be distributed to the poor," wrote Sir Walter Calverley in his *Diary*, of the funeral already mentioned, ". . . to have 3*d.* a piece, but they finding them very numerous gave them but 2*d.* a piece and in so doing distributed all that and 10*s.* more."[1] Religious changes prevented these "towards 700 poor persons that had doals" from praying for the dead lady's soul, as they would have done before the Reformation, but no doubt they thought kindly of her and wished her well as they drank the burnt ale usually provided at such times and returned home with the little extra money that must have been a very welcome addition to the low wages of that time.

[1] *Diary of Sir Walter Calverley* (Surtees Society).

Chapter VII

THE THINGS OF THE SPIRIT

RELIGION in the sixteenth and seventeenth centuries was no mere matter of personal inclination or conventional weekly observance. It was a fierce and vital flame that illumined every phase of private and public life, a favourite subject of discussion wherever men congregated, and a customary topic in news-letters, broadsheets and writings of every kind. A man's chosen faith coloured his opinions on political as well as spiritual concerns and influenced his daily habits, his choice of friends, his speech and, in extreme cases, his dress. Indifference was so rare a state as to be almost non-existent, and tolerance was regarded as a weakness rather than a virtue. "Religion," said John Selden, "is like a fashion; one man wears his doublett slashed, another lac'd, a third plaine, but every man has a doublett."[1] And by its fashion he was usually judged, for most men considered their own to be the only Christian wear and thought of those who went dressed in another mode as hardly to be trusted in this life and almost certainly in danger of Hell-fire in the next.

It could not fail to be a matter of intense interest to every thinking individual, for the swinging tides of the Reformation had swept away most of the old landmarks and forced men to find their own way as best they could by those that remained, or to set a new course over unfamiliar seas. How they went was a matter of supreme importance, not only ultimately in another world but more immediately in this one. Religion was for nearly two centuries inextricably mixed up with politics, and a man's beliefs might well be his undoing though he had every other advantage of birth, brains or wealth on his side. For simple people the changes of the sixteenth century must have been bewildering indeed. In one short lifetime, honest citizens had seen their services altered in form and language, their shrines defaced, their clergy deprived first for one reason and then for another. They had seen men well known and respected accused of high treason in one reign because they would not take the Oath of Supremacy, and destroyed as heretics in another for refusing to acknowledge the Pope. Even the Elizabethan settlement did little more at first than provide moderate men with some shelter from the storms that had blown unceasingly over England since

[1] *Table Talk of John Selden*, 1892.

Henry VIII developed his surprising scruples about a twenty-year-old marriage. Elizabeth desired primarily to unite her people, and her settlement blended ancient Catholic ritual and new tenets with deliberate vagueness designed to offend as few as possible. In actual fact it settled very little but, like many English compromises, it worked. The great majority of her subjects accepted it with thankfulness and the beliefs and ceremonies then laid down were the foundation of the Anglican Church as we know it to-day.

But there were many who could not accept it. Catholics and extreme Protestants alike stood outside it; the latter were destined in the seventeenth century to come within an ace of destroying it altogether, and the former were popularly regarded as its secret and implacable enemies. Even within the Church there were shades of opinion which sometimes caused trouble in parishes, and between men of different denominations there was often bitter enmity. Friendship and understanding did exist between men of opposing views; during the worst periods of persecution many a Catholic owed the retention of his property and occasionally his life to the disinterested kindness of his Protestant neighbours. But tolerance was not a general virtue, and more than a century and a half was to pass before the raging fires of religious hatred began to flicker towards their unlamented extinction.

"We quarrel about the trimmings," said John Selden, and quarrel they did with a ferocity unimaginable in this indifferent age. Yet this intolerance was but the darker side of something beautiful and fine. Along with a widespread interest in the finer points of theology and ritual went a genuine piety which influenced every department of daily life and was to be found in all sects and in practically every social class. Men saw God's finger in every occurrence, from the most important to the most trivial. Good fortune was a matter for thankfulness in its literal sense, disaster a reminder that our hope is in another world than this. Disease was a visitation from on high, good health a mark of heavenly mercy, and sin an offence against an all-seeing, ever-present God. "This love and kindnes is from God,"[1] wrote Ralph Josselyn in his *Diary* when a friend made him a present of a breast of veal, and Henry Newcome recorded how "my great security hath moved the Lord to lay my wife somewhat low this day by distemper and great pains upon her."[2] Theirs was a simple unquestioning faith which supported them through every change

[1] *Ralph Josselyn's Diary*, ed. E. Hockcliffe (Camden Society, 1908).
[2] *The Diary of Henry Newcome* (Chetham Society).

of fortune and turned even major troubles to good account. "If God be pleased to favour you with a longer life," wrote William Blundell to a London friend during the Plague of 1665, "the memory of this dismal time will be an antidote for your future against all temptations to sin. It seems to me that every day at London is now (as it were) a Day of Judgement and that all your thoughts are placed on death, on Hell, on Heaven and upon eternity."[1]

Family prayers were customary in most houses (30, 31). In Elizabeth's reign Archbishop Grindal approved a form of daily prayer consisting of thirty collects which "the master kneeling with his family in some convenient place, perfumed before with Frankincense or some other wholesome thing, as Juniper, Rosemary, Rose water and Vinegar, shall with fervent heart say or cause to be said . . ." in the presence of his servants and children. In great houses the chaplain was expected to prepare lectures and direct the household in spiritual exercises. Anne Murray tells us that the Howards at Narworth Castle "had an excellent preacher for there chaplaine, who preached twice every Sunday in ye chapell and dayly prayers morning and evening." And speaking of her own childhood in the early seventeenth century, she records that

> . . . my mother's greatest care, and for which I shall ever owne to her memory the highest gratitude, was the great care that she tooke that even from our infancy, wee were instructed never to neglect to begin and end the day with Prayer, and orderly every morning to read the Bible, and ever to keepe the church as offten as there was occation to meet there either for prayers or preaching. So that for many yeares together I was seldome or never absent from divine service, at 5 a'clocke in the morning in the summer and 6 a'clocke in the winter till the usurped power putt a restraint to that publick worship so long owned and continued in the Church of England; where I bless God, I had my education, and the example of a good Mother who kept constantt to her owne parish church, and had allways a great respect for the ministers under whose charge she was.[2]

Theology was the most important item in every child's education. Parents of all persuasions considered it a first duty to see that their children were grounded in the elements of their faith as soon as they were capable of learning anything. Babies hardly out of the nursery were taken to hear sermons that often lasted an hour or more, and older children were expected not only to listen to the minister's words but to be able to discuss them

[1] M. Blundell, *Cavalier.*

[2] *The Autobiography of Lady Halkett.*

30 The Chapel, Haddon Hall, Derbyshire

31 The Chapel, Ightham Mote, Kent

Both from lithographs by Joseph Nash

FAMILY CHAPELS

32 A Tudor Bedroom: the Inlaid Chamber at Sizergh Castle, Westmorland

From a lithograph by Joseph Nash (1849)

intelligently afterwards. The Catechism was thoroughly taught both at home and in church. Clergymen were required to instruct children, apprentices, and servants, every Sunday after Evening Service, and such instruction was normally supplemented by further lessons from parents and tutors. "My sons have been very towardly," wrote Oliver Heywood with great satisfaction, "plyed their book, read chapters, learned Chatichismes, got some chapters and psalmes without book, John repeated the 12th, Eliezor the 10th of Revelation last night in bed; blessed be god." On 24 August 1671, he spent the morning in prayer with his family, "beginning at youngest, Eliezor prayed first very sensibly, tho short, John prayed both a long time and exceeding pertinently and affectionately weeping much."[1]

Private fasts were not unknown amongst very religious people. "Saturday I devoted to a family humiliation and religious fasting with my wife and most of our people,"[2] wrote Simmonds d'Ewes in his *Diary*, and this was by no means the only occasion on which he did so. Public fast-days were held in times of trouble, as when epidemics were sweeping the country, or to mark some particular disaster such as the Massacre of St. Bartholomew's Day in 1572, or the discovery of the Babington Plot in 1586. Pepys refers to a fast-day "for the plague" on 2 August 1665. Such days were definitely religious in origin and were specially called for when necessary; the statutory meatless days of Elizabeth's reign, on the other hand, were expressly stated to be secular in intention, and it is perhaps for this very reason that they failed to grip the popular imagination.

Sermons were extraordinarily popular. Great crowds flocked to hear the better-known preachers at Paul's Cross and other places, and volumes of sermons formed a large part of every private library, where they shared the shelves with devotional treatises and such favourite works as Foxe's *Book of Martyrs*. John Manningham, a barrister of the Middle Temple, made a habit of hearing as many sermons as he could and recording them almost word for word in his diary for 1602 and 1603, with an occasional trenchant comment on the manner or appearance of the speakers. "One Clappam" he describes as "a blacke fellow with a sower looke, but a good spirit, bold and sometymes bluntly witty"; another, apparently less attractive, had "a long browne beard, a hanging looke, a gloting eye, and a tossing, learing jeausture."[3]

[1] *Oliver Heywood's Diaries*, ed. J. Horsfall Turner, 1872–85.
[2] *Autobiography of Sir Simmonds d'Ewes*, ed. J. O. Halliwell, 1845.
[3] Harleian MSS., 5353.

Puritans regarded the sermon as the most important part of the service and expected their ministers to be both eloquent and long-winded. One of the charges brought against an unpopular vicar at Penistone in 1647 was that his sermons were not always his own, and he tended to repeat the same one too frequently. Under the later Tudors the rage for preaching was so great that both Mary and Elizabeth were forced to issue licences to preach, and to restrict those not so licensed to reading printed homilies. But no regulations could entirely silence those who felt they had something to say, and if the unlicensed Anglican usually obeyed the law, members of other sects did not. There were constant complaints of their unorthodox teachings, their abuse of resident parsons, and their not infrequent lapses into downright sedition. Anabaptists urged the levelling of all ranks, Adamites preached a return to the primitive simplicity of Eden, the early Quakers in the seventeenth century went about deliberately affronting the susceptibilities of their hearers and made almost as many enemies for themselves as the Catholics.

Presbyterians also had their message to deliver, and suffered for it, except during the Commonwealth. Oliver Heywood tells us how, after the Restoration, he "went to George Horsmans house at little Woodhouse, there preacht and before I had done was apprehended by constables, carryed to the Mayor who sent me to the common prison."[1] All such preachers were liable to arrest and imprisonment if the local constable took his duties seriously, yet all had their hearers; and if some listeners were of that idle type whose descendants are now to be found every evening in Hyde Park, many more were genuine seekers after some more exciting form of truth than could be found within the boundaries of the Established Church.

During the Commonwealth the Anglican clergy in their turn suffered persecution and were driven from their parishes, forbidden to preach, and denied the right to minister to their people. This was the heyday of extreme Puritanism. In its milder form the Puritan spirit had long existed both within and without the Church, and showed itself chiefly in a desire for greater simplicity of ritual and a genuine striving after self-denial and austerity of living. But its more violent manifestations took the form of an extreme Protestantism whose professors not only detested anything which might, by the widest stretch of the imagination, be thought tainted with popery, but also struck at many of the ordinary decencies of public worship. To wear a surplice, to use a ring in marriage or the sign of the Cross in baptism, to receive

[1] *Oliver Heywood's Diaries.*

Holy Communion kneeling, were all alike anathema to them, and so were many of the customary pleasures of the time, which they described as "rags of popery" and "the dregs of Anti-Christ". Such Calvinistic tendencies had been slowly growing in England since the early years of Elizabeth's reign when the Marian exiles first returned from Geneva, and during the Interregnum they came into their own.

Though Cromwell favoured religious freedom, at least in theory, his followers did not, and under their influence forms of worship in parish churches were drastically altered, secular marriages were enforced, and the use of the Book of Common Prayer forbidden under pain of fine or imprisonment. From 1650 to the Restoration the word "baptized" disappeared almost entirely from the parish registers, and children's names were entered under the date of their birth instead of that of their christening. Anglican children had to be secretly baptized by their own deprived clergymen, or by their parents. "I pray you give no offence to the State," wrote Ralph Verney nervously when discussing the christening of his little boy, "should it bee done in the old way it may bring more trouble upon you than you can imagine, and all to noe purpose, for soe it bee done with common ordinarie water, and that these words 'I baptize thee in the name of the Father and of the Son and of the Holy Ghost' be used with the water, I know the child is well baptized."[1]

Everyday life was darkened by a flood of edicts prohibiting amusements of various kinds and imposing punishment upon a host of minor transgressions. A strong effort was made to abolish Christmas both as a religious and a secular festival, and if it did not entirely succeed, this was due more to the tough conservatism of the people than to the tolerance of the Government. Plays, May-day ceremonies, church-ales, and Morris-dances, were all forbidden, the first being especially detested by the authorities, as were also cards and dice and most other games. Even the great Lord Fairfax was fined 5*s*. in 1655 "for that it hath been proved that he was present when Tho Carlton, Anth Chapman and others acted a comedy or stage play at Gillinge at Christmas last."[2]

If the Puritans could point to a time of prosperity as well as persecution, those who clung to the older religion could hope for nothing better than comparative quiet, and that only when nothing occurred to inflame the constant suspicions of their

[1] *Verney Memoirs*.
[2] *North Riding Quarter Sessions Records*, Vol. V, quoted by E. Trotter in *Seventeenth-Century Life in the Country Parish*, 1919.

neighbours. To be a Catholic was to be outside the ordinary life of the community, unable for conscience sake to accept the new dispensation and suspected for that reason of disloyalty to the State. For the average Englishman, fed on the fiery doctrines of Foxe's *Book of Martyrs* and the bitter teachings of extreme divines, a Catholic was not simply a man who held another faith than his. He was a friend of Spain or France, an enemy of English freedom, a plotter who sought constantly to overthrow the Establishment and relight the fires of Smithfield. The very word conjured up horrific visions in simple minds of papal intrigues, foreign invasion, and all the terrors of the Inquisition. That only a small minority had ever taken part in any Elizabethan conspiracy or in the Gunpowder Plot, that the majority had proved their loyalty in every national crisis, and that hundreds fought and suffered for an Anglican King in the Civil War—all this went for nothing against the memory of old grievances and constantly fanned alarms. "I deny as in the presence of God," wrote William Blundell, the Cavalier, in 1679, "that I have ever entertained any design whatsoever contrary to the duty of a subject against that King or this. And as for invasions, it hath ever been my professed principle that all Catholic subjects of a lawful Protestant King (such as King Charles the 2nd) are obliged faithfully to adhere to that King in all invasions whatsoever, though made by Catholic princes or even by the Pope himself."[1] But few would have believed such a statement in spite of much evidence supporting it, and nothing was easier at any time than to inflame the smouldering anti-Catholic feelings which were shared by almost every section of the community.

By the Act of 1584 the very presence of a priest in England was made high treason, and to harbour him was a felony. To hear Mass or receive the Sacrament according to Catholic rites was a perilous undertaking which could only be carried out with the utmost secrecy, in upper rooms and at odd times, in constant fear of the informer. Nevertheless such services were held whenever possible. Devoted clerics risked their lives to minister to their people and their hosts cheerfully faced imprisonment and ruin to shelter them. A sudden search might be made at any moment, and it was on such occasions that recourse was often had to secret hiding-places contrived in the thicknesses of ancient walls and chimneys by the famous "Green Man" and his assistants. Such "priest-holes" are still to be seen in many old country houses. They vary in size from very small rooms to spaces hardly large enough to permit an inmate to stand erect. In these

[1] M. Blundell, *Cavalier*.

cramped quarters the hunted priest had to remain for hours, and sometimes for days, while the pursuivants tramped about the house, tearing up floorboards, wrenching away panelling, and tapping on walls in search of any suspicious hollow sound. In *The Life of Father Gerard* we read how in one house which is not named he was forced to take refuge for four hours in an underground hiding-place which was "covered with water at the bottom, so that I was standing with my feet in water all the time."[1] Yet hideously uncomfortable as these secret holes were, and harrowing as was the experience of waiting in them which the pursuers raged ever nearer, they undoubtedly saved hundreds of lives during the worst penal times. Royalist fugitives sometimes sheltered in them as well as priests, and one, at Moseley, preserved the Crown of England for the nation when Charles II was hidden there after the Battle of Worcester.

Catholics were debarred from membership of the Universities and, like Sir Francis Throckmorton when he went to Cambridge in 1654, could only live on the fringe of the academic world. An irritating and inconvenient regulation forbade them to travel more than five miles from their homes without a licence, and though this was not always enforced, it was liable to be revived whenever some fresh trouble broke out. Their property was constantly diminished by fines for recusancy which sometimes amounted to as much as £20 a month. Every Englishman was required to attend Divine Service each Sunday in his parish church and was fined 1*s.* if he stayed away without sufficient excuse. Continued absence meant presentation at the visitational court and a much heavier punishment. Such absence was enough in itself to rouse suspicions of recusancy. In the *Calendar of State Papers*, 1580, it is recorded that "Sir Piers leighe, a Justice, never communicateth, his famylie greatlie corrupteth, and come not to churche, and is a Cherisher of Masse prestes and such others," and this in spite of the fact that Sir Piers had conformed and had caused Disley Church to be re-consecrated for Protestant worship. In 1606 Richard Mennel was fined £80 at Richmond, Yorkshire, for allowing his servant to stay away from Church for eight months; his own absence for the same period would have cost him twice as much. Eighteen years later William Green paid £100 in the same court for omitting to have his child baptized in the parish church within a month of its birth.

These heavy fines must have ruined most of the old Catholic families if they had been constantly levied, but much depended upon individual justices and the general state of feeling at any

[1] Rev. J. Morris, *The Life of Father Gerard.*

particular period. During the Commonwealth and the frenzied time of the Popish Plot, and again at the accession of William III, every anti-Catholic law was put into active execution, and known Catholics suffered severely, as they had done before in Elizabeth's reign. But there were intervening periods of comparative serenity when they were able to travel like other men and live undisturbed lives so long as they did nothing to attract the attention of the authorities. Sir Miles Stapleton, of Carlton, was able to maintain a private chapel in his house and to pay £5 a year to a priest who secretly ministered there. He was even strong enough to protect his people to some extent and to save them occasionally from being listed as recusants.

The constables were obliged to provide the Quarter Sessions with lists of persistent absentees from church, and could themselves be fined if they failed to do so, but evidently they were not above taking bribes now and then. In his household accounts Sir Miles notes the payment of 2*s.* to "Christopher Ward, our constable of Carlton, for not giveing in the names of the Cath(olics) at Waikfield Sessions in January 1676", and also, as a further precaution, the payment of 3*s.* 6*d.* for "John Sotheby's chardges to Waikfield Sessions Jan the 12 1676 for goeing along with the constable to prevent giveing in names."[1] But even this powerful landowner was accused of high treason during the Popish Plot, though he was acquitted by a York jury, and further trouble fell upon him in 1688. A strong wave of Protestant feeling swept over the country at this time, and by an Act of Parliament then passed, every Catholic became liable to have his house searched for arms and to forfeit to the King's use any horse in his possession over £5 in value. Sir Miles relates how on 16 December a mob of excited men armed with guns and pitchforks burst into his home and, after turning the house upside down, carried him off a prisoner. In his carefully kept accounts he notes the cost of this night's violence. The intruders "stayed all night in the house and drunke above half a hogshead of wine and as much ale with bread and chese and what other meat was in the house and carryed mee and all my Catholicke men prisoners to Ferry bridge where wee were released and stayed all night, wch cost me in £4 10*s.*"[2]

Perhaps the saddest result of all this intolerance was the division which it caused between friends and still more between members of the same family. There are few more pathetic stories

[1] J. C. Cox, *The Household Books of Sir Miles Stapleton, Bart.*, 1658–1705, published in *The Ancestor*, No. 2, July 1902.

[2] *The Household Books of Sir Miles Stapleton.*

than that of the little Falkland children who followed their mother when she became a Catholic and were taken from her in consequence. They were sent to their eldest brother's house to be brought up in the Protestant faith by their devout sister-in-law, Lettice, and their tutor, Mr. Chillingworth. Young as they were, the two boys and their four sisters resisted the gentle but persistent pressure put upon them by their guardians and remained faithful to their religion, but it must have been a sad life for children, separated from their mother and from everything they had been taught to hold sacred. Eventually Lady Falkland, who was then living in London, sent word that she could receive her sons and arrange an escort for them if they could contrive to escape from the house.

The story of their flight is recorded in the account of Lady Falkland's life afterwards written by her daughter. The children had no one to help them and had to rely entirely upon their own wits. Since the boys slept with their tutor who was a light sleeper it was impossible for them to rise without his knowledge. They therefore expressed a wish to wake early, and at three o'clock next morning began to play noisily about the courts and passages with their sisters, so that everyone knew they were there. Then, aided by the girls, they ran out to meet the men who had been sent to fetch them. It was not safe for their escort to come too near the house, so the two little boys, aged ten and eleven respectively, had to make the first part of the journey by themselves, "they running all alone that mile" as their sister tells us, "(it being not yet light) to meet men that were entirely strangers to them, whose persons were no way promising nor apt to encourage children to have confidence in them."[1]

With these guides they set off along the road to Oxford and London. Every time a coach passed them the little company was forced to hide for fear the hue and cry had already been raised. When they came to Abingdon the watermen who were to have taken them on were too drunk to travel, and while they waited, a rumour spread through the town that they were stolen children. Only the fact that the constable knew one of the men saved them all from arrest, but even so they dared not go on until nightfall, "but were fain to take water at 10 o'clock at dark night, with watermen not only not able to row, but ready every moment to overturn the boat with reeling and nodding." Nevertheless, they came to their mother at last and were hidden by her until she was able to send them to safety on the Continent. "She was fain," says her daughter, "to put them in some private

[1] *The Lady Falkland, her life, by her daughter.*

places in London, often removing them, and for to be able to pay for their diet and lodging . . . she and her household were constrained for the time she stayed in town to keep more Fridays in the week than one." A mother then had no rights whatever over her children, and had they been found they would certainly have been sent back to their Protestant brother. But for once in her unhappy life Lady Falkland triumphed, and the adventure which began with two nervous children running down a darkened road to meet their unknown guides ended peacefully on the Continent where, one hopes, both boys led a more cheerful life than they had ever done during their Oxfordshire childhood.

If religion was constantly in men's thoughts, so were the darker manifestations of the spiritual world. Nearly everyone believed in witchcraft. A few intelligent individuals here and there refused to subscribe to that ancient faith, and some like Reginald Scot and Johann Weir, derided the grosser superstitions of the age in their books. They were, however, in advance of their time. The majority of Englishmen had no doubt at all that witches existed in large numbers and were both able and willing to harm their enemies and assist their friends by magical means. Not only simple folk but learned men and judges, clergymen and magistrates, all agreed that sorcerers could and did afflict their neighbours with misfortunes of every kind, from ordinary domestic mishaps to serious illnesses, madness and death. Joseph Glanvil, whose *Saducismus Triumphatus*, published in 1681, did more than any other book to confirm the general credulity, was a member of the Royal Society and Chaplain-in-Ordinary to the King. Roger Boyle and Sir Thomas Browne were both men of great learning, yet both believed in witchcraft, and so did many other scientists and philosophers of equal intellectual standing. Sir Matthew Hale voiced the general opinion in 1664 when he declared at Bury St. Edmunds that he could not deny the existence of witches because "the Scriptures had affirmed so much", and because "the wisdom of all Nations had provided laws against such Persons, which is an Argument of their confidence in such a Crime."[1]

The religious teaching of the period favoured the spread of these terrifying beliefs. The preoccupation of the more extreme Puritans with Hell and the Devil drove them to look upon every trafficker in magic as a servant of the Evil One, every practising witch as a member of some satanic coven. Old charms known

[1] *A Tryal of Witches at the Assizes Held at Bury St. Edmonds for Cy of Suffolk: on the* 10 *March* 1664 *before Sir Matthew Hale, Kt. Taken by a Person then attending the Court,* 1682.

and used for centuries, old customs, innocent and otherwise, thus became tainted in the eyes of devout people with all the horrors of paganism and worse. In the early seventeenth century the ancient aversion to the witch flared up into a widespread persecution which for a short time endangered the lives and liberties of hundreds of men and women. Prickers and witch-finders went from town to town subjecting their victims to "tests" of the most illegal kind, on the strength of which they declared them guilty and handed them over to a "justice" almost as brutal as their own illicit proceedings. It took considerable courage, during the height of the frenzy, to stand out against these wretches, and even judges were subjected to a sort of moral pressure for, as Roger North tells us, "if a judge is so clear and open as to declare against that impious, vulgar opinion . . . the countrymen cry, 'This judge hath no religion, for he does not believe in witches.'"[1]

The Law acknowledged sorcery as a crime punishable by imprisonment or the pillory and, in extreme cases where murder was involved, by death. In 1542, 1563 and again in 1580, Acts of Parliament forbidding every kind of magical practice were passed; in 1604 an even harsher Act extended the death penalty to all cases of bodily harm caused by witchcraft, and also to treasure-seeking with the aid of spirits and charms to cause unlawful love, if these offences were committed for a second time. Such laws could only have sprung from a general belief in the possibility of such crimes, and there is no doubt that this belief did exist in every district and in every class of society.

Nor was the acknowledged witch the only person who dabbled in the secret arts. The Tudor Acts forbade divination, necromancy, image-making, and conjuration of spirits, not on general principles alone but because such things were very far from uncommon. In 1532 Sir William Neville involved himself in a network of sorcery by seeking the aid of Richard Jones, an astrologer. Sir William simply desired to find some missing spoons, but from this small beginning he was led on to spirit-raising and the preparation of a "ring of power" which would enable him to gain the King's favour. Twelve years later Lord Henry Nevell, desiring money for gambling, embarked upon a course of crystal-gazing and image-making that finally landed him and his associates in the Fleet Prison. In 1562 Arthur and Edmund Pole were accused of invoking spirits as part of a plot against the Queen, and, though they denied all treasonable intentions, they admitted that they had tried to ascertain the date of the Queen's death by conjuration.

[1] R. North, *Lives of the Norths.*

In both the sixteenth and seventeenth centuries astrology was a favourite study of learned men whose known characters raised them far above all reasonable suspicions of witchcraft. Dr. Dee and Thomas Vaughan both studied magic without any fear that in so doing they were transgressing the laws of Christianity, and Dr. Nepier, a physician, made it a rule to consult spirits before he prescribed for his patients. Queen Elizabeth herself called in Dr. Dee on several occasions, and in 1558 he was officially asked to find an auspicious date for her coronation. Elias Ashmole was another innocent student of the occult, and Aubrey tells that a certain Mr. Marsh, of Dunstable, "did seriously confess to a friend of mine that astrology was but the countenance; and that he did his business by the help of the blessed spirits; with whom only men of great piety, humility and charity could be acquainted."[1]

It is true that towards the end of the seventeenth century increased scientific knowledge was beginning to turn men's minds away from these alluring edges of a dangerous world. The more enlightened gradually perceived the mistaken notions upon which magic and astrology were based, and with this perception came the realization that most of the accusations hurled against suspected witches were absolutely impossible. But this change came only very slowly. The passionate interest in spiritual matters that inspired so much true devotion and so many quarrels extended to the shadows as well as the light; and as far as witchcraft was concerned, they were closely associated, since to doubt the existence of witches was thought to be equivalent to doubting the truths of the Bible. Even those courageous men who stood out against the persecutions of the early seventeenth century did so more because they believed innocent persons were condemned upon unsatisfactory evidence than because they questioned the possibility of their guilt. For them, as for the more ignorant, the charm and the amulet existed to counteract the spell, the white witch to cure the diseases caused by the sorcerer, the conjurer and the exorcist to deal with devils that invaded men's souls. Many years were to pass before the world of magic and sorcery finally ceased to impinge upon our own; to the men of that simpler and more credulous age such a state of affairs would have seemed incredible and, with its necessary negation of so many ancient beliefs, perhaps not altogether to be desired.

[1] J. Aubrey, *Miscellanies.*

PART II (1700-1800)

Chapter VIII

THE GEORGIAN HOME

THE dawn of a new century does not usually bring with it any immediate or startling changes in everyday life, and even a change of dynasty need not necessarily affect the comings and goings of the ordinary man. Manners and customs alter very slowly, and most periods in history merge so imperceptibly into their successors that it is often hard to define where one ends and another begins. Yet every century has its own peculiar flavour which cannot be mistaken for that of any other. England during most of the eighteenth century was in many ways much the same as it had been in preceding years. It was still a green and lovely country whose skies were only faintly darkened by factory smoke towards the end. It was still predominantly rural in outlook, drawing most of its wealth and nearly all its traditions from the soil. In the villages the old customs and beliefs persisted, and ancient superstitions lingered in men's minds, in spite of the slow spread of knowledge. The people had the same vigorous faults and virtues as their ancestors, and were usually quite as lively and courageous, as cruel, coarse, and boisterous, as their great grandparents had been. But there was one supremely important difference between Stuart and Georgian England which even the most unobservant could not fail to notice. The latter was a far happier and less troubled place in which to live.

For the first time for many years there was almost unbroken internal peace. Occasional upheavals did occur, like the two Jacobite risings and the Gordon Riots, but these touched only a small section of the population and had nothing like the far-reaching effects of earlier religious and political feuds. Men were no longer faced with the necessity of shedding each other's blood in support of King or Parliament, or threatened with the loss of their property through sequestration by the winning side or heavy recusancy fines. Religion had ceased to be a reason for persecution or for hatred between neighbours, and the priest-hole was henceforth to be tenanted only by the spider and the mouse.

Certain disabilities, it is true, attached to those outside the Anglican fold. Dissenters and Catholics alike were debarred from holding national or municipal office or entering the Universities unless they took an oath repugnant to their consciences. The penal laws remained upon the Statute Book, though they

were rarely enforced, and as late as 1788 Nonconformists were still trying to get the Test and Corporation Acts repealed. Catholics were still vaguely distrusted for political reasons and were denied a number of civic rights enjoyed by others. A Parliamentary attempt in 1780 to relieve them of their worst disadvantages provoked the most serious riots of the century when for four days the London mob ran wild under the irresponsible leadership of Lord George Gordon, burnt a number of Catholic chapels, and indiscriminately attacked and plundered any house whose owner had incurred their easily roused dislike. But in general no one greatly cared to what faith a man belonged, and chapels of every denomination were openly built and filled with worshippers. Life in the villages and smaller towns may not have been very exciting in the eighteenth century, but it was pleasant and friendly, and it was more free from outside alarms and disturbances than it had been since the Wars of the Roses.

The bitter divisions of the Stuart period were already dying when George I came to the throne, and not even the most bigoted lover of old things regretted their passing. The Forty-Five was the last flicker of those ancient fires, and it failed principally because the English Jacobites discovered, when it came to the point, that their devotion to the exiled Royal House was more romantic than actual. In the North there were many who believed, or thought they did, in the Stuart cause, and regularly drank their toasts to "the King over the water", and some of these came forward when there was a chance of restoring that King to his throne. A few towns like Manchester and Macclesfield received him with wild enthusiasm and provided a number of eager young men to fight under his banner. That ardent Jacobite, Elizabeth Byrom, records in her *Diary* how she put on her white gown, presumably her best, and went to Mr. Fletcher's house in Manchester to see the Prince ride out. "A noble sight it is," she says, "I would not have missed it for a great deal of money; his horse had stood an hour in the court without stirring and as soon as he got on he began a-dancing and capering, as he was proud of his burden, and when he rid out of the court, he was received with as much joy and shouting almost as if he had been king without any dispute, indeed I think scarce anybody that saw him could dispute it."[1] But most of the Jacobite associations contented themselves with holding meetings at which they prudently decided to do nothing, and at Derby the Prince was forced to turn back for lack of adequate support. The truth was that he had come too late. Prosperity and security had

[1] *Diary of Elisabeth Byrom* (Chetham Society), Vol. XLIV.

33 An Eighteenth-century Interior

From a painting by A. W. Devis (1742)

34 The Minuet *From a painting by John Zoffany*

35 A Music Party (1733): the Prince of Wales and his Sisters at Kew

EIGHTEENTH-CENTURY MUSIC-MAKING

already quietly killed much that had seemed of vital importance half a century before, and new interests were daily crowding over the horizon to take the place of older loyalties and desires.

What strikes us most in looking back upon the bright scene of Georgian England is the cheerful independence of most of its inhabitants. The well-to-do did what they liked without troubling themselves about other people's opinions; the poorer citizens expressed themselves freely and occasionally with some violence, but certainly without servility. Class privilege was very strong and democratic government still a dream of the future, but a common passion for freedom checked the excesses of the great and gave even the voteless majority an undeniable power. At elections, as at other times, the ordinary people could make their voice heard even without the ballot box, and narrow as the franchise was, the results of those elections did usually represent the wishes of the country as a whole. The rural labourer treated his betters with respect, but otherwise did pretty much as he pleased, for he had something more than his wages to depend upon, and was correspondingly independent in his attitude towards employment. He saw the wealthier farmer, not as a master to be placated at all costs, but simply as a larger edition of himself, for he too usually had his plot of ground on which he worked two or three days in the week, and his common rights which enabled him to keep a cow for his own use. Often his wife could earn money also by making lace or following some other local craft in her own kitchen in the intervals of housework. His cottage was small but it was trim and warm, and his table was usually well supplied. A young French traveller in 1784 noticed with interest how in Norfolk villages "the houses are clean and have an appearance of cosiness in which ours in France are lacking."[1] All this gave the poorest worker a standing above that of a mere employee, and made the feeling of respect and kindliness which existed between gentle and simple a genuine thing, untainted by patronage on one side or servility on the other.

What finally undermined the countryman's security was not the conscious will of a powerful aristocracy but the crippling effect of large-scale enclosures in the latter half of the century. There was nothing new about enclosures which, as we have seen, had been going on for the past two hundred years. In the eighteenth century, however, the movement was greatly accelerated both by the growing needs of an expanding country and by the new method of tillage and breeding introduced by men like

[1] *A Frenchman in England*, ed. J. Marchand, 1933.

Coke of Norfolk and Robert Bakewell. Their efforts placed British farming on a far better footing, and even if they had never existed, the old open-strip system was already doomed. But the changes meant the extinction of many ancient rights, and in the end they were paid for by a vast increase in rural poverty and a decay of village life never contemplated by those who so enthusiastically promoted them.

Towards the end of the century, when the Napoleonic wars brought steeply rising prices and much new taxation, there was widespread distress in both town and country. In the last decade, after a series of bad harvests, the price of bread rose so violently that the poor could hardly afford to buy it, and patriotic citizens were urged to deny themselves flour in any form. The shadow of the Industrial Revolution, too, was beginning to throw its ugly length over the land, and the machine was already slowly ousting the independent craftsman who worked in his cottage during the winter and on the land in summer. Yet in spite of these and other troubles, Georgian England was on the whole a prosperous place whose inhabitants had a great belief in themselves and in their country and were not unjustified in that belief. Freedom was their passion and a sturdy independence their chief characteristic, and they respected that independence in others even when it was expressed, as it not infrequently was, by eccentricity. It was indeed a golden age for individualists who pursued their cheerful way through a world as yet unshackled by bureaucracy and equally untroubled by the violent upheavals of the previous era, or the introspective doubts and self-questionings of our own day.

The houses in which they lived were an outward expression of their characters, for they were solid, dignified, well-made, and admirably suited to their purpose. This was a period of great activity in domestic building; as in Tudor times, new houses were springing up everywhere, while older ones were being refaced and altered to suit the prevailing fashion. Every educated man considered himself something of an architect, with at least enough knowledge to appreciate the work of the great designers and to understand the numerous books on architecture then published. Many designed their own houses and either directed and advised the professional architect or personally superintended the erection of the building. The very rich lavished their wealth upon magnificent country mansions in the Palladian style, some of which were more like palaces than ordinary homes. Such houses were designed with an eye to dignity rather than comfort and they were often more splendid than convenient, particularly in

36 A Family Group of *c.* 1750

From a painting by Francis Hayman

37 A Tea Party of the early Georgian Period

From a painting by an unidentified artist

38 The Two Ladies

From a silhouette by W. Wellings (1782)

39 "The Sitwell and Warneford Families"

From a silhouette by Forond

EIGHTEENTH-CENTURY SILHOUETTES

the first half of the eighteenth century when the fashion for grandiose building was at its height. But they were undoubtedly beautiful both within and without and, in an age when the rich were not ashamed to display their wealth, their magnificence amply repaid the owners for such trifling disadvantages as long draughty corridors or awkward interior arrangements.

Everything was sacrificed to the state apartments, and if these were sufficiently splendid no one minded if the other rooms were somewhat cramped in comparison. They were planned on princely lines and beautified by painted ceilings, delicate plasterwork, and furniture that was often specially designed by the architect to set off their lovely proportions. In mansions of this type the Great Hall, though it had ceased to be the main living-room, was still important and was frequently the finest room in the house, where concerts could be held, or meals served on special occasions when there were too many guests to be accommodated in the dining-room. Libraries, music-rooms, boudoirs, studies, and withdrawing-rooms, now replaced the old Long Galleries and winter parlours of an earlier time. A more exclusive way of living demanded numerous sitting-rooms as well as a host of bedrooms which made it unnecessary for any guests or members of the family to share a room. Dressing-rooms also were beginning to make their appearance. This was an idea introduced by travellers who had seen such rooms in France and improved upon by English builders who made them larger than the French *cabinets de toilette* so that they might serve as additional sleeping-chambers when the occasion called for it.

The kitchens were kept as far away as possible and were often placed in an outlying pavilion connected with the central block by covered passages. This arrangement allowed the family to live untroubled by the noise and smells of cooking, an advantage which may or may not have compensated for the fact that the food must frequently have been half cold after its long journey to the dining-room. Flanking pavilions joined to the main house by curved corridors were extremely popular with eighteenth-century architects. The kitchen wing was often balanced by a second pavilion containing the stables or perhaps a chapel, and in a few houses such separated buildings formed a private wing to which the family could retire when there were no guests to entertain.

The gardens which surrounded these great mansions were adorned with classical temples and summer-houses, wide lawns and ornamental canals, and occasionally a model dairy with marble walls, fine porcelain vessels, and fountains to cool the air in summer. They steadily became less formal as the taste for

straight walks and topiary declined. The geometrical patterns of the previous century gave place to "natural" gardens; winding paths replaced the pleached alleys, wildernesses became fashionable and with them what Miller in his *New Principles of Gardening* calls "Serpentine Meanders, Precipices" and "Rude Coppicies". In the latter part of the eighteenth century, when the Gothic style was once again in vogue, private grounds were further diversified by grottoes, hermitages, and artificial ruins intended to produce a pleasantly romantic melancholy in the beholder. A crumbling tower, a broken arch, or a hermit's cell, added just that touch of pleasing gloom which was so much admired at this period, and verisimilitude was sometimes added to the hermitages by a stuffed figure dressed in the traditional garments and set in the darkest recesses of the hut. One landowner at Pain's Hill even went so far as to hire a living hermit whose painful duty it was to live in a cell of logs and roots heavily overshadowed by trees, wear a camlet robe and allow his hair, beard, and nails, to grow unchecked after the manner of ancient anchorites. By the terms of his engagement he was to remain for seven years in his depressing surroundings without speaking to any of the servants or going beyond the boundaries of the gardens. His literature was to be the Bible alone, his timepiece an hour-glass, his pillow a simple hassock and, what must have seemed the hardest of all in that heavy-drinking period, his only beverage plain water. But this experiment was not a success. The hermit was a true son of his age and preferred comfort to romance. After three weeks spent amid his Gothic glooms he abandoned the contemplative life for good and all and returned without regret to the noisier but more cheerful world of his own day.

The great country mansions were necessarily rare, since the expenses of building and maintenance were colossal. Less wealthy people contented themselves with substantial, pleasant homes containing three or four good-sized sitting-rooms besides the kitchen and its satellite apartments, a sufficient number of bedrooms and attics, and a trim coach-house and stables to accommodate their travelling carriage and perhaps a gig as well. Such dwellings, with their spacious rooms, finely ornamented doors and tall graceful windows, were quite as lovely in their own way as the Elizabethan or Jacobean houses that were so often destroyed to make room for them, and they were far more convenient. Their design and interior arrangements were essentially modern, and indeed many of us are fortunate enough to be living in them to-day with only the addition of a bathroom and electric light to mark the passage of nearly two hundred years.

Changes in custom modified house-planning quite as much as the novel conceptions of professional architects, or the fresh ideas brought back by young gentlemen who had recently made the Grand Tour. Except in the most palatial mansions, the Great Hall of mediaeval and Elizabethan days had shrunk to its present position as an entrance chamber only, for the communal spirit which dictated its use as a living- and dining-room was dead. Servants ate by themselves and hospitality, though it was still lavish, was far less indiscriminate. If poor travellers and humble folk were entertained it was in the kitchen, and there were no longer seats at the table above and below the salt, for those who would normally sit below it were not admitted to the family's presence at meals. The Great Chamber, too, had disappeared. It was not now customary to receive guests in bedrooms, or to house even the best bed in any parlour or sitting-room. A drawing-room and a dining-room were essential in any dwelling whose owners had the slightest pretensions to gentility, and most houses had one or two other rooms as well. In *Northanger Abbey* Jane Austen describes a comfortable parsonage of the late eighteenth century, with its handsome dining-parlour, its pretty drawing-room, and a third room "belonging peculiarly to the master of the house" which he used as a study. And in *Sense and Sensibility* we get a glimpse of what was then considered a really small house, only just large enough to accommodate a gently bred woman and her three daughters in decency and comfort. "Barton Cottage," we are told, "though small, was comfortable and compact . . . a narrow passage led directly through the house into the garden behind. On each side of the entrance was a sitting-room about sixteen feet square; and beyond them were the offices and stairs. Four bed-rooms and two garrets formed the rest of the house."

The "offices" usually comprised a kitchen, pantries, and china-closets, with a wash-house and perhaps a brewery, for much beer and ale was still brewed at home. In larger houses there was a still-room and buttery and probably a servants' hall. At night the staff slept in attic dormitories under the roof, if they did not, like Sir John Verney's footboy, "lie in a hole within the passage over the scullery".[1] There were, of course, no bathrooms, except in very large houses, and before 1770 no water-closets. The eighteenth century saw the dawn of our modern drainage system, and for the first time country houses were furnished with pipes and cesspools. But privies remained scarce for a long time, and one or two tucked away in odd corners were considered sufficient

[1] *Verney Letters.*

even in big establishments. Night commodes were provided in bedrooms, and baths were usually taken there also before the fire. A daily bath was not then the usual custom that it has since become, and if the preparations involved much tedious carrying of water up and down stairs, nobody thought anything of that in an age when servants were plentiful and easily replaced.

In the smaller farmhouses the old communal life continued for many years, though the parlour was gradually gaining in importance as a sitting-room specially dedicated to the women of the family. The great kitchen, flanked by a dairy, scullery, cheese-room, and larder, was the principal room, in which the farmer and his workers ate together at long uncovered tables, and sat round the hearth on winter evenings. The fireplace was of the old open type, with a chimney crane to carry pots, fire-dogs, and spits, and hams or flitches of bacon hanging from the roof above. Upstairs the bedrooms still led inconveniently out of each other, and the labourers who slept in climbed to their quarters in the loft by a steep wooden ladder. In large farmhouses the interior arrangements were much the same as in the smaller houses of the gentry, but even here the kitchen was the chief room, though the family did not always eat in it, preferring the privacy of a dining-parlour to the rough and ready company of their servants and hinds.

Cottagers lived mainly in their kitchens also, though many owned a neat parlour, used only on great occasions unless the size of the family dictated its use as a sleeping-chamber, as in earlier times. The front door opened directly into the kitchen, out of which led the short, steep stairs to the rooms above. The floors were usually flagged, or made of earth mixed with bullocks' blood and beaten to a hard, smooth surface. Over this rushes were strewn and renewed at festivals such as Easter and May-day, when sprigs of lavender and rosemary were mixed with the reeds. Before the fire there was often a settle with a high back which provided shelter from the draughts that came through the door, and a wooden arm-chair for the master of the house. Sometimes there was a scullery or back-kitchen as well as the two main rooms, and nearly always an outhouse of some kind for stores. The upper storey consisted of two or three small bedrooms, frequently unceiled and open to the rafters, with low windows which the ideas of the time usually kept hermetically sealed from one year's end to the next.

Not every cottage, unfortunately, was as comfortable and commodious as this. In the North of England both small farms and cottages were often much more primitive than their prosperous counterparts in the South. In the "clay biggins" that had

40 The Cottager and his Family (1790)
Reproduced by permission of the Trustees of the Royal Holloway College

41 A Pedlar at a Cottage Door (*c.* 1785)
Both from paintings by George Morland

42 "Christmas Gambolls"

43 The Allemande Dance (1772)

once been built before a marriage by the bridegroom's friends on land allotted by the Lord of the Manor for the purpose, there was usually no parlour and very poor sleeping accommodation. Even in some farmhouses it was often difficult to dispose a large family and the men and women servants with due regard to decency in the space available. As late as the mid-nineteenth century Canon Atkinson inspected a Yorkshire farm in which the only bedroom was a long, low chamber divided into four compartments like loose boxes, with open backs giving on to a gangway along which all had to pass. In a cottage in the same moorland district he found no bedrooms at all, no loft, and only a single living-room along the sides of which were ranged cubicles where all the family slept. "We entered," he writes, "on a totally dark and unflagged passage. On our left was an enclosure partitioned off from the passage by a boarded screen between four and five feet high and which no long time before had served the purpose originally intended, namely, that of a calves' pen. Farther still on the same side was another dark enclosure similarly constructed, which even yet served the purpose of a henhouse."[1] These visits were made during an attempt to mitigate the worst housing evils in the parish and they were welcomed by the parishioners concerned, yet the Canon records how, when he had prevailed upon the lady of the Manor to improve her cottages by the addition of a decent bedroom, the old habit of overcrowding died so hard that the new room was not used. Instead it was set aside as a guest-chamber, not to be profaned by children and servants who were still herded together in the cramped spaces provided by the original, unaltered house.

The furniture in well-to-do homes was lighter in design and more comfortable than that of the previous century. Upholstered chairs and settees were now usual and were often beautifully embroidered by the women of the family who, like their predecessors, spent long hours in needlework and took great pride in it. The graceful rooms were never overcrowded as they were later, in Victorian times, but there was a sufficiency of furniture for everyday needs. Wooden stools were no longer wanted to supply the lack of chairs, and chests were used simply as receptables for goods and not as seats or supplementary couches. In the dining-room a single well-made table, chairs, a sideboard or smaller table, and a wine-cooler provided all that was necessary for the service of meals, while in the parlour there were arm-chairs, a sofa for resting, tables for tea, a writing-desk, and the harpsichord which had replaced the earlier virginals.

[1] Rev. J. C. Atkinson, *Forty Years in a Moorland Parish*, 1892.

Carpets and rugs had superseded the earlier woven floor-mats, and towards the end of the eighteenth century printed oilcloths were sometimes used. Many fine carpets were still imported from the East or from the Continent, but an increasing number were now made in England. In 1745 a factory was established at Wilton and a few years later Thomas Whitty founded the Axminster carpet industry. From these and other works came large unseamed carpets in brilliant colours, some plain, and others patterned with designs of flowers, baskets, and fruit. Walls were still panelled in many houses, but wallpapers were increasing in popularity and produced in more varied designs. Stucco walls painted in delicate colours and decorated with plaster were also fashionable, and in some houses the principal rooms were panelled with damask silks in pale and lovely hues.

Half-tester beds began to be used in the latter half of the century, but the four-poster, with its draught-proof curtains, was still a favourite, and was sometimes piled so high with feather mattresses that the night commode had to be made in the form of steps to enable the owner to go to bed at all. A cheaper form of couch was the tent bed, with curtains flung over a light iron framework finished with small brass finials. Low wooden beds without curtains were provided for children and servants, but the truckle bed that could be pushed under the four-poster by day was now less usual. Nervous mistresses sometimes had their maids with them at night, but the increasing desire for privacy relegated most servants to their own quarters, and even the personal servant more often slept in some small chamber near the employer's bedroom than in it. Small washstands and dressing-tables were customary articles of furniture, as well as chests-of-drawers and wardrobes for clothes, and there were usually two or three chairs, now plentiful enough in most houses to allow their use even in small bedrooms. A really well-furnished chamber might also contain a tallboy and a writing-desk as well as a swinging mirror and perhaps a smaller glass on the dressing-table. A stand for wigs was an essential adjunct in an age when few men appeared in their own hair and there were also candle-sticks, and occasionally a rushlight holder, for those who disliked sleeping in total darkness.

During the eighteenth century the old open hearths slowly gave place to fire-grates, as these improved in design and convenience, and coal became a more usual fuel. The first grate appeared in Queen Anne's reign in the form of an iron basket set in the ordinary fireplace, but it was not satisfactory since the wide flues intended for wood fires did not adequately draw away the coal

smoke, so much more disagreeable than that of wood. In later designs this inconvenience was eliminated by a shield introduced into the opening, or by the building up of the hearth itself, with the result that the grate became extremely popular and advanced through various stages of improvement to something very like the fire-grate we know to-day. Coal was brought by sea, river, and canal, and carried to inland houses in slow carts driven from the nearest wharf. It was a far more expensive fuel than wood, and only the well-to-do could afford to buy it in large quantities at a time; in towns it was often bought from itinerant hawkers who were willing to sell it in comparatively small amounts, and in farms and cottages it was rarely used at all. Even in wealthier houses it was usually reserved for the living-rooms, cooking being still done with wood on open hearths as it had been for centuries before.

Candles provided most of the illumination and were made at home or bought from chandlers in large quantities. Every house was supplied with a good number of brass, silver, or pewter candlesticks, and in some, where the rooms were large, there were handsome chandeliers of carved and gilded wood suspended from the ceiling. Fine branched candelabra were used for dining-tables or set upon the walls of parlours and living-rooms. Striking a light was a cumbersome business, for though tapers of wax and phosphorous were known in the late seventeenth century, they were both expensive and dangerous, and phosphorous matches were still hidden in the future. Small tinder-boxes were generally used, containing a steel and a piece of flint, and underneath a mass of charred timber to receive the spark. Into this, when it was glowing, a thin match tipped with brimstone was thrust. To maintain an adequate supply of tinder was one of the housewife's many duties. It was made of pieces of linen rag slowly charred without being set on fire, and large quantities of linen were annually used in this way.

Cottages were lit by rushlights made from long rushes which were gathered in the summer while they were still green, peeled, dried in the open air, and soaked in scalding fats in a grease-pan just long enough to hold them. Gilbert White thought very highly of this form of lighting which he considered the most economical of all, especially for labourers who rose and went to bed by daylight in summer and rarely tried their eyes with print. "The careful wife of an industrious Hampshire labourer," he wrote, "obtains all her fat for nothing, for she saves the scummings of her bacon pot for this use,"[1] and if she lived near any stream

[1] Gilbert White, *History of Selborne*, 1789.

or fenny meadow, her rushes also were free. The light given by these prepared reeds was not brilliant, but it was clear and steady if good fats were used; it was the inferior watchlights made from tallow which gave this form of illumination such a bad name and caused some wit to describe it as "darkness made visible". Rushlights were certainly cheap even when fat or rushes had to be bought, for each light burnt for a long time, and one man told Gilbert White that a pound and a half supplied the needs of his family throughout the year. They were kept in bark containers fixed against the wall and burnt in special rushlight holders made of iron or wood and fashioned in various designs. Some were simple upright pieces of metal set in a wooden block and having a movable jaw to hold the rush in position. Others were more elaborate and had sockets so that they could be used for candles as well as rushlights. There were also perforated tin canisters for use on tables, and long holders with ratchet adjustments that could be hung from beams. For lights set on the floor there were tall holders with wood or metal feet and springs which enabled the rush to be fixed at varying heights along a central rod. Rushlights are now nothing more than a memory, but they were for centuries the universal illumination of the poor and they persisted in some districts until the late nineteenth century. There are still a few people living to-day who can remember their clear small flames from the days of their remote childhood and who have seen in ordinary use the iron holders that are now preserved only as curiosities.

Chapter IX

KITCHEN AND DINING-ROOM

GEORGIAN households were usually somewhat smaller than their predecessors in Tudor and Stuart days. Fewer servants were employed, both because wages had risen and because changing notions of accommodation made it impossible to house as many dependents as formerly in an ordinary establishment. Moreover, though much varied work had to be done by the mistress and her maids, the average country house had ceased to be an almost entirely self-supporting unit. Capable housewives still did their own baking, brewing, preserving, spinning and churning, and made their feather-beds, their soap, ink, and candles, at home. Winter stores were still a matter for careful thought, and the dairy and poultry-yard were as necessary adjuncts to the kitchen (44, 46) as they had been in earlier years. But far more necessities could now be bought from tradesmen, or from the itinerant vendors who travelled up and down the country and visited every considerable house at regular intervals. New methods of feeding cattle and better trade organization made it easier to obtain meat in winter without the trouble of salting it down in autumn, and while the still-room remained one of the busiest rooms in the house, the mistress was no longer altogether dependent upon it for the cordials, juleps, aromatic waters, and medicines, that she needed for her family's use.

Nevertheless, the staffs employed were generally much larger than they are in homes of the same size to-day. Most comfortable householders of middle-class status had at least one indoor man and a couple of maids, with perhaps a house-boy as well, a gardener and, if they kept a carriage, a coachman. In a great house, of course, there were many more. Numerous footmen, a butler, a French chef, a valet for the master and a personal maid for the mistress, coachmen, grooms, gardeners, and an ostler, were all essential to the service of a man of rank, with as many chambermaids and kitchen helpers as the size of the house demanded. Two or three dairy-maids were also required, and there was usually a housekeeper who superintended the work of the indoor women. Over all these reigned the Steward who was responsible for the whole vast establishment, while other high officials looked after the accounts, the stables, and the myriad ramifications of a great estate. Such men were often of gentle

birth, as were the waiting gentlewomen who still assisted the mistress in some houses. In many cases they were related to their employer, or were the sons of neighbouring gentlemen or yeomen who had been sent as children to be trained as pages and later to be placed in some good position in the same or another nobleman's household. This method of providing for likely lads was quite usual in the Middle Ages and persisted until the beginning of the eighteenth century. But it was a custom based upon a conception of service that was fast dying out, and it was already declining when the Georgian era began; by the end of the century it was practically extinct.

Black servants (47) were very fashionable in the reigns of the first two Georges. These curious additions to English family life were slaves, bought in slave-trading countries and brought to England in childhood or early youth to serve as personal attendants or pages. They remained in bondage here in spite of the fact that slavery was not legally recognized in this country. They were not allowed to leave their masters or seek fresh employment for themselves; if they ran away, as they sometimes did, they could be brought back by force and returned to their irate employers as the personal property they in fact were. Usually they were well treated, and sometimes even pampered, but they were unpaid, and such money as they received came to them by the generosity of their owners and not by right. It was not until 1772 that this evil state of affairs was finally ended by the judicial decision of Lord Mansfield in the "Somerset" case. By this it was laid down that every slave automatically becomes free by the mere act of landing upon English soil. Henceforward no owner of a negro servant had the right to keep him against his will and, while some of those thus freed chose to remain in what was the only home they knew, many others sought a wider liberty and took to the road as showmen or pedlars.

These nameless captives are mostly forgotten now, but one at least is remembered in Dorset tradition, for his skull is preserved at Bettiscombe Manor House, and his angry ghost is said to fill the house with tumult whenever the skull is moved. This unhappy man was brought to England from the West Indies by Azariah Pinney when he was already full-grown and the less likely in consequence to settle down easily to a totally new life. What sort of welcome his strange black face and alien ways won him from the suspicious Dorset peasants around him we can well imagine, but he did not live to endure it long. He died of consumption contracted from the damp English airs, a fate that must have befallen many such children of the sun in our cold northern

climate. With his last breath he asked that his body might be sent home to the West Indies, and tradition has it that he threatened to haunt the house if this was not done. But needless to say, no one troubled to fulfil his request, and so the memory of this poor homesick creature is kept green for us by a horrific ghost-legend and part of an old skull still carefully kept in a box under the Manor House roof.

Wages were considerably higher than they had been when John Dee paid his Lettice 20*s.* for twelve months' work. A well-trained maid capable of taking a certain amount of responsibility was paid from £4 to £5 a year, and less experienced girls could ask from £2 to £3. Menservants in large houses received anything from £6 to £10 and their livery, and these sums they were usually able to supplement very considerably by the heavy "vails" which guests were then expected to give for the slightest service. In small establishments an indoor man might have £4 or £5 with a certain amount of free clothing, usually a coat, waistcoat, and hat. Parson Woodforde's wage-bill for five servants in 1783 came to £22 10*s.* 6*d.*—£5 15*s.* 6*d.* for his head maid, £2 0*s.* 6*d.* for the second maid, £4 4*s.* for his manservant, 10*s.* 6*d.* for the boy and £10 for the outside man who worked on the farm.

In addition to these sums, he had to pay a tax of £2 10*s.* for the indoor man and one of 10*s.* for each of the maids. The Napoleonic wars brought an ever-increasing number of new taxes in their wake, and by the end of the eighteenth century we hear of charges upon land, houses, incomes, horses and carts, windows, and dogs. "Willm Bidewell and James Pegg called on me this morning," writes Woodforde in his *Diary* on 19 July 1796, "to know how many Dogs I intend to pay for, two only." On another day in the same year he records that he "paid Mr. Corbould £3 3*s.* to get three Receipts for the Powder-Tax from Norwich on Saturday next."[1] This last was a tax on hair-powder levied in 1795 at the rate of £1 1*s.* a head. It largely defeated its own object by causing a revolution in fashion, for after its introduction only the most conservative clung to their powdered hair, and by doing so earned for themselves the nickname of "guinea-pigs". The rest evaded payment by wearing their hair unadorned, an innovation which must, one imagines, have been welcomed by all who had to clean the bedrooms or powder-closets where heads were dressed.

In ordinary houses servants were normally engaged through the recommendation of friends or by personal application, and their wages were fixed in each case by agreement between

[1] *The Diary of a Country Parson*, ed. J. D. Beresford, 1924–31.

employer and employed. It is interesting to note that in many instances tea is specially mentioned in such agreements. This beverage, once so expensive a luxury, had now descended to the servants' hall, but it was still sufficiently rare to stand outside the customary diet provided there. Parson Woodforde's various maids all seem to have expected it; one engaged in 1776 was to be given it twice a day as part of her wages, and another had an extra allowance paid to her to find herself in tea and sugar. The clothes allowed to each servant were renewed once a year, and wages also were paid annually, on or near the anniversary of the original engagement.

Farm servants and labourers were usually hired in public at the Michaelmas or Statute Fairs held in every considerable market town. These fairs derived from the ancient Statutes of Labourers by which Justices of the Peace were authorized to fix the current rates of wages and to proclaim them annually at Michaelmas. The Statutes themselves had been passed at various times to deal with the disorganization caused by the Black Death and other plagues, and when, in Elizabeth's reign, they were repealed, the Michaelmas fairs were specially retained, for they were considered too useful to be abolished with the laws from which they sprang. Legally they were not fairs at all, since they had no charter and were merely gatherings of would-be employers and employed. But the large crowds they attracted soon brought booths and stalls in their wake, as well as amusements of all kinds to fill the hours after the hirings were ended, and where the paraphernalia of a fair existed, the name soon followed. Hither came farmers seeking labourers, and their wives in search of maids, and here also came the servants, to stand in lines until they were chosen, each one bearing a symbol of his particular calling—a crook or tuft of wool for a shepherd, a whip for a horseman, and so on. Once they were engaged, and the bargain clinched by the traditional "luck-penny", they were expected to stay a full year on the farm, and only for unusually serious misdemeanours were they dismissed before their twelve months had passed. If, however, the farmer said nothing towards the end of the time about renewing the engagement, his hinds and maids knew they would have to seek another master at the ensuing Statute Fair.

In this, as in most other periods, we hear a good deal in letters and diaries about the idleness and unreliability of servants and occasionally of exasperated masters and mistresses beating or otherwise punishing them for their faults. Footmen were noted for their insolence, and maids too were sometimes impertinent

44 The Kitchen of a London House, *c.* 1820

From a water-colour by G. Scharf

and careless. "I gave Eliza warning," wrote young Mrs. Freemantle in her first year of wifehood, "she is a giddy, impudent thing."[1] Drunkenness was a constant fault amongst the men, for heavy drinking was the principal vice of the age, and working-men were no freer from it than their masters. "My servants were both rather in liquor," wrote Parson Woodforde indignantly on 17 April 1777, "and as for Will, he behaved very surly and went to bed before I supped, a pretty return for giving him half a guinea last week."[2] Mr. Newton, Secretary of the Royal Academy, had a still more unpleasant experience in 1794 when he "dined with some magistrates in the neighbourhood of his House at Barton in Somersetshire, and was a little effected by liquor, but on coming to his carriage He found his servants much more so, which caused him to put them into the carriage and He mounted the Coach Box." He was not the only employer to suffer such a mishap after the coachman and footmen had been entertained in too hospitable kitchens, but in this case the results were, unfortunately, fatal. The night was wet and the coachman's box afforded no shelter to a driver who was not dressed for the work. "He neglected," writes John Farington, "when he got home to use any precautions against cold, the consequence was an immediate fever which killed him in two days."[3]

Yet in spite of much grumbling in the parlour and, no doubt, corresponding grievances in the kitchen, the old paternal feeling persisted in most houses. It did not occur to Parson Woodforde to dismiss Will for his surly behaviour and probably, if he had lived, Mr. Newton would have retained his drunken coachman after a suitable reprimand. Servants were still regarded as junior members of the family and as such were allowed a great deal of freedom both in speech and action. If they were sometimes punished in a way which would not be tolerated to-day, they also received many gifts and treats from indulgent masters. Mr. Woodforde notes in his Diary several small sums of money paid to pedlars for trifles for his maids, and also a supper party given by his servants to those of a neighbour for which "a couple of rost Fowls and some good Punch" were provided. He also arranged with the village schoolmaster to give his two men lessons in reading and writing and paid him 4*s.* 6*d.* a quarter for doing so.

Other contemporary writings reflect the same kindly spirit. Some servants remained from childhood to old age in one household and were loved and respected by the children who had

[1] *The Wynne Diaries*, Vol. II, ed. A. Freemantle, 1935–40.
[2] Woodforde, *op. cit.*
[3] *The Farington Diary*, Vol. I, ed. J. Grieg.

grown up round them. Even without years of service behind them, they took a very genuine interest in their master's affairs and were allowed to do so without any suggestion of presumption on their part. When Claver Morris quarrelled with his daughter for marrying against his will, the maids joined with his wife in urging him to forgive her. "My daughter, with my wife, Mrs. Evans and all the maid servants came into my chamber," he writes, "while I was putting on my clothes. I refused to see her and ordered her to be had down and going into my closet I shut the door."[1] But, supported as she was by the open sympathy of her stepmother and the whole household, she finally persuaded him to pardon her; and we can well imagine the excited chatter that went on in the kitchen during these proceedings and the eager congratulations of the friendly maids when all was satisfactorily concluded.

The day did not begin quite as early as in the previous century. The normal hour for rising in an ordinary household was about seven o'clock, though fashionable ladies sometimes slept much later after the fatigues of parties, and one diarist confesses with remorse that he frequently lay in bed till noon. Breakfast was coming into its own as a regular meal, but it was not served immediately as it is to-day. The housewife had already discharged many of her varied duties, and her children had spent two or three hours in study or exercise before the family gathered in the dining-parlour at ten o'clock or thereabouts. At the beginning of the Georgian period the meal was a light one, consisting of toast, bread, rusks and butter, with tea, coffee, or chocolate, instead of the ale that had once been customary. In the country meat was sometimes eaten as well, but the heavy breakfasts of the early nineteenth century were not yet usual. It was the steady advance of the dinner hour which made them so. The noonday meal was gradually moving forward, at first to two o'clock, then to three or four, and so by slow degrees to five, six and even, in very fashionable circles, seven o'clock. "In my memory," wrote Richard Steele at the beginning of the century, "the dinner hour has crept from 12 o'clock to 3." Sixty or seventy years later the ordinary citizen sat down at five or six, and only the more conservative clung to the three o'clock dinner which had seemed so very late to Steele when it was first introduced.

Dinner and supper were the only considerable meals of the day, the latter served about half-past nine or ten at night, and consisting of a great variety of cold meats, bread, fruit, sweets,

[1] *The Diary of a West Country Physician*, ed. E. Hobhouse, 1934.

45 A Card Party

From an illustration by Thomas Rowlandson

46 A Farm Kitchen of *c.* 1800

47 "The Merry Thought"

48 "Telling Fortunes in Coffee Grounds"

From prints of c. 1790

and wine. Luncheon did not exist except in the form of a light snack taken about noon or, for townsmen, a cup of coffee or chocolate at one of the numerous coffee-houses. Morning visitors were offered a glass of wine, with cake or biscuits; in a wealthy house cold meat might be provided, and occasionally a country picnic called for such substantial dishes as chickens, pies and salads. But on ordinary days only very slight refreshments were considered necessary between breakfast and dinner, and the morning hours were left free for work, exercise and visiting without the interruption of a set meal in the dining-parlour.

Afternoon tea began to make its appearance towards the end of the century, but only amongst those who dined fashionably late. In most households tea (37) was provided immediately after dinner in much the same way as coffee is provided to-day. Sometimes it was accompanied by thin bread and butter or toast, foods which seem to have been peculiar to England at that time, since foreign visitors so often remarked upon them. "The slices of bread which they give you with your tea," wrote Pastor Moritz in 1782, "are as thin as poppy-leaves—But there is another kind of bread and butter usually eaten with tea, which is toasted by the fire and is incomparably good. This is called toast."[1] It must have seemed to him excellent indeed to call forth such praise from the critical German pastor, for in general he thought little of English cooking. He declared that we lived chiefly upon half-boiled or half-roasted meat and cabbage leaves boiled in plain water, with a sauce made of flour and butter that he evidently did not admire. As for our coffee, he considered it atrocious. "I would always advise those who wish to drink coffee in England," he wrote, "to mention beforehand how many cups are to be made with half an ounce, or else the people will probably bring them a prodigious quantity of brown fluid."[2]

There is something familiar about this last complaint which has occasionally been echoed by foreigners in our own day. Probably there was less criticism of tea, for here the English housewife was on her own ground, and there was scarcely a woman in the kingdom who was not experienced in its making. One of the most remarkable changes of the age was the steady rise to favour of this exotic drink, which had once been far less popular than chocolate, and was now fast displacing both that and coffee, and even threatening to shake the supremacy of ale. Although the price had fallen considerably by the middle of the eighteenth century, it was still expensive, much more so, indeed, than coffee, which cost about 4*s.* 6*d.* or 5*s.* a pound. In 1757

[1] C. P. Moritz, *A Journey to England*, 1782. [2] C. P. Moritz, *op. cit.*

green tea could be bought for 12*s.* a pound and Hyson tea for 14*s.* or 16*s.*, while Bohea sometimes cost as much as 30*s.* or 35*s.* Such prices, however, were not enough to check its widespread consumption, nor had the fulminations of those who considered it a harmful drug or the complaints of old-fashioned people who thought it effeminate any effect whatever upon the growing fashion. The manner of serving to some extent offset the cost. Both from preference and from motives of economy it was made extremely weak, and a little probably went a long way. Moreover, those who had no scruples about using contraband goods —in other words, the majority of the population—generally found it possible to obtain supplies more cheaply. A very large quantity was smuggled into the country every year and this, since it evaded the heavy tax of 5*s.* a pound, could be sold at prices considerably lower than those obtaining in the ordinary markets.

Tea was by no means confined to the tables of the rich in spite of its high cost. The poor drank it quite as often as the well-to-do and much preferred it to the cheaper coffee or cocoa. Sir Frederick Eden tells us in *The State of the Poor* that cottagers in southern England took it regularly three times a day, and we have already seen that maids expected it when they went out to service. "Your very Chambermaids," wrote Jonas Hanway disgustedly in 1757, "have lost their bloom, I suppose by sipping tea."[1] Social reformers constantly deplored the use of such luxuries by working-men who, they thought, would do better to make barley broth and other nourishing soups instead of spending money upon tea and its accompanying sugar. But hard words rarely alter habits, and in fact the sums so spent cannot have been very large. Needless to say, the poorly paid labourers of those days could not afford to buy tea, or anything else, at 12*s.* a pound. They bought the cheapest smuggled varieties and husbanded them with the utmost care, using the leaves a second and third time whenever possible and mixing them with other herbs to make them go further. Sometimes they eked out their supplies by buying used tea-leaves for a few pence from the cooks of the well-to-do who regarded such remainders as their perquisites. If nothing better could be had, they drank sage-tea, a substitute for the true tea imported from China that was used by economical housewives of all classes, while infusions of rosemary, dandelions, cowslips, nettles, and violets, were freely taken as tonics and medicines.

Dinner was both the main meal and the central point of the day in that leisurely age when so few people had to hurry off to

[1] *An Essay on Tea*, by Mr. Hxxxx, 1757.

office or factory. A dinner engagement was then no mere matter of a few hours away from home but a lengthy entertainment covering most of the afternoon and evening. It was quite usual to spend an hour or so upon the meal itself, and to follow it by tea in the drawing-room and later on a quite substantial supper before the guests departed. Two courses only were served in most houses, but each contained a great variety of dishes which were all placed on the table at once. It was not yet customary to have the food handed round by servants. This was a fashion borrowed from the Continent which first appeared amongst more travelled people in the early nineteenth century. During most of the Georgian period the diners waited upon themselves and upon each other. Each man helped himself from the dish before him and offered some of it to his neighbours; if he wanted something beyond his reach he sent a servant for it, or called across the table in friendly fashion to the man nearest the particular dish he fancied.

No one then insulted his host by bringing a delicate appetite to table. Regardless of their figures, both men and women ate heartily and drank deep, and the results, somewhat exaggerated, may be seen in the pot-bellied gentleman and overblown ladies of contemporary cartoons. The amount of food consumed every day in the eighteenth century was prodigious. Enormous quantities of beef, pork, venison, mutton, and veal, were eaten, with poultry of all kinds, fish, cheese, tarts, good solid puddings and elaborate sweetmeats made with generous supplies of eggs and cream. Fruit was fast losing its evil reputation as a breeder of fevers and was now very popular. Plums, apricots, gooseberries, cherries, apples, pears, and quinces, could be had from native gardens, and large quantities of oranges, lemons, limes, and melons, were imported, as well as bananas which were cooked in tarts and dumplings and very rarely eaten raw. Vegetables also, in spite of Pastor Moritz's remarks upon our devotion to cabbage, were much more plentiful and varied than they had been in the previous century. We hear of asparagus, French beans, peas, mushrooms, turnips, "frill'd potatoes", and celery, as well as the older carrots and coleworts and a variety of salads. The only food which, compared with modern usage, was eaten in small quantities was bread. What there was was usually made of wheaten flour. The maslin and other mixed breads of earlier times had largely disappeared, and even the poor thought themselves hard done by if they could not have wheat loaves, except in the North of England where oatcakes were more usual in cottage homes than bread of any kind.

Our ancestors often noted in their diaries what they ate in their own and other people's houses, and the menus they have preserved for us show how little they believed in stinting themselves. Catherine Hutton records how on one occasion "we sat down to dinner, which consisted of three boiled chickens at top, a very fine haunch of venison at bottom; ham at one side, a flour pudding on the other, and beans in the middle. After the cloth was removed, we had gooseberries, and a remarkably fine dish of apricots."[1] Parson Woodforde was another who was interested in his food and not ashamed to say so, and he tells us of many excellent meals, both those he ate when he was alone and the various dinner-parties at which he was host or guest. "A boiled Leg of Mutton and Capers, a Duck rosted and one of Nancy's Puddings, with Jelly," sufficed for himself and his niece on one occasion; on another they had "boiled chicken and a pig's face, a bullock's heart roasted and a rich plumb pudding." On Good Friday, being a fast day, he ate no meat at all and did not dine till five, when he had fritters and toasted cheese and Nancy had eggs.

When he entertained, this simple clergyman whose income was not more than £400 a year, really let himself go. For five guests in 1770 he provided "a dish of fine Tench . . . Ham and 3 Fowls boiled, a Plumb Pudding; a couple of Ducks rosted, a rosted neck of Pork, a Plum Tart and an Apple Tart, Pears, Apples and Nutts after dinner; White Wine and red, Beer and Cyder." After this meal, which began at four o'clock, there was coffee and tea and, in case the guests should feel hungry going home, "Hashed Fowl and Duck and Eggs and Potatoes, etc., for supper" at ten. At a really elegant dinner to which he was invited by the Bishop of the diocese in 1783, there were two courses of twenty dishes each, and a further twenty dishes of dessert afterwards, all served upon a table decked with urns of artificial flowers and a miniature garden with a temple and shepherdesses which Woodforde describes as "one of the prettiest things I ever saw."[2]

In hotels and wayside inns also the variety and cheapness of the food provided at short notice was astonishing. Viscount Torrington paid 4*s.* 5*d.* at Broadway in 1787 for a chicken, an apricot tart and "liquors"; at Basingstoke he had a rabbit and a sole, and in the little village of "Nesscliff" he "made a glorious repast" of roast veal, peas, and potatoes. Arthur Young, whose travels through England and Wales made him a connoisseur of

[1] *Reminiscences of a Gentlewoman of the Last Century*, ed. Mrs. C. H. Beale, 1891.
[2] Woodforde, *op. cit.*

inns, thought one Newcastle hotel "extravgantly dear" because he was charged 2*s*. 6*d*. there for a boiled fowl, oysters, and a woodcock. At Penrith he paid 1*s*. for roast beef, apple pudding, potatoes, celery, potted trout, and sturgeon, and even a very disagreeable and dirty inn at Rotherham could provide hashed venison, potted mackerel, cold ham, tarts, cheese, and a melon, for the same modest sum.

All this food was washed down with plentiful supplies of varied drinks, from herbal teas and cordials to imported brandy. Countrymen drank ale and small beer made in their own homes, and cider or perry from their own orchards. Townsmen, who had not the same facilities, depended on the breweries whose products were not always by any means as pure as the country varieties. The gentry drank wine of all sorts, especially port which was extremely cheap in the early part of the century since the duty on it was very low. Eighteenpence was then the usual price for a quart bottle; in later years, when the duties were raised, the price increased very considerably. Spirits also were generally popular. The London poor drank so much bad gin that the Government was forced to take steps to suppress the innumerable gin-shops that plied their trade in every back street and undermined the health of the people by selling adulterated liquor as harmful as it was fiery. The well-to-do drank rum and brandy, much of which was smuggled. Few people, however respectable, had any objection to using contraband goods provided that they could escape detection. "Please tell her," wrote Henry Paschall in 1723, sending a message to his daughter, Lady Fermanagh, "that Vand-vord, as things now are, will not be capable of furnishing any Brandy, there being so strict a watch set on the river."[1] Even so genuinely religious a man as Parson Woodforde had no scruples about receiving tea and spirits from Richard Andrews and John Buck, the local blacksmith, both of whom were "free traders". "Andrews the Smuggler brought me this night about 11 o'clock a bag of Hyson Tea 6 Pd. weight," he tells us in 1777, "he frightened us a little by whistling under the Parlour Window." How well we can imagine the good old parson and his niece looking at each other in the candle-lit room and nervously wondering whether anyone else had heard that tell-tale whistle.

On another night in 1786 a thump on the door brought him out to find a tub of gin and another of brandy standing unattended on the step. Once he had a bad fright when Buck was betrayed by some enemy to the excisemen, but soon afterwards,

[1] *Verney Letters.*

the alarm having died down, he was again buying goods from the same illicit source. Smugglers, indeed, like the highwaymen of the previous century, were rather admired than otherwise in spite of the really horrible crimes committed by the more lawless among them. Hardly anyone considered it morally wrong to cheat the Government of taxes on necessities, and even luxuries like India muslin, cambric, silk, and tobacco, were cheerfully bought by many who would have resented fiercely any imputation of dishonesty.

In all this plenty the poor shared until hard times came at the end of the century. Foreigners were astounded to see how well they lived, how much ale they drank, and how varied was their diet compared with that of peasants in other countries. Most cottagers in those prosperous early years had their butcher's meat once or twice a week, their pork and bacon from their own pigs and eggs from their own hens. When meat could be bought for 2*d.* or 3*d.* a pound, cheese for 2*d.* and butter for 5*d.* or 6*d.*, there was no reason why the labourer should not eat as heartily as he wished. He could still vary his diet with rabbits snared in the fields or fish from local streams, and an occasional poached bird did not come amiss, though the game laws had already robbed him of much wild food that his ancestors had enjoyed. In the north of England less meat was eaten, but there was plenty of oatmeal, milk, and cheese, and everywhere there were good supplies of ale to go with the solid puddings and fat pork that working-men preferred.

It was this bounty in the first half of the century that made the later shortage seem so hard. Between 1764 and 1776 a series of bad harvests forced up the price of bread and with it that of many other necessities. When the quartern loaf reached the unprecedented price of 1*s.* 6*d.*, as it did once in 1777, the poor man was hard hit indeed. Enclosures also were slowly but surely depriving him of his pig or his cow, and even greater hardships befell him when the long wars with France sent the cost of living rocketing upwards without any corresponding rise in wages. It was then that the labourer really felt the pinch, and families that had been accustomed to good meat at least once or twice a week were lucky if they saw it even on festival occasions. In times of dearth the local authorities did what they could by relieving individual households and subsidizing wages out of the rates but, in default of a national organization, they could only touch the edges of the problem. The bugbear of high rates was always in their minds, and many magistrates and overseers were more concerned with moving on the paupers who did not belong

to their parish than with giving adequate help to those who did. Economists in general took a somewhat unsympathetic view of the poor man's distress. They urged him to eat less, to give up tea and butter, to substitute rye bread for wheaten loaves; they did not suggest that wages might be raised to meet the increased cost of living. One West Country parson, John Acland, advocated a system of insurance not unlike our own, but he was before his time, and no one took any notice of so revolutionary a suggestion.

Yet in spite of the harsh doctrines disseminated in the writings of the time, there was much real charity and a genuine desire to relieve suffering wherever it was found. If the wealthy failed to do all they might have done, it was more from lack of imagination than from unwillingness. Farmers allowed the villagers to glean in their fields at harvest-time, and so to gather enough corn to keep them a long time in bread. On St. Thomas's Day country women went "a-Thomassing" and received gifts of wheat which the miller ground for them without charge so that they might have sufficient bread and cakes on Christmas Day. The squire in nearly every parish gave food, coals, and blankets, to his people at this season, and Parson Woodforde annually entertained seven poor men to a dinner of beef and plum pudding. He records many other small charities in his diary, gifts of food or money to poor parishioners, to discharged soldiers and wandering beggars, as well as collections made in his church during the bad years. In general the wealthy and the comfortably-off, though they rarely thought of paying better wages, had a strong sense of responsibility towards those less fortunate than themselves. The care of the poor was then almost entirely a personal matter, for the State did little or nothing for them, and the children of the manor house were trained from a very early age to take a real interest in their welfare. Jane Austen's *Emma* provides a good example of the prevailing outlook, for that spoilt and rather frivolous young woman never failed in this respect, and we are told that she not only helped those who needed it with money and good food, but also "entered into their troubles with ready sympathy, and always gave her assistance with as much intelligence as good will."[1]

The labourer himself faced all his difficulties with a courage and independence that testified to the fine stock from which he sprang. The generations of good living behind him stood him in good stead when food was scarce, and through lean years and fat, he continued to raise his large family, to eat heartily when things

[1] Jane Austen, *Emma*.

went well, and to tighten his belt when they went badly. "Probably no workman in Europe," said Lecky in his *History of the Eighteenth Century*, "could equal the Englishman in physical strength, in sustained power and energy of work, and few, if any, could surpass him in thoroughness and fidelity in the performance of his task, in general rectitude and honesty of character." These words were written of the labourer in the prosperous early years of the century, but they were no less true of him at its end. His inherited toughness could not be undermined by a few bad seasons, and it took many years of scarcity and bad conditions to impair the magnificent bodily and mental health that was perhaps the finest possession of eighteenth-century England.

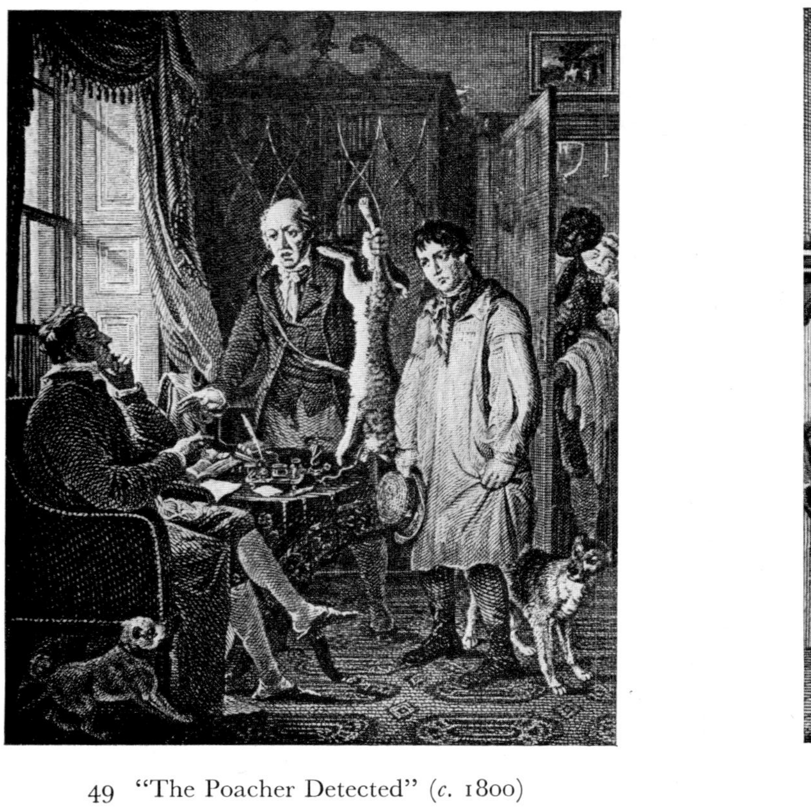

49 "The Poacher Detected" (*c.* 1800)

50 Round the Fireside (*c.* 1775)

51, 52, 53 At a Private School, a Public School, and at the University *From prints by Thomas Rowlandson (1802)*

Chapter X

GROWING-UP

GEORGIAN nurseries were usually as well filled as those of Stuart times and in many ways they were much more cheerful and natural places in which to start one's life. At all events, their inmates were not hustled out of them and into the schoolroom quite so quickly, though they were often hustled unwittingly into the grave by an excess of misplaced care. Infant mortality was still extremely high, so high indeed that it was generally regarded as something tragic but inevitable. There were few parents who had not to face the loss of one or two children in the course of their lives, and parish registers everywhere provide sad lists of infant funerals. The same infectious diseases that carried off the Stuart children attacked the eighteenth-century baby and were fought with almost the same degree of ignorance till vaccination put a check upon the worst of all towards the end of the century; and if happily the child escaped these scourges, he not infrequently fell a victim to the curious notions of dressing and feeding which then prevailed.

Chills were the principal terror of the careful mother, and to avoid them she wrapped the baby in tight swaddling-bands and kept him in over-hot rooms from which the sunlight was excluded so far as possible for fear it should injure his eyes. These swaddling clothes were also supposed to keep his limbs straight, though in fact they prevented him from exercising them naturally and freely. His diet varied according to the circumstances of the household. The most fortunate children were those whose mothers fed them in infancy; the rest were nourished mainly on soft paps made from flour and milk and administered through a horn or an earthenware "bubby-pot" with a glove-finger over one end to act as a teat. Sometimes a piece of sponge was put inside the finger to regulate the flow of liquid. If the nurse was conscientious and well-trained it was constantly renewed, but if she was not, it might be left where it was for an indefinite time, to provide a perfect paradise for germs which the unfortunate baby absorbed with his food.

Wet nurses were often employed in families where the mother was unable to look after her own children, but there was a growing prejudice against them. It was still believed that the nurse's vices could be absorbed with her milk, and there was also a more

reasonable objection in some cases to her ministrations. When gin was cheap and easily obtainable, as it was in the early part of the century, nurses, like other people, sometimes drank too much of it, and a few were not above quietening their charges with little sips of spirit. Cows' milk was distrusted by many mothers as too heavy a food, and they preferred to make a pap of rice-flour or arrowroot mixed with asses' milk. "Augusta is the name of the Youngest," wrote Mrs. Drake of one nursery brood in 1783, "she has had three Wet Nurses and none gave satisfaction, so the old Lying-in nurse came here with her, and she is fed with pap made of Asses' milk, and it seems to agree with her for she looks extremely healthy and well."[1]

Doctors and parents occasionally disagreed on the subject of diet, for the more advanced physician deplored the use of these paps and the habit of putting babies much too early on to heavier foods. "They are fed on meat before they have got their teeth," wrote Sir William Fordyce in 1773, "and what is, if possible, still worse, on biscuits not fermented, or buttered rolls, or tough muffins floated in oiled butter, or calves-feet jellies, or strong broths, yet more calculated to load all their powers of digestion."[2] A few pioneers, like William Cadogan, went so far as to stress the virtues of air and sunlight and to urge the substitution of loose clothing for swaddling-bands. Such revolutionary notions had little effect upon established custom, nor were they supported by every practising physician or indeed, by the majority. And so great is the toughness of even infant humanity that many babies persisted in living and growing to healthy manhood in spite of all the disadvantages with which their careful and loving parents surrounded them.

Once out of their nurses' arms, the children of leisured families could look forward to a few carefree years before school or tutor curtailed a precious liberty. Absolute obedience and respect for parents was still expected, but it was no longer considered unnatural for a child to love play, or even to prefer it to study. In the Russell household accounts there are several pleasant entries of sums spent on toys for little Lord Tavistock and his sisters. A book of drawings for Lady Caroline cost 5*s.* in 1753 and a battledore and shuttlecock for her brother cost 4*s.* 6*d.* Some whips and tops were bought on another occasion for sixpence, and the same sum was paid for a new door to a cherished dormouse's cage.[3] In the *Verney Letters* there is a very charming account of

[1] *Dear Miss Heber . . .*, ed. Francis Bamford 1936.
[2] Sir William Fordyce, *A New Inquiry into the Causes, Symptoms and Cure of Putrid and Inflammatory Fevers*, 1773.
[3] G. Scott Thomson, *The Russells in Bloomsbury*, 1669–1771.

Ralph Verney's life at Claydon when he was not quite seven years old. He had been left in the Rector's charge while his family were in London, and in 1721 his temporary guardian wrote to his father:

> I can no longer contain my Joy for our good Success hitherto with that dear Pledge you have left in our Hands. He is in perfect Health and seems well-content with his Company, and the sweetness of his Temper and Vivacity of Spirit, joyn'd with the Innocency of his Age, renders him the delight of all about him. He lyes in a little Room hung with Paper, which is a sort of Alcove within ours, so that we are near at hand upon any occasion; and he has a Bedfellow, as my Lady directed, but I hope his good Angel, or rather that Eye of Providence, which neither slumbers nor sleeps, will be his continual Guard. After Prayers and Dressing, betwixt the Book and the Top and other Diversions, the hours pass smoothly and not unprofitably away; so that tho' he is everyone's Care and concerne, he is a Trouble to none. He pleases himself with imagination of his Brother's being cooped up in a little house whilst he has the liberty of ranging the Garden and the Fields, and on Church-Days has the sole Ringing of the Bell, and the whole property of the News-Papers. He was in great expectation of the Drum and Fiddle on Thursday night, and when the Carrier delivered the one broken and the other lyeing at the bottom of the Waggon, could not be come at, he bore the Disappointment with the Temper of a Philosopher.

All this is a long way removed from Sir Henry Slingsby's anxious ponderings on his child's deplorable love of play, or the harsh training of that other Verney child whose great-grandmother pleaded for him in vain. A later age of marriage permitted a longer childhood, and the general decline of religious fervour had at least this one advantage that children were less often regarded as creatures of sin whose soul must be saved as fast as possible at whatever cost to their natural high spirits. "The Innocency of his Age", spoken of a child of seven, is not a seventeenth-century phrase. John Wesley, it is true, held that children were born wicked and needed to be driven to grace by frequent beatings, but this harshness in a man not otherwise unkindly was probably due quite as much to his own stern upbringing as to religious beliefs. His mother, he tells us, strove always "to conquer the will of her children betimes", and brought them up "to fear the rod and to cry softly". Severity and not indulgence was her rule and if, as her son says, "the odious noise of the crying of children was rarely heard in the house",[1] it was

[1] *The Journals of John Wesley* (Standard edition), 1910.

probably because tears would bring further punishment rather than because there was never anything to cry about. Many worthy people, doubtless, approved of Mrs. Wesley's methods, but such notions were far less common than they had once been. In spite of the instant obedience still theoretically demanded, the average boy or girl was allowed much more liberty than formerly, and it must be admitted that the children depicted in Jane Austen's novels were often quite as spoilt as the most pampered modern infant.

A boy's education usually began at home under a tutor (55) who gave him a good grounding in the classics and taught him the elements of mathematics and history. Where there was no resident tutor, the local clergyman sometimes coached the squire's sons, or a series of visiting masters came from the nearest town to give instruction in different subjects. There were then no preparatory schools in the modern sense, and home teaching was almost the only convenient method of preparing for public school or university. The grammar schools, where boys of all classes had once studied together, had greatly deteriorated in many districts, and it was no longer customary for the children of the gentry to attend them. Less wealthy parents who could not afford a tutor, or the heavy costs of the larger public schools, sometimes sent their sons to private academies where a classical education could be obtained more cheaply. Such private establishments were becoming increasingly popular, and by the middle of the century there was a fair number to choose from round London and in other parts of the country (56). Arthur Young noticed one at Scorton in Yorkshire where "the method of teaching is the same as at Eton", but the fees were considerably lower. "Boys are boarded," he tells us, "in a very proper manner for £10 10*s*. a year. The tutorage is £2 2*s*. more; and all expences do not rise to £15."[1] We do not, of course, know what his ideas of "proper" board were, and certainly in some schools the diet was very poor and the accommodation rough. But fifteen pounds cannot be regarded as unduly expensive when we remember that holidays were then both few and short, and the children had to be fed, housed and taught through terms which lasted for five or six months at a time.

In the public schools the charges were much higher. Young Lord Tavistock's board at Westminster in 1755 cost £25, with £10 for his room, and an extra £5 for a fire. He paid a guinea for sitting in the Abbey and 6*s*. for the cleaning of his shoes. His books cost £11 7*s*. 11*d*., and there were a good many other items

[1] Arthur Young, *A Six Months' Tour through the North of England*, 1771.

54 A Dame School

From the painting by John Opie

55 The Tutor and his Pupil

From the painting by John Zoffany

56 A Break between Lessons at the Salvadore Academy, Tooting (1787)

57 The Classroom of a Village School, *c.* 1800

in his account, including one of £1 3*s.* 3*d.* "for washing 93 waistcoats".[1] Besides the ordinary subjects taught in the school he learnt fencing, dancing, and French, which were paid for separately, and there were also writing lessons, the fees for which amounted to £8 8*s.* a year.

This separation of writing from the general curriculum, which seems so curious to us, was then quite usual. Amongst educated people great attention was paid to calligraphy, and special writing-masters were engaged to instruct children in the art. To write a good hand was a mark of culture; in many humbler schools the subject was omitted altogether, and the pupils, if they wished to learn it, went to special writing-schools. Thus little Catherine Hutton studied reading and needlework in one place and calligraphy in another, while in a higher social sphere Lady Caroline Russell and her brother were taught by a visiting master who charged £2 12*s.* 6*d.* for thirty lessons in handwriting.

School life did not begin quite so early as it had done in the previous century, and the usual age for entrance to the Universities were correspondingly later. Ralph Verney, who had no resident tutor, went to his private school at Brentford when he was not quite eight years old, but Lord Tavistock did not leave home for Westminster until he was fourteen, and both lads were eighteen—grown men by their grandfathers' standards—when they went up to Cambridge. The cost of University residence had risen considerably since the days when Sir Peter Legh maintained his two sons at Oxford for £139 in James I's reign. Not only was everything rather more expensive but the students, being older, expected larger allowances, nor could their expenditure be as carefully supervised and checked as in the earlier years when the average age of undergraduates was thirteen or fourteen. "With good management they may doe with £200 a yeare," wrote Lady Cave in 1721, "and their servants' wages and board wages payd besides, but not under; My Lady sent me a particular of Sir Humphrey Moneaxes expenses in the College at first setting out, and I find the same cant be done for Verney under £200, which is a deal for us, but I hope he'le deserve it."[2] Such a figure was too high for many people, but it did not altogether exclude the brilliant poor scholar who was determined to try for his degree. There were still free places open to him in most colleges; and if he failed to win one of these, he could go up as a Servitor or a Sizar and pay his way by personal services instead of ordinary fees.

Really wealthy parents finished their sons' education by sending them abroad with a tutor to make the Grand Tour. This

[1] G. Scott Thomson, *The Russells in Bloomsbury*, 1669–1771. [2] *Verney Letters.*

usually lasted for six months or a year, during which time the young men travelled in some state with their own servants and carriages, visited the different Courts of Europe, and gained a first-hand knowledge of foreign languages and manners. Only the rich, naturally, could afford to pay for such tours, but in those prosperous times there were enough of them to make the travelling Englishman well known on the Continent. When he returned he brought with him a variety of fresh ideas which flowed slowly outwards from the greater houses through the more insular and conservative homes of those who could not travel themselves. The Grand Tour was in part responsible for the renewed wave of interest in the arts which swept over the aristocracy in the first half of the eighteenth century, and the memorials of this now extinct habit may still be seen in the surviving Palladian mansions and the paintings and sculptures they contain.

Farmers and the smaller professional men who could not aspire to public schools or tutors, sent their sons to a grammar school if there was one within walking or riding distance, or a dame-school in the village where they could gain the rudiments of knowledge for a very small sum. Claver Morris paid 6*s*. 6*d*. a quarter for his little son's first lessons at one such establishment, and there were many others where reading, spelling and, occasionally, writing could be learnt for a few pence a week. A little arithmetic was sometimes included in the curriculum, but not always, and there was usually some handwork and, of course, sewing for the girls. No particular qualifications were demanded from the teachers at these places. Almost any one who could keep a little ahead of the pupils was considered competent to run them, and the tuition was naturally of the most elementary description. Nevertheless, hopelessly inadequate as they were, the dame-schools kept the torch of knowledge burning, however faintly, in many places where but for them it would have been altogether extinct; and not a few intelligent children whose parents would not or could not rise to the expenses of better schools must have lived to thank the ancient widow or broken-down schoolmaster who first taught them the art of reading and so opened to them the treasure-house of the world's literature.

The really poor, if they went anywhere, went to charity schools founded by the Society for the Promotion of Christian Knowledge, or to the older Free Schools which still existed in many districts. In the latter the grounding was often sound, if narrow, but much depended upon the character of the individual master. We hear of many schools declining because the master was a drunkard or incompetent, or because he was so poorly paid that

he was forced to undertake other work in order to live at all. Walter Gale at Mayfield had only £12 a year, and this meagre salary he supplemented by a number of other paid occupations which naturally caused him to neglect his pupils. He was a particularly bad example of a country schoolmaster, often drunk and, on his own confession, idle. "Began my school at noon," he writes on one occasion, and on another "Left off school at 2 o'clock, having heard the spellers and readers a lesson apiece, to attend a cricket match of the gamesters of Mayfield against those of Lindfield and Chailey."[1] He did not escape without stern reproof from the trustees and eventually he was dismissed, but unfortunately he was not the only master to whom the cricket pitch and the alehouse were more congenial than the schoolroom. Even in the middle of the nineteenth century the rural teacher was often a man of little ability, though at all times there were honourable exceptions. When Canon Atkinson asked why an obviously unsuitable man had been chosen to run the Free School at Danby, the senior churchwarden replied: "Wheaa, he could do nowght else. He had muddled away his land, and we put him in scheealmaster that he mou't get a bite of bread."[2]

Very often the children of the poor received no education at all. To send a child to school when he might be earning a few pence to add to the scanty family budget meant a very real sacrifice for a labourer, and he was hardly encouraged to make it by the prevailing ideas of his time. The love of knowledge for its own sake which shone so brightly in Elizabethan days had declined very considerably by the middle of the eighteenth century. Even prosperous yeomen were often quite content if their sons had mastered the three R's, and their daughters could sew and perhaps paint a little by the time their studies were ended, and what was enough for them was considered rather too much for those they employed. Many people thought education for the poor a dangerous experiment or at best an entirely unnecessary luxury. The fine, generous spirit that drove the Tudor magnate to spend his wealth on schools where poor scholars could learn Latin and mathematics had died away and the most that was now offered outside the ancient Free Schools was a little reading and handwork and the elements of religion.

There were, it is true, nearly two thousand charity schools in the country which had come into being since the Society for the Promotion of Christian Knowledge was founded in 1698, and these were followed later by the Sunday Schools that sprang from

[1] *The Diary of Walter Gale*, Sussex Archæological Collections, Vol. IX.
[2] Rev. J. C. Atkinson, *Forty Years in a Moorland Parish.*

Robert Raikes's pioneer foundation at Gloucester. To such schools the charitable freely gave their money and their approval, and the good work done in them was clearly seen by comparison with the state of ignorance amongst poor children in districts where no such establishments existed. But they were concerned more with useful work and religious teaching than with general education. Their promoters were usually satisfied if, at the end of their time, the pupils could read a little of the Bible, speak civilly, use their hands to good purpose, and repeat their Catechism. Nothing further was considered necessary or even desirable in an age when most men honestly believed that wider knowledge could do little good to manual workers and would probably lead to discontent. In view of the general low level of wages, it is not altogether surprising that labourers sometimes deprived their children of even these limited opportunities and sent them to work instead at a horrifyingly early age. Few people then thought it shocking that a child should toil for long hours in the fields, or even in the mills, from the moment it was able to use its hands, and in the bad years, when every penny counted, the children and their education were all too often sacrificed to the general needs of their impoverished families.

In well-to-do households the education of daughters was usually supervised by a governess who taught them when they were children and acted as their chaperon when they were old enough to need one. In many houses their lessons were supplemented by others from visiting masters who gave instruction in special subjects, such as writing, French, or dancing. A well-brought-up girl had normally some knowledge of history and geography, and could speak one or two languages; she could draw and paint a little, sing, play the harpsichord and perhaps the guitar, and do a variety of more or less ornamental fancy-work. She could also sew and embroider, though in the latter art she was not as skilled as her great-grandmother, and she was acquainted with the finer work of the stillroom and the dairy. In all that concerned housecraft she was thoroughly well trained, and her knowledge of music and poetry was often extensive. If she was seriously inclined towards learning she studied Latin with her brother's tutor, and might even have a smattering of Greek and mathematics. But unless she was a professed blue-stocking she did not parade her knowledge. "The second caution to be given her," wrote Lady Mary Wortley-Montagu in 1753 when giving advice on her granddaughter's education, "is to conceal whatever learning she attains, with as much solicitude as she would hide crookedness or lameness; the parade of it can only

58 A Doll's House of the early Eighteenth Century

59 A Visit to a Boarding School (1788)

From the painting by George Morland

60, 61 Children's Samplers of the Eighteenth Century

serve to draw on her the envy, and consequently the most inveterate hatred of all the he and she fools, which will certainly be at least three parts in four of all her acquaintance."[1]

This was perhaps a little exaggerated, the bitter comment of one who was herself a highly educated woman, brought up in the later Stuart period when women's minds were encouraged to a freer flowering than at the time in which she wrote. There were many eighteenth-century women whose minds were quite as highly trained as those of their brothers and husbands, and some who presided over *salons* unsurpassed in any later age in their brilliance and wit. But in general the Georgian girl was not as well taught as her Tudor or Stuart ancestress. Her spelling was certainly better than her grandmother's, and her housewifely attainments quite as good, but far too much of her time was spent in learning polite accomplishments, to the detriment of real education. All that was normally expected of her when her training was finished was that she should be able to express herself in her own language and perhaps French and Italian as well, sing, play, and draw, with some taste, and comport herself gracefully in society.

If she wished to add Latin or mathematics to her list of accomplishments, she was generally allowed to do so, but no one considered this really necessary, and some parents looked with suspicion upon too much devotion to learning as likely to frighten off possible husbands. To be charming abroad and capable at home was her main duty in life, and anything which did not actually help towards this end was of only secondary importance, if indeed it was not regarded as a disadvantage. Lady Mary Wortley-Montagu drew up an excellent course of study for her grand-daughter which included English literature, Latin, Greek, mathematics and modern languages, but when she had sent it she was seized with misgivings. In her next letter to the girl's mother she says:

> I cannot help writing a sort of apology for my last letter, forseeing you will think it wrong, or at least Lord Bute will be extremely shocked at the proposal of a learned education for daughters, which the generality of men believe as great a profanation as the clergy would do if the laity should presume to exercise the functions of the priesthood. I desire you would take notice, I would not have learning enjoined them as a task but permitted as a pleasure if their genius leads them naturally to it.[2]

Some girls were sent to finish their education at boarding-schools. Of these there was a fair number of all kinds, from

[1] *Letters of Lady Mary Wortley-Montagu.* [2] *Ibid.*

fashionable seminaries for the daughters of the nobility to the more homely establishments that catered for the children of farmers. In many such schools far more attention was paid to deportment than to any other subject, but some gave a good training in housewifely matters and all provided instruction in the accomplishments then thought necessary for a young lady. Painting upon glass, shell-work, waxwork of all sorts, lace-making and mould-work, are listed in the prospectus of one school, and it is perhaps worthy of note that these come before writing and arithmetic, which appear at the bottom of the list. Dancing, of course, was essential and in most good schools music was thoroughly taught. A general grounding in ordinary subjects and a complete training in social conventions and good manners were what was chiefly desired by parents, and if there was sometimes rather too much stress laid upon the frills of education, most girls came away from these seminaries more or less fitted for their future careers as elegant young ladies and competent wives. Jane Austen, in *Emma*, gives us a pleasant picture of a good middle-class school in the late eighteenth century where forty girls were brought up on common-sense lines and were amply fed and housed for fairly moderate fees. "Mrs. Goddard," she tells us,

> was the mistress of a school—not of a seminary, or an establishment, or anything which professed, in long sentences of refined nonsense, to combine liberal acquirements with elegant morality, upon new principles and new systems, and where young ladies for enormous pay might be screwed out of health and into vanity, but a real, honest, old-fashioned boarding-school, where a reasonable quantity of accomplishments were sold at a reasonable price, and where girls might be sent out of the way and scramble themselves into a little education, without any danger of coming back prodigies.

The end of all this feminine education was, of course, marriage, then almost the only desirable career open to a gently bred woman. A girl who did not marry might sometimes lead as full and interesting a life as her sisters, provided she had money and an independent mind, but for most women the wedding ceremony represented the only gateway to happiness and freedom. To marry well it was necessary to have an adequate dowry, for alliances were still largely a matter of arrangements between financial equals, and portionless girls had little hope of finding husbands of their own rank, however attractive or well-educated they might be. Their position was far from enviable, and to escape from it many were glad to take some comparatively poor man who could not aspire to the hand of an heiress. If they could

not do this, they had nothing before them but a rather dreary existence at home, without outside interests and with very little money, or poorly paid work in one of the only two professions possible for them, that of a governess or a waiting gentlewoman. Neither career was particularly attractive. Of the two, the waiting gentlewoman probably led the happier life since her service was usually in the homes of relatives or friends who might be expected to take some interest in her outside the terms of her employment. Many superfluous daughters were disposed of in this way, and though their work was sometimes hard and occasionally distasteful, it was at least less lonely than that of the governess who was forced to spend so much of her time amongst strangers.

More fortunate girls, whose parents were not hampered by lack of means, usually married at about eighteen or nineteen, or at latest in their early twenties, since to be still unwed at twenty-five was to be in serious danger of becoming an old maid. In all matters pertaining to marriage the father's authority was very great and both sons and daughters were expected to bow to his will in this as in other family concerns. Love, however, was beginning to be more seriously considered as a ground for choice. The purely mercenary marriage was much less common than it had been, and even girls were allowed to follow their own hearts provided that the men they chose were suitable in other ways. When they were not, or when a son was too much attracted by a pretty face unsupported by wealth or position, the match was sternly forbidden, and in most cases the young couple complied, however unwillingly, with their families' wishes. But not always. We read of many eighteenth-century elopements and clandestine weddings, most of which ended in the erring pair being forgiven by their parents, since what was done could not be undone even by the most outraged parent. Secret marriages were fairly easy to arrange in the first half of the century when banns and licences were not as essential as they became later. If the bride was under age, the officiating clergyman was liable to punishment, but the ceremony itself, though irregular, was looked upon as binding. When Claver Morris's daughter married John Burland in 1718 without her father's knowledge, the minister concerned was severely punished by the ecclesiastical authorities, but no one questioned the validity of her marriage, and in the end her father was forced to accept the position since nothing could be done to alter it.

Nor did runaway couples always need to ask some parish priest to run a risk for them. There were several private chapels in

London where weddings could take place without the formality of banns or licences, and where everything was done to ensure the utmost secrecy. In the Fleet Chapel hundreds of such marriages were annually performed without any sort of inquiry, and many more were solemnized, if such a word can be used in this connexion, in the notorious Mayfair Chapel. The scandal of these irregular ceremonies, which sometimes included the unwilling union of an abducted heiress to some penniless adventurer, eventually grew to such proportions that the Government was forced to take notice of it. In 1753 an Act of Parliament put an end to the activities of the Fleet and similar chapels by declaring all future marriages null and void if they took place without banns or licences, or in any building except an authorized church. Needless to say, this did not prevent elopements, though it made them slightly more difficult; there were still ways of getting married secretly in this country, and for those who could afford the journey there was always Gretna Green where the marriage laws of England did not apply.

An elopement, however, was but the last resort of the desperate, and no girl in that or any other century would have chosen a runaway marriage in preference to the pleasant ceremonies, and feastings, the music, dancing, and pretty dresses, of an orthodox wedding (62, 83). "Sir George and my Sister look'd beautiful," wrote Mary Curzon of one such family occasion in 1778. "She was dress'd in a white figur'd sattin gown, a fring'd silk petticoat, white fring'd slippers, a beautiful white hat trimm'd with blond, a long figur'd white sattin cloak trimm'd with fur, & arm-holes, & really you never saw a more elegant creature than she look'd."[1] In conservative households the cheerful old custom of bedding the bride, drinking sack possett, flinging the stocking and waking the bridal pair next morning with music were still customs sometimes observed, but they were gradually dying out. Instead honeymoons were coming into fashion. The newly married pair set off soon after the ceremony to spend a few weeks at Bath or some other watering-place, or to make a prolonged round of visits to their relations. In most cases they were accompanied by one of the bridesmaids, usually a favourite sister, cousin, or particular friend of the young wife.

When the wedding-trip was over, the husband took his bride home to be welcomed by his tenants and family and to receive the keys that marked her new status as ruler of his household. Young Mrs. Wrightson wrote very happily to her sister in 1788 about her first home-coming and "our cheerful reception at

[1] *Dear Miss Heber* . . .

62 A Fashionable Wedding in a London Church (1729)
(St. Martin-in-the-Fields)

From a painting by William Hogarth

63 Gentlemen Commoners of Christ Church, Oxford

From the painting by John Zoffany

Doncaster, thro' wch place our carriage was the whole way surround'd by people paying their compts: the Bells had been ringing the whole Day. I really cd. not help laughing to see how much I was the object of curiosity; every window was crowded with people, to whom Wrightson had nothing to do but Bow & say 'Howdy' & laughing too all the way. I am sure they must have thought us a very merry couple."[1] And so, laughing all the way, this cheerful little bride, like many another, passed into her kingdom. Doubtless she ruled over it with all the efficient care expected of her, and brought her children up to love and admire, as she did, the gentleman she probably addressed as Mr. Wrightson, in the formal fashion of the age, to the end of her days. Whatever happened, she had to make the best of it, for there was no divorce except in very extraordinary circumstances, and few people in any case cared to avail themselves of so difficult, expensive, and public a remedy for private ills. Unhappy marriages naturally, there were now and then, but most couples acquired the art of living together in amity, even where there was no deeper affection; and far more could have echoed the words of Lord Egmont when he wrote in his diary for 1732:

> This day I have been married twenty-two years & I bless God that I have lived so long with the best Wife, the best Christian, the best mother and the best mistress of her servants living; and that not only the world thinks so but that I am myself sensible of it.[2]

[1] *Dear Miss Heber . . .*
[2] *Diary of Viscount Percival, Earl of Egmont*, H.M.C., Vol. I, 1920.

Chapter XI

PASTIMES AND PLEASURES

A COUNTRY landowner's life in the eighteenth century was filled with a number of varied interests, from the management of his estates and the proper discharge of all the traditional duties that went with landed property, to the field sports and games that played so large a part in every countryman's existence. He was the head of a considerable household in which his word was law, and the ruling spirit, patron, and principal employer in the village outside his gates. He was the landlord of a mixed tenantry of farmers and cottagers, most of whom he knew personally, and in whose affairs he was expected to take an active and benevolent interest. Upon his friendship and good feeling depended much of the comfort and well-being of his tenants, upon his generosity and kindness that of the local poor. In an age when social services were practically non-existent, it was to him that the sick and impoverished looked for material aid, the ignorant for advice, and those in trouble for protection and help. At Christmas he usually gave gifts of food and clothes to all his cottage tenants; when the church needed new furniture or structural repairs, it was to him that the incumbent first applied, and at all times he was the natural leader in every charitable enterprise that might be set on foot within the boundaries of his own locality.

Nor were his customary duties confined to purely material concerns. As patron of the living he was expected to show a good example in religious matters and, when necessary, personally to reprove the drunken, the idle, or the immoral. In this he was supported by the parson and tolerated by the culprits, for what would probably be resented to-day was then regarded as a quite natural and praiseworthy action for a man in his position. Regular church-going was also expected of him, and in most cases he not only went himself to church at least once a week but saw to it as far as possible that his people did the same. Sir Roger de Coverley, we are told, "found his parishioners very irregular, and in order to make them kneel and join in the responses, he gave everyone of them a hassock and a Common Prayer-Book."[1] He also made it a rule to rise in his seat during the service and note the absentees with a view to admonishing them later for their non-attendance. Progressive squires sometimes founded

[1] *The Spectator*, No. 112.

charity schools in their own villages and took a genuine interest in the pupils' progress, and many left money in their wills to pay for religious or other instruction for a certain number of poor children. A really good landlord had plenty to do, and usually he did it to the best of his ability. There were, of course, men who neglected the duties laid upon them by custom, and some who allowed too much power to turn them into petty tyrants. Sometimes they failed through lack of imagination, or through inherited prejudices too thick to be pierced by pity or understanding. But in the great majority of cases the country landowners were kindly and conscientious men who looked after their people according to their lights, and did a great deal to make life easier for those in their care.

Frequently the squire was also a Justice of the Peace, and in that case he had much extra business to transact. He was responsible for remedying local abuses of all sorts, for relieving the poor, superintending the work of parish officials, trying minor cases, and enforcing the law generally in his own locality. Before the Petty Sessions system was extended from the towns to country districts, the main bulk of this work had to be done in the Justice's own home. Hither came women demanding affiliation orders, wayfarers wanting passes, men wishing to swear an affidavit, cripples who could not work asking for licences to beg and paupers complaining of harsh treatment by the overseer. The parish clerk brought his accounts to be signed, the surveyor came to discuss the state of the roads and demand more workers for their repair; and very often the constable came with some wretched vagrant to be moved on to another parish, or a petty criminal whose offence was slight enough to be dealt with immediately. All this and much beside could be settled by a single magistrate; there were other tasks, such as fixing the poor rate or issuing alehouse licences, which could only be done by two Justices acting together, and for these a conference had to be arranged with a brother magistrate in the house of one or the other. The extension of the Petty Sessions system eventually relieved the Justice of this constant invasion of his home, but even so, there was still a great deal of work to be done locally, as well as periodic attendances at Quarter Sessions which might keep him away from home for two or three days together.

The land itself provided the country gentleman with a never-failing source of interest and occupation. Some landowners left the management of their estates almost entirely to bailiffs or agents, but many preferred to take an active part in directing the work and were qualified to do so by a sound practical knowledge

of farming. A few were ardent experimenters in the new ways of agriculture which were beginning to revolutionize rural life. Such men as Coke of Norfolk and "Turnip" Townshend were leaders in a movement that led eventually to a general increase in crop-production and a much higher standard of stock-breeding. Faced with indifferent herds and ancient, uneconomic methods of tillage, they set themselves to enrich the soil and improve breeding strains. They adopted new ideas with enthusiasm and experimented boldly, with results that not only improved their own estates out of all recognition but helped to raise the level of farming in almost every part of the country.

They enclosed land wherever they could and thereby brought hardship upon many poorer men, but they did not hesitate to spend time and money lavishly upon the lands so enclosed. Thomas Coke is said to have spent nearly half a million pounds on his experiments and improvements during the course of his lifetime. He started with little knowledge, but he took the trouble to learn from experienced farmers and to travel through England in order to observe the agricultural methods of other counties. He was an exceptionally brilliant man whose attainments the ordinary squire or farmer could hardly hope to equal, but there were many who followed in his footsteps, if only at a distance. The keener spirits spent money freely on the betterment of their lands. They built roads and cottages and model farm-buildings. They manured the soil and experimented with roots and clover; they enclosed wastelands and converted them into good grazing-grounds or crop-producing fields, grew corn where only rye would grow before, and developed the rotation system which made it unnecessary for land to lie fallow for one year in three, as had been customary in open-field farming. Naturally they prospered, and their outlay was repaid by the increased value of their estates. But in most cases they were inspired more by a genuine love of the land than by commercial considerations and, whatever their individual motives may have been, it was largely through their collective energy and pro-pressive ideas that agriculture was able to make the great advance which was one of the distinguishing features of the eighteenth century.

Yet in spite of all this varied activity, the country landowner did not need to work as hard as his modern descendant, and his life was far more untroubled. His estates kept him in comfort; only rarely did he have to look outside for other sources of income. If he spent money on his property, it was to improve it and not, as now, to save it from disintegration. It is true that some of the

64 A Lost Kite

From the painting by George Morland

65 Shooting

From a print by S. Howitt (1784)

66 Hunting

From a print by J. V. Sartorius (1795)

EIGHTEENTH-CENTURY FIELD SPORTS

smaller squires and yeomen were being slowly squeezed out by new economic factors, but the majority were able to live very well on the revenues of their lands, and the larger landowners were men of considerable wealth. Taxation was comparatively low and wages lower still; labour was easily obtained, and much of the material needed for new buildings or repairs came from the estate itself. If the squire wished to put new roofs on his cottages, or give a pulpit to the church, he could use his own timber and reeds and employ his own craftsmen; if he desired a road across his fields he seldom had to import the stones and his own men laid them. His rents came in regularly from farming tenants as yet untroubled by foreign competition; his table was largely supplied from his own herds and fields, and the surplus was sold without difficulty. The work of household and farm went on steadily and without discontent, for the large number employed made the work light, and there was no particular hurry as a rule to bring any individual task to an end. The whole pace of life was slower and more leisured. Holidays for servants and labourers were few and generally dependent upon local customs and celebrations, but the working-day was not very strenuous. The hours were long but they were filled with familiar and unhurried tasks. Farmers, too, however busy, could usually find time for a day's hunting or a cricket match, while the squire and the parson had plenty of leisure for outdoor amusements and other occupations, for reading, study, or music, if their tastes led them in that direction, for occasional visits to London and such fashionable watering-places as Bath, Bristol, or Tunbridge Wells.

Hunting and shooting (65, 66) were the principal pastimes of the gentry; poaching, cock-fighting, sparring, and bear-baiting, those of the simpler country-folk. The increasing severity of the Game Laws steadily diminished the legal sports open to poor men, with the natural result that poaching became more and more general. The independently minded peasant of those days regarded hares, rabbits and birds as wild creatures and could not see why he should not have his share of them in spite of man-traps, steel-guns, and the threat of transportation. In the early years of the century, when the countryside still teemed with game of all sorts and preserving had not yet become fashionable, a certain amount of poaching was more or less tolerated by all but the sternest landlords, but this attitude changed as the century advanced. The Act of 1671 had authorized the employment of gamekeepers and these unpopular functionaries gradually became more and more common on the big estates. They certainly earned their wages fully. They were usually disliked by the villagers

who regarded them as their natural enemies and their work was not without its physical dangers. The sturdy poacher (49), surprised in his nocturnal activities, frequently showed fight, and affrays sometimes ended fatally for one side or the other. But no repressive measures or watchful keepers could stamp out poaching altogether. The serious penalties attaching to it only added spice to an occupation that the countryman refused to regard as morally wrong. "'Tis my delight on a shiny night", says the old song, and delight it was for many a poor man who took his secret pleasures in the squire's woods and added the results to his larder or sold them to dealers who were perfectly willing to buy them without asking too many inconvenient questions.

Fox-hunting (66) was beginning to take the place of the older deer- and hare-hunts. All three were popular, but the fox provided faster sport and greater opportunities for displaying skill in horsemanship. Mixed packs of hounds which would follow any quarry gradually fell into disfavour. Thomas Fownes of Stapleton formed one of the first packs of true foxhounds in 1730, and ten years later the Belvoir Hunt was founded by the Duke of Rutland. The Cottesmore and the Pytchley were started soon afterwards, and numerous other packs began to make their appearance in different parts of the country. The rage for this form of sport was shared by all classes. The gentry devoted most of their winter leisure to it, clergymen often came to church with their riding-clothes under their cassocks, ready to start off as soon as the service was finished. The poor who had no horses or scarlet coats to bother about followed the chase on foot whenever they could. Even women were sometimes seen in the hunting-field, though this was considered very unfeminine by old-fashioned people. The prejudice against them was not enough, however, to keep away the more intrepid spirits. Lady Salisbury actually became Master of the Hatfield Hounds in 1793, a post which she held for several years and only resigned because, at seventy-eight, she began to find the pace a little too hot for her. The fox was still legally a pest for whose carcass parish officials would pay along with those of polecats, hedgehogs, and other vermin. At Ovington in Hampshire one shilling was paid "for every fox caut in the parish", and similar payments were made in other districts. But the creature's growing popularity as a hunting-quarry protected it to a large extent. Most countrymen were willing to forgo the shilling for the pleasure of the chase, and even if they were not, it sometimes took a great deal of courage to risk the disapproval of the local landlords by killing or trapping a fox in a hunting county.

67 Easter Monday in Greenwich Park

68 A Game of Skittles at The Swan Inn, Chelsea

69 A Match, with a wicket of only two stumps, in 1743

70 A Match at Islington in 1816

CRICKET

Hawking was dying out fast and archery had become little more than a graceful exercise for women. Shooting was legally confined to those who had freeholds of £100 or more or leaseholds of £150; such men were allowed to shoot at will over their own lands but no one else could do so without their permission. Greyhound-coursing was another popular amusement, and for those of more philosophic temperament there was plenty of good fishing in rivers as yet unpolluted by factory effluents and still teeming with fish.

There were also games of all sorts. Quiet men played bowls on smooth greens, and skittles (68) in covered alleys; the well-to-do played tennis on their own courts and nearly everyone took a hand now and then at fives against the church tower or some convenient wall. Golf was known but it was not yet popular, and football was still regarded as too rough for all but young and boisterous labourers. Cricket (69, 70), which in one form or another had been known for centuries, was now coming into its own and was rapidly surpassing the older games in popularity. It was played at first with curved bats varying in size and shape according to the fancy of the owner; there were only two stumps, and the score was kept by notches cut in a piece of wood. In 1744 definite rules were laid down and variations smoothed out, but long before that time county cricket as we know it had begun to take shape. In 1711 and again in 1746 Kent played against all England, and a few years later the famous Hambledon Club was formed. Here moved such giants as John Small, the first man to use a straight bat, and William Beldham; and here in 1777 the All-England team was defeated by the Hambledon men on Broad Halfpenny Down. To such matches as these flocked gentle and simple, squires, farmers, cottagers, and noblemen. They came to cheer on their own side and to enjoy themselves, but most of them were not content to be spectators always. In hundreds of little villages there were active teams in which landlord and tenant played together throughout the summer; and many an inter-parish rivalry was first fought out in some vigorous match on the green and then washed away in copious draughts of home-brewed ale sent down from the manor or the inn.

Boxing was everybody's delight, from village lads sparring at home to young sprigs of nobility who were proud to learn the noble art from the hands of established champions. Public contests attracted enormous crowds who came from all parts to watch the savage fighting without gloves and without the restraints of Queensbury Rules which were not introduced until the following century. Severe injuries were sometimes suffered

by the contestants, but no one minded that. In spite of superficial refinements, it was a rough and brutal age, with an almost total indifference to human or animal pain. Great crowds assembled to see a hanging and windows with a good view were hired by young men of fashion as they would be to-day for a coronation, while few spectacles were so popular as a bull- or bear-bait, or a fight to the death between savage dogs or gamecocks specially trained for the purpose.

At a bait it was quite common for several dogs to be killed or injured and bets were freely laid upon their endurance. Prizes were sometimes given to their owners. "I gave a collar to be played for," wrote Nicholas Blundell in 1712, "but no dogg cld get it fairly so I gave it to Rich. Spencer, of Leve: being his dogg best deserved it."[1] Spencer, being from "Leve", probably had well-trained animals, for Liverpool people were devoted to bull-baiting, and a great contest was held there every year until 1772 on the occasion of the Mayor's Election. At Stamford the famous Bull-running took place on 13 November, when everyone turned out to hunt an unhappy bull through the streets until it was killed, after which the meat was sold to the poor at a low rate. This brutal sport was supposed to date from the reign of King John and was associated with certain common rights in the town, a fact which made its suppression extremely difficult. The churchwardens contributed annually to its cost and in 1756 a Mayor of the town left money in his will for its encouragement. When in 1788 a later Mayor and the Earl of Exeter tried to abolish the hunt, they were both insulted by an infuriated crowd and the bull-running went on as before until 1839. At Tutbury an even more barbarous form of bull-running formed part of the Minstrels' Festival in August until it was suppressed in 1778 by the Duke of Devonshire.

Yet in fairness to our ancestors, it must be admitted that there was often a wide gulf between private and public practice where animals were concerned. The same men who laughed and cheered at a cock-fight and derided those who strove to put down bear-baiting took the greatest care of their horses and usually had a number of dogs which they treated quite as kindly as any modern dog-owner. Dr. Johnson sat up all night with his pet cat when it was ill and fed it with oysters. Fielding records how when a kitten fell overboard on the way to Lisbon the captain of the ship ordered the sails to be slackened and all hands to turn out and rescue the little creature. Parson Woodforde has left us a vivid picture of his own tender care for one sick pet. "I had a poor little cat," he says,

[1] *Crosby Records: Blundell's Diary*, ed. Rev. T. Ellison Gibson, 1895.

> that had one of her ribs broke and that laid across her belly, and could not tell what it was, and she was in great pain. I therefore with a small pen knife this morning opened one side of her and took it out and performed the operation very well, and afterwards sewed it up and put Friars Balsam on it, and she was much better after, the incision was half an inch. It grieved me much to see the poor creature in such pain before, and therefore made me undertake the above, which will preserve the life of the poor creature.[1]

Horse-racing increased steadily in popularity throughout the eighteenth century as breeding-strains improved and more definite rules were laid down. The smaller country meetings tended to disappear after 1740 when the stakes were raised, but those which survived were never without large and happy crowds of spectators, and many new ones were founded. Newmarket remained for a long time the principal centre, as it had been in Charles II's reign: it was to regulate the racing there that the Jockey Club was first formed in the middle of the century. At Chester, York, Stapledon Leys and many other places there were important meetings, that at Chester being one of the oldest in the kingdom, springing directly from the mediaeval Guild Homages due on Shrove Tuesday. Regular racing at Epsom began in 1730 and at Ascot in 1713; in 1776 the St. Leger was founded and in 1780 the Derby. Steeplechasing was coming into fashion amongst the country gentry who organized their own contests and rode across country towards an agreed mark in the manner of a modern point-to-point. Such races at first attracted little attention outside the districts in which they were held; it was not until the following century that steeplechasing became, like flat-racing, an organized spectacle for the enjoyment of vast crowds.

Much money changed hands at every race-meeting, as indeed it did on almost every occasion when it was possible to lay a wager. Gambling had long been a national passion, so widespread in Queen Elizabeth's time that strong efforts had to be made by the government to suppress it at least amongst labouring folk and students. In the eighteenth century it was even more general. Almost anything served as an excuse for a bet. Men backed their fancy on the race-course and the cricket fields; they laid wagers on the size of the bag after a day's shooting, on the results of boxing-matches, cock-fights and bear-baits, on the probable course of a hunted fox, on the speed at which a new cabriolet could be driven, and even on such domestic matters as the end of a courtship or the sex of a coming child. In fashionable circles whole fortunes were sometimes lost or won in a single game of

[1] Woodforde, *op. cit.*

cards. Lotteries were extremely popular with all classes and were sanctioned by Parliament which introduced a Lottery Bill every year from 1709 to 1824. No chance was too big or too small to interest the risk-loving people of the time, and it was this speculative spirit that was responsible for the rise of numerous Assurance Companies and for the frenzied buying of stocks which led to the ruin of so many at the time of the South Sea Bubble.

Women's amusements were not so numerous as those of their husbands and brothers. Most outdoor pastimes were only for men. Women, as we have seen, did occasionally appear in the hunting-field, and many rode or walked long distances for pleasure, but the world of sport was considered too rough for them, and it was still almost entirely a masculine preserve. Country life, however, was far from dull even for the feminine half of the population. Every married woman had her household to superintend, with all its changing interests, so much more varied than they are to-day. The squire's lady shared to some extent in her husband's work in the village, and the products of her stillroom and her medicine chest were carried by her or her daughters into many cottage homes. There was a close intimacy between neighbours which led to a great deal of pleasant entertaining. Dinner-parties, balls, and the occasional visits of touring players diversified the winter months, and in the summer there were often guests who came to stay for two or three months together. Morning calls were usual in every district where distances did not forbid them, and during these visits informal dances for six or eight couples were frequently arranged, or card-parties for whist, quadrille, picquet or loo.

Cards (45) were a favourite indoor amusement for all above the rank of labourer; even clergymen did not disdain them, though strict Methodists regarded them as snares of the Devil. Long ago Sir John Harington had said in their defence that "Man cannot allways be discoursing, nor women allways pricking in clowts", and most eighteenth-century people heartily agreed with him. "Pricking in clowts", by which he meant embroidery, was still a necessary accomplishment for every well-educated girl. "I think it as scandalous," wrote Lady Mary Montagu, "for a woman not to know how to use a needle as for a man not to know how to use a sword."[1] Such a state of affairs, however, was rare. Little girls were carefully taught to make elaborate samplers and pictures in wool from an early age, and their elder sisters whiled away a good many quiet hours working at their tambour-frames or drawing floral patterns for embroidered fire-screens and

[1] *Letters of Lady Mary Wortley Montagu.*

cushions. Many made their own dresses and trimmed their own hats. But great skill in needlework was not as common as it had been in the seventeenth century. The much wider choice of tapestries, silks, and figured velvets, that could be bought for household use made much of the old fine work unnecessary, and the Georgian miss, though she could sew well enough when she wished, spent far more time upon less enduring forms of handicraft like shellwork, netting and painting upon fans and little boxes.

Dancing (43) was a favourite diversion with young people, music (35) its close rival with both young and old. Almost everyone in a leisured household could sing and play the harpsichord or the pianoforte which succeeded it towards the end of the century. Many could play the harp as well or the violin which had displaced the older viol. "We have a man here that plays most admirably upon the Violin & accompanies us most days," wrote Mary Curzon in 1777. "It's vastly pleasant with the Bass as that is no trouble to one. Our Concert last night was both Vocal and instrumental & some delightful Catches. . . . We had a flute too besides the Violins."[1] Poorer people, if they could not play so often for lack of instruments, had their own songs and country dances, and there was always the village fiddler to provide music at every private or public festival. Most parishes had at least one fiddler who played at weddings and May-day dances, or at the "merry-meal" to which the anxious rural father invited his friends while the midwife upstairs ushered his son or daughter into the world. Sometimes he played for informal dances at the Manor, or in the church choir where he took his place alongside the sturdy yeomen with bassoons, flutes, and serpents. Music was never far to seek in eighteenth-century England, whether in the alehouse with its roaring choruses and ancient folk-songs or the music-rooms of great houses where the family gathered to sing glees for their own amusement and entertained their guests with the lovely strains of Mozart and Handel.

Much time was spent in keeping journals and in letter-writing which was then more of an art than a casual occupation. Men wrote at length to air their views on politics or the arts, women to send one another favourite receipts for puddings or herbal remedies, and both to pass on local news and all the gossip of the countryside. It was then the pleasant custom of most householders to exchange gifts of food and drink, and to send such country riches as hares, birds, and eggs, to town relatives in return for the more sophisticated products of the city. "Aunt Adams

[1] *Dear Miss Heber . . .*

neither wants mony nor presants," wrote the Reverend Mr. Vickers of one well-loved lady, "her knocker is worne out with the Carriers comeing to the Doore—hogsheads of strong Bear—Brawn, Turkeys, Geese, with Fowls, etc. come to her from Calflande."[1] Such gifts must have been a pleasant addition to anybody's larder, though bad roads and slow carriers' carts made their state on arrival somewhat uncertain. "The codling was very good," wrote one householder in acknowledging a present, "but the oysters, half of them were black as ink and the other half poisoned with the stench, for they were all of a ffroth, and your ffishmonger should give you your money again."[2]

With all these varied occupations went the never-failing pleasures of reading. Many great houses contained fine private libraries which included volumes of all sorts. Here could be found the sermons inherited from seventeenth-century ancestors and the works of popular Georgian divines, books on philosophy and history, drama, natural history, and travel. Serious reading was not only an essential part of religious and secular education; it was the cherished pleasure of every cultivated person. Even humbler folk read much that would not be accounted popular to-day, as Pastor Moritz observed on his travels. He remarked that English people of every degree read far more widely than his own compatriots, and related how he had seen his landlady, a tailors' widow, reading Milton. "This single instance," he wrote, "would prove but little; but I have conversed with several people of the lower class, who all knew their national authors, and who all have read many, if not all of them."[3]

Books were far more plentiful than they had been in the seventeenth century when legal restrictions limited the permitted number of printing-presses. Newspapers also abounded. Many were published daily or weekly in London, and most provincial towns had their local prints which were widely read by men and women in the surrounding villages. Then as now varieties of political opinion were represented in the Press. The Whig or Tory householder could always find a paper to suit his particular views, over which he could drowse in the evenings and work up a pleasant fury against governmental iniquities as described in the editorials. There were also numerous periodicals like the *Spectator*, the *London Gazette* or the *Gentleman's Magazine*, and even a few published specially for women. The circulation of newspapers and reviews was often quite small, for not everyone could afford twopence or threepence for a daily paper, or sixpence for

[1] *Verney Letters.* [2] *Purefoy Letters* 1735–53, ed. G. Eland, 1931.
[3] C. P. Moritz, *op. cit.*

a magazine. But those who could not buy could usually borrow from their neighbours, and it was generally possible to see a copy of some paper at the local inn or in a coffee-house.

Of all the books published in the Georgian period, the novels were undoubtedly the most popular. What the best of them were like we know for ourselves, for the works of Richardson, Smollett, Fanny Burney, and Jane Austen, are still widely read to-day. In the eighteenth century they were new in two senses, for the novel as we understand the term only came into being with Richardson and Fielding. Such books as *Clarissa Harlowe*, *Tom Jones*, and *Pamela Andrews*, were widely read, and so were the works of Mrs. Radcliffe and Monk Lewis, which were the ancestors of the modern thriller, and quite as popular. "Do you not think *Udolpho*[1] the nicest book in the world?" asked Catherine Morland in *Northanger Abbey*, a question that might have been put with equal sincerity by nearly all the women of her time and a good many men.

There were, of course, some who disliked fiction and considered its influence pernicious. Polite young ladies sometimes affected to despise novels and preferred, at least in public, to read more serious books. But reading for amusement as distinct from instruction had come to stay. Visitors to London were constantly charged to bring back the newest volumes, and carriers' carts everywhere lumbered along with two or three novels for parsonage or manor tucked away amongst their more prosaic parcels. Circulating libraries first appeared in 1740 and thereafter sprang up in most of the larger centres. The best were to be found in watering-places and spas, but smaller ones existed in many market towns. In Bath, books could be had for a guinea a year or half a crown a week; in less fashionable places the charges were lower. Those who lived too far from any town to avail themselves of libraries sometimes formed book-clubs amongst themselves, the books being brought down by coach and sent round from house to house in rotation. What pleasure they must have given to all, and particularly the women, it is perhaps difficult for us to realize in this age of easy amusements. A really good novel must have been a boon indeed in isolated country houses, especially on winter nights when there were no guests and all the family resources of gossip, needlework, and newspaper-reading, had been exhausted.

[1] *The Mysteries of Udolpho*, by Anne Radcliffe.

Chapter XII

HOLIDAYS AND TRAVEL

THE great pleasure centres of the eighteenth century were the inland spas and watering-places. They were, of course, primarily health resorts, dependent for their renown upon the healing properties of their wells, but in their heyday they were much more than that. For every visitor who came in search of health there were nine or ten more who came simply to enjoy themselves, to meet their friends and note the latest fashions, to display a daughter's beauty to the social world or find a wealthy bride for a son. "Here was the same specimen of company as usual," wrote John Byng at Cheltenham (72) in 1784, "widows wanting husbands, old men wanting health and misses wanting partners."[1] All these things a well-regulated watering-place could usually provide, besides a constant round of balls, concerts, plays, picnics, and parties of every kind.

The fashion for visiting spas was by no means new when the Georgian era began. Charles II's subjects had gaily travelled over appalling roads to Epsom, Harrogate, and Buxton, or followed his Queen to Tunbridge Wells. They had crowded into inferior lodgings at Bristol or Astrop and penetrated into the depths of the country to some new spring lately discovered by an enterprising landowner or physician. The old urge for holiday travel, once satisfied by religious pilgrimages, had broken out afresh when the turmoils of the Civil War and the Commonwealth subsided, but now the excuse was the body's health rather than that of the soul. Ancient healing or saints' wells, deprived of their sacred associations by the Reformation, blossomed anew as health resorts, and many a remote village won a sudden and short-lived prosperity because of some medicinal quality in its waters.

Yet in spite of the fashionable people who patronized them, these early watering-places were often very primitive, with little to offer but the well itself. Lodgings were generally scarce and very dear, and there were few amusements to fill the hours after the morning bath had been taken. In Buxton, visitors were charged inordinate prices for rooms where they were sometimes obliged to sleep three or four in a bed, and conditions in some of the lesser spas were probably much worse. Even Bath, the most famous of all, could provide only poor accommodation and

[1] *The Torrington Diaries*, ed. C. Bruyn Andrews, 1934-35.

71 "The German Spa and Pump Room, Brighton", *c.* 1800

72 The Royal Wells, Cheltenham, in 1823

THE COUNTRY SPA

73 A Georgian Street Scene: the entrance to Ranelagh Gardens, London

From a painting by Francis Hayman

hardly any diversions other than private entertainments. In the morning a band played while the patients bathed and at night there were dances at the Town Hall, but as yet there was no theatre and no assembly room. The streets were narrow and dirty, the houses mostly too small and cramped for the number of visitors they were called upon to shelter. Rapacious landladies and sedan chairmen almost as surly as the notorious Thames watermen added little to the amenities; and even amongst the guests the standard of courtesy was somewhat rough and ready, so that it was not unknown for men to appear at balls with swords and heavy boots, and occasionally to brawl amongst themselves in the presence of ladies. The town's future glory as a centre of elegance and good manners was as yet undreamt of, and much the same conditions prevailed in the other health resorts of the time.

It was not until the beginning of the eighteenth century that the watering-place, as that term was understood in the Georgian period, began to take shape, largely through the influence of Richard Nash. He came to Bath in 1705 and at once set to work to supply its deficiencies. In a few years he had built an assembly room and a playhouse, rebuilt the Pump Room, and laid down a strict code of manners which every visitor had to observe. Some of his rules were so elementary that it seems incredible they should ever have been necessary, but apparently he found them so. Gentlemen were expressly forbidden to crowd before ladies at a ball, and both sexes were adjured not to take offence if someone else danced before them. Indecorous speech was rigorously suppressed, duelling prohibited, the price of lodgings controlled, and a high standard of etiquette and dress enforced. The regulations were set out in the Pump Room for all to see and all alike had to obey them, from the shyest country girl newly come from her rural village to the most sophisticated lady of the Court.

High rank was no protection from public reproof when such reproof was needed. When the Duchess of Queensberry wore a morning apron at a ball, Nash tore it off with his own hands and threw it down in a corner. This extraordinary man, of uncertain lineage and still more uncertain means, reigned like a king for many years and no one dreamt of disputing his authority. He came into the town with hardly any money and died in comparative poverty in 1762, supported by a small allowance from the Corporation. But during the interval he had made and spent a fortune and had not only made Bath the undisputed queen of watering-places but, in so doing, had enormously raised the tone of every other spa in the kingdom.

Life in such resorts was colourful and gay, a pleasant, leisurely round of friendly meetings and public and private diversions. London was, of course, the centre of the fashionable, literary and political worlds and the Mecca of the ambitious, but there was an intimacy about these little towns which was lacking in the capital. Bathing began early in the morning. Men and women walked together in the water, dressed in stiff canvas robes which completely covered them, while their friends lounged along the sides or in the gallery above. Ladies were provided with little trays to carry posy and handkerchief which floated in front of them, lightly attached to their waists. After the bath the company adjourned to the Pump Room to drink the waters, a custom observed by many who did not really need it for the sake of the cheerful meetings and conversation that accompanied it. Breakfast followed and, at Bath, a service in the Abbey to which nearly everyone went. At Cheltenham a public breakfast was given every Monday, a habit approved by Lord Torrington who tells us that "there is a gaiety in a public breakfast in a summers morning, with music, that is to me very pleasing; every one then looks fresh and happy; the women are more in their natural looks, not disfigured by over dress and paint, and the men are civil and sober."[1]

The rest of the morning was devoted to visiting, riding, shopping, and expeditions of all sorts, and at night there were balls, card-parties, and visits to the theatres. It is not surprising that every young girl looked forward with longing to her first visit to Bath or Tunbridge Wells, and that people of all types flocked every year to these cheerful little towns where they were certain of finding interesting company, good shops and circulating libraries, and an opportunity of meeting the great ones of their time.

The fashions alone must have been a great attraction for simple country squires and their families whose lives were spent in remote villages where changes in the mode penetrated only very slowly. At the spa the men could note the varying forms of wigs worn in the early years of the century, the later powdered hair, and the studiously negligent styles of head-dressing introduced by Fox at the time of the French Revolution. They could see the newest thing in cravats and ruffles, in satin coats and waistcoats, and walking-sticks with long tassels. It was probably at Bath or Cheltenham that the countryman first realized, towards the end of the century, that the once effeminate umbrella was now permissible for men. Umbrellas had been known in the seventeenth century, but they were rare and used only by women. In

[1] *The Torrington Diaries.*

1708 Kersey's *Dictionary* defined them as "a kind of broad fan or screen, commonly used by women to shelter them from the rain." When Jonas Hanway carried one in 1778 he was hooted in the London streets, and for many years afterwards a cry of "Frenchman" sometimes followed the bold user of the new-fangled thing. Sedan chairman particularly hated umbrellas since their owners were less likely to call for a chair in a sudden shower of rain. But their opposition and the prejudices of the old-fashioned were fruitless; after 1780 the umbrella steadily gained ground, and by the beginning of the nineteenth century even the hero of a novel was not ashamed to carry one on the off-chance of rain, as Captain Wentworth did in *Persuasion.*

For wives and daughters the changing pageant of fine clothes must have been still more exciting, even in that colourful time when men were not afraid to dress as beautifully as their sisters. All the extravagances of the powdering age were displayed before the wondering eyes of country misses at the health resorts: the hoops of varying size, so wide at one period that carriages had to be specially made to accommodate them, the silks, velvets, sarsanets, and taffetas, the French riding-habits that so scandalized the prudish when they were first introduced, and the towering headdresses of horsehair pasted over with powder and crowned with feathers, flowers, and little model ships. These erections were so elaborate and took so long to build that they had to be left in position for weeks together, their owners sleeping uneasily at night with their elongated heads enclosed in special cases. Such exotic fancies were only for the rich and, it must be supposed, for the determined, for the cost was great and the discomfort almost equally so, especially in hot weather. The fashion was not unnaturally short-lived, and even the most elegant female must surely have seen its passing without regret, and welcomed with relief the simpler styles that followed it.

Headgear was a constant source of feminine interest, for women of all ages usually covered their hair both indoors and out. In the street they wore large hats lightly poised upon their abundant hair or, in the later years of the Georgian era, bonnets; in the house they wore lacy caps or turbans made of silk and feathers. "After Dinner we walked to a Milleners Shop," wrote kind old Parson Woodforde when he was in London in 1782, "and I bought 3 dressed Caps for Nancy, for my Sister Pounsett and her little girl, with about 10 Yards of Ribband besides—pd there 1.10.6."[1] No doubt the ribbon was used to trim other caps or to renovate a favourite hat, for much millinery work was done

[1] Woodforde, *op. cit.*

at home by the deft fingers of young girls or ladies' maids. When poor tactless Anne Steele offended her sister, she was much distressed by the latter's instant refusal to help her in this most important matter, but Lucy relented later on. "She vowed at first she would never trim me up a new bonnet," confided Anne to Elinor Dashwood, "nor do anything else for me again, so long as she lived; but now she is quite come to, and we are as good friends as ever. Look, she made me this bow to my hat, and put the feather in last night."[1] And a very gay confection this hat must have been for we know that in addition to the feather it was liberally trimmed with pink ribbons specially chosen to catch the eye of one of Anne's admirers.

Towards the end of the eighteenth century women's fashions were revolutionized by the introduction of India muslins and light China silks. Before these washable fabrics were known heavy velvets, silks, cloth, and linen, were the principal materials. They were far from cheap, and only the rich could hope to possess many new dresses at a time. Gowns were made to last and were often handed down from mother to daughter and even to grand-daughter in economical families. Silks that stood up by themselves, stiff brocades, and good hard-wearing woollens, were the favourite stuffs, and these were usually of rich rather than delicate colours. Pale shades were hardly practicable, except in the case of linens, because of the difficulties of cleaning. The new silks and muslins changed all this. Henceforward young ladies could have several gowns in a year without undue extravagance. It was possible to buy a good muslin for nine or ten shillings a yard and sometimes even less, and the dresses, once made, could be washed and retrimmed as often as was necessary. White and soft pale colours became the accepted hues for young girls, both for day and evening wear. If dowagers clung to their dark satins and richly figured brocades, their daughters preferred the fresh, white, posy-trimmed and be-ribboned frocks that did not last so long but looked so pretty while they did. We hear of a variety of muslins, spotted, sprigged, tamboured, and plain, for the well-to-do; and though these dainty stuffs were beyond the means of cottage girls, they too could have their washable Sunday gowns, made of the cheap coloured or sprigged cottons which pedlars carried with them on their rounds.

Sea-bathing began to be popular about the middle of the century. In 1750 Dr. Russell wrote in glowing terms of its healing properties, and when George III took to visiting Weymouth regularly, the seal of fashion was set upon this hitherto neglected

[1] Jane Austen, *Sense and Sensibility*.

74 "The Preposterous Headdress"

From a satirical print of 1776

75 In the Garden

76 Tea and Talk

Both from plates by Nicholas Heideloff

FASHIONS OF THE EARLY REGENCY PERIOD

pastime. Scarborough, Margate, Brighton (71), and Lyme Regis, were filled with visitors every summer, and loyal subjects flocked to Weymouth to cheer their King when he went bathing and watch him eat with his family at the public breakfasts. All the gaieties of an inland spa were reproduced at the seaside resorts, with the added delights of regattas and reviews, the pleasant sight of frigates and fishing-boats in the bay, and the opportunity, unknown to inland dwellers, of buying really fresh fish straight from the sea. John Byng seems to have been more interested in the Weymouth fish-market than in anything else in the town; the joys of buying large soles for 1*s.* 6*d.* a pair and mackerels for three halfpence or twopence each intrigued him more than routs and balls, or the fashionable tea-drinkings at which he found "nothing but form and grimace". Less serious-minded citizens, however, found plenty to amuse them. They bathed, they went sailing and racing on the water, they made expeditions to Upwey and Maiden Castle, they went to Royal Fêtes, and danced or gambled away the evening hours. "The great plague of the place," wrote Elisabeth Ham, who lived there, "was the 'Season' to all sober Housewives. Our country connection was large, and no sooner was the King come than country Cousins came too. The influx of visitors at such times was very great . . . and Weymouth was all the fashion."[1] Her mother, she declared, was made quite desperate by all this enforced entertaining; and doubtless other ladies suffered similar inroads in all the smarter resorts, even without a visiting King to act as a magnet.

Once indeed, in 1804, the Weymouth visitors were sharply reminded of a sterner world by a rumour that the French Fleet was close at hand and likely to land its men at any moment. "In a few minutes Drums were beating to arms," wrote Miss Ham many years later, "Officers galloping about in all directions. The horses being put to the Royal Carriages and everybody standing at their doors asking everybody for news. . . . That there was real cause for alarm no one could doubt, who witnessed the anxious looks of the hurrying Field Officers, and saw the Royal Carriages drawn up in front of Gloster Lodge ready to start at a moment's notice."[2] A thick fog added mystery to the flying rumours, and while the Dorset Yeomanry clattered through the town with a great noise of shouted orders and jingling harness, anxious women packed their trunks and dressed their children in readiness for instant flight. But it all turned out to be a false alarm. The mists lifted and disclosed an empty ocean, and within a few hours the gowns and plate had been unpacked again,

[1] *Elisabeth Ham, by herself*, ed. Eric Gillett, 1945. [2] *Ibid.*

the waiting carriages dismissed, and the customary round of entertainment resumed with undiminished vigour.

Travel for its own sake was becoming much more usual than it had been in the seventeenth century, when the would-be traveller was often hampered by the necessity of obtaining a licence or explaining his movements to a suspicious village constable. Englishmen were beginning to appreciate the varied beauties of their own country and to think time well spent in seeing them. Men like John Byng, Pennant, Defoe, and Arthur Young, toured England assiduously and wrote long accounts of their adventures; others, like John Gay and Jonas Hanway, set out lightheartedly on trips lasting for several days for no particular reason except a desire for change and diversion. The gentry travelled in their own carriages as a rule, in heavy coaches drawn by two or four horses on long journeys and in fast-moving gigs, phaetons, and curricles, on short pleasure-trips. When they were pressed for time, or unable to take their own carriages for some reason, they used the post-chaise, the fastest form of public travel which only the well-to-do could afford. Post-chaise passengers had the advantages of speed and freedom from undesired company, but the charges were high, and most innkeepers raised their prices for rooms and food to those who journeyed in this way. Parson Woodforde recorded in his diary for 1774 how he came from Oxford to Ansford, nearly a hundred miles, in a single day. He left Oxford at half-past five in the morning, and the total cost of his journey, including meals and tips, came to the not inconsiderable sum of £4 8*s.* 0*d.*

Men covered long distances on horseback, as their ancestors had done in the days when stage-coaches were unknown. The indomitable John Wesley sometimes rode as much as sixty miles in a day, in good and bad weather and over all sorts of roads. No coach could equal this performance, even in the heyday of coaching, and it must be admitted that Wesley had few peers as a courageous and determined traveller. Riding appealed to the fit man as the most manly and convenient method of getting about. "My wish is riding," wrote Lord Torrington, after many long journeys on horseback, "and that I would indulge in all weathers, were my fortune ever so excessive, by purchasing the very best hacknies; for the pleasure and convenience of such a journey, for the opportunity of going in any roads, for the preservation of health, and for the procuration (if to be had by any means) of old age. Most of the old men I know, have been great riders."[1]

[1] *The Torrington Diaries.*

Coaches ran regularly from London to all the principal centres, their guards playing lively tunes upon the horn as they bowled through the quiet streets of little market-towns. On May-day, or when some great victory had been gained in the French wars, they were decked with flowers and greenery, and at Christmas time with mistletoe and holly. The fastest vehicles travelled at about six or seven miles an hour, stopping at recognized inns for meals and the necessary changes of horses. A "Flying Coach" could travel from London to York in four days, if it was not delayed by mud and weather, from London to Chester in six. The journey to Edinburgh took ten days in 1751 during the summer months and twelve days in winter. When the era of speed began in 1784 with the establishment of John Palmer's Royal Mail Coach which covered the distance between Bath and London in sixteen hours, speeds of ten and even twelve miles an hour were not unknown, and the time taken on a journey was further reduced by night travelling. Until the last two decades of the century all coaches put up at some inn for the night and started out afresh in the early hours of the following morning. About 1780, however, certain enterprising owners broke this rule, and a little later all mail-coaches began to run through the hours of darkness, halting only for supper and breakfast and depositing their sleepy passengers at the London termini about six o'clock in the morning.

All this increased speed and volume of traffic was made possible by the slow but steady improvement of the roads, an improvement largely due in the first instance to the work of the Turnpike Trusts which paved the way for the great innovations of Telford and Macadam. These last were to raise English highways in the early nineteenth century to an undisputed position as the best in the world, but this high eminence was only slowly achieved. For the greater part of the Georgian era even turnpike roads were far from good in summer and truly appalling in winter. Pitfalls of all sorts awaited the intrepid traveller and some coach-owners wisely advertised their vehicles to cover a given distance in a certain number of days "if God permits". Arthur Young constantly inveighed against the terrible tracks over which he had to pass. "Of all the cursed roads that ever disgraced this kingdom in the very ages of barbarism," he wrote in 1768, "none ever equalled that from Billericay to the King's Head at Tilbury",[1] and the road from Newport Pagnell to Bedford he described as "a scandal to the country".[2] But far worse was to come when he

[1] Arthur Young, *A Six Weeks' Tour through the Southern Counties of England and Wales*, 1768. [2] Arthur Young, *A Six Months' Tour through the North of England*, 1771.

toured through the northern counties. The Great North Road, itself, he tells us, was "execrably broke into holes, like an old pavement; sufficient to dislocate ones bones",[1] and as for the way from Preston to Wigan, it was almost too bad for adequate description. He declares that

> I know not, in the whole range of language, terms sufficiently expressive to describe this infernal road. To look over a map, and perceive that it is a principal one, not only to some towns, but even whole counties, one would conclude it to be at least decent; but let me most seriously caution all travellers, who may accidentally purpose to travel this terrible country, to avoid it as they would the devil; for a thousand to one but they break their necks or their limbs by overthrows or breakings down.[2]

Yet these were main highways, leading to important centres and carrying a heavy load of traffic. The secondary roads were often infinitely worse. In Sussex, where the tracks were notoriously foul, the mud was so deep in bad weather that shire horses had to be used to draw carriages, and one traveller in 1703 complained that it took him six hours to go nine miles. The King himself was overset and thrown into the road in 1727 when driving to Kew, and Mrs. Freemantle, travelling in 1800 from Kington to Swanbourne, records in her diary how

> from Stoney Stratford we ventured to go the cross road to Swanbourne, which we found very bad indeed. A little before Beckington we had to go through a very deep water indeed, & from Nash to great Harwood we met with a great disaster, one of the horses fell, we were obliged to get out sunk in the mud and snow up to our knees. It was just getting dark, we were obliged to find our way across a common in Whaddon chase to Little Harwood, where we at last arrived, & did not get to Swanbourne till near eight o'clock, much fatigued & very cold, & quite cross at having had such a miserable journey full of alarms.[3]

A journey by coach was a somewhat arduous undertaking at the best of times. The traveller had to be up betimes, ready to start from the advertised inn at five or six o'clock in the morning. When the coach was full he might find himself rather cramped for space, with five other passengers beside him and another six opposite. If he was too poor to pay for an inside seat, he climbed on to the roof and found a precarious perch there, holding on to a strap or handle fixed to the side. It was possible for the economically minded to ride in the straw-filled luggage basket,

[1] Arthur Young, *A Six Months' Tour through the North of England*, 1771.
[2] *Ibid.*
[3] *The Wynne Diaries*, Vol. III.

but few did so, for the shaking was extreme, and there was always the danger of being struck by a falling box as the coach lurched through a pot-hole or over the uneven stones of the highway. Until the last years of the eighteenth century the outside passengers had a hard journey which called for a good deal of physical and moral fortitude. His place on the roof was uncomfortable, dangerous, and exposed to all the changes of weather, and when he arrived at the inn he was usually treated with scant civility. Innkeepers took it for granted that only poverty drove a man to travel thus, and consequently the unfortunate "outside" was kept waiting for his food while his betters were served, forced to dine at a separate table, and sometimes even herded into the kitchen to eat with post-boys and servants.

In the golden age of coaching, however, these absurd and snobbish distinctions were broken down. Young men of fashion then preferred a seat next to the driver before all others, for it often carried with it the privilege of driving the coach for a few miles in open country. It was, of course, illegal for the coachman to allow the reins out of his own hands, but he could sometimes be persuaded or bribed to do so, and the fact that it was forbidden only added spice to the pleasure. In the course of time the seating accommodation on the roof was greatly improved, and eventually it became possible even for ladies to ride there in comfort. Bewildered innkeepers were forced to revise their ideas when they saw the quality thus mingling with the once despised "outsides", and henceforward all their guests were treated alike, regardless of their places on the coach that brought them.

Delays were frequent on winter journeys when the heavy coaches had to force their way through snowstorms, fogs, floods, and deep mud-filled ruts. It was no uncommon thing for the passengers to be forced to alight in a morass or a snowdrift while guard and driver struggled to extricate the vehicle or strove to repair a wrenched-off wheel. There were also highwaymen. These gentry were not quite as numerous as they had been in the previous century, but there were enough of them to be a serious nuisance. Coach-guards went armed with blunderbuss and sword, and most travellers considered it prudent to carry pistols on a night journey.

Highwaymen usually confined their activities to particular districts where they could bribe or terrify the local people to silence and were sometimes sheltered by the more dishonest innkeepers. Dick Turpin, who infested the roads of the Home Counties until he was hanged in 1739, is said to have relied for much valuable information on the owner of one hostelry, and to

have been warned by him whenever a wealthy guest was about to leave the inn. Round Knutsford a series of unexplained robberies were at last brought home to a respected citizen of the town, Edward Higgins, who lived there unsuspected by any one for many years before he was caught and hanged at Carmarthen in 1767. Rewards were offered for the apprehension of road-thieves and were not infrequently claimed, for the romantic age of highwaymen was passing, and there was no longer the same sympathy for their exploits, except in a few cases. When they were convicted they were hanged, and their corpses afterwards swung in chains on hill-side gibbets as a grim warning to other marauders and a reminder to nervous travellers of possible perils on the road.

The pleasantest part of a winter journey must often have been the arrival at the inn. Here all was bustle and hurry as the coach or post-chaise drove into the yard, the host waiting to greet his guests, ostlers standing ready to tend the horses, and maids running about with food, blankets, and candles. Good fires and generous meals were the hallmarks of the coaching inn; there was no shortage of servants, and in the best houses the service was excellent. The food was both plentiful and varied and, by our standards, very cheap. The average price paid by Lord Torrington for a night's board and lodging, with fodder for his horse, was seven or eight shillings, rising occasionally to eleven or twelve shillings in the more expensive places. When Joseph Farington stayed at the Granby House in Harrogate he recorded that the expenses of his party were

> . . . Breakfast, Dinner, Tea, Supper, Six Shillings a day. Lodgings I conclude very reasonable. Seven Shillings & 6*d.* only was charged for 3 beds,—viz: Mr. & Mrs. Offley—Miss Waring & mine for five nights.—We had also occasionally a sitting room.—The Lodgings are not usually charged, and I know not how this small sum of 7*s.* 6*d.* came into the bill.[1]

Travellers were expected to take wine, brandy or ale with their meals, and to give generously in tips. In winter they were lighted to bed with wax candles for which an extra charge was made. These candles were a great feature of inn-life; if a guest was bold enough to refuse them and content himself with the cheaper lights, he was regarded as mean or poverty-stricken and his stock fell accordingly, with disastrous effects upon the attention he received. Innkeepers usually made little pretence of treating all their visitors with equal deference. The wealthy and important

[1] *The Farington Diary.*

came first in their estimation and those of lesser consequence had to take second place. A few houses catered only for post-chaise travellers and the owners of private vehicles; the majority depended largely upon the stage-coaches for their trade, but even here those who travelled post or in their own carriages were given the lion's share of attention.

Pedestrians and poor people who travelled in the long canvas-roofed wagons that trundled along at two or three miles an hour were hustled into the kitchen and treated with indifferent civility. Some innkeepers refused to receive them at all. When Pastor Moritz toured the country on foot, he often found the door shut against him, and he sadly records that "in England, any person undertaking so long a journey on foot is sure to be looked upon and considered as either a beggar or a vagabond, or some necessitous wretch, which is a character not much more popular than that of a rogue."[1] In a comfort-loving and ostentatious age no one walked or went by wagon who could afford anything better, and pedestrians were too few to break down the prejudices of the average innkeeper. The poor rarely travelled except from necessity, and many never went more than a few miles from their native villages throughout the whole of their lives.

If the best inns were good, there were many that did not rise to the high standard they set. Cleanliness was not always a conspicuous feature of the rambling rooms and passages, and even beds were not always above reproach. It is true that much was cheerfully endured then by visitors that would not be tolerated to-day. "I was bit terribly by Buggs last night," wrote Parson Woodforde when he was staying in London in 1782, and on the following day he recorded that he "was terribly swelled in the face and hands by the Buggs."[2] But this did not prevent him from describing the inn as a "very good House", and on subsequent visits to London he did not hesitate to go there again. Fastidious travellers who wished to wash the grime of the journey from their hands and faces often found it difficult to obtain hot water, and if they were only stopping for a meal, they sometimes had but scanty opportunity for ablutions. When the coach halted for dinner or breakfast, delays in service frequently curtailed the short time allowed so that the unhappy passengers had only time to swallow a few mouthfuls before the guard came to urge them outside again. In theory the dishes were set upon the table as soon as the guard's horn was heard in the distance, but in practice this did not always happen. Dishonest innkeepers were quick to see the advantage of these hurried meals, and a few bribed the

[1] C. Moritz, *op. cit.*

[2] Woodforde, *op. cit.*

guards to cut down the allotted time so that the food, already paid for by one set of guests, could be saved and served anew to a second coach-load.

Contemporary diaries are full of complaints of hard beds, badly served meals, and disrespectful servants. Overcrowding and the billeting of soldiers sometimes caused difficulties, and Catherine Hutton's adventure at one inn was doubtless not altogether exceptional. She and a friend were put into a small room without locks on the door. During the night they were disturbed by two drunken post-boys to whom the room had been assigned before the two ladies arrived, and only with much trouble were they able to persuade the intruders to depart. "The imposition in travelling is abominable," wrote John Byng in 1781, "the innkeepers are insolent, the hostlers are sulky, the chambermaids are pert, and the waiters are impertinent; the meat is tough, the wine is foul, the beer is hard, the sheets are wet, the linnen is dirty, and the knives are never clean'd."[1] After this one wonders that he had the courage to travel at all, especially as he had no need to do so. But he did, for the sheer pleasure of seeing the countryside; and so did many of his contemporaries who found the changing adventures of the road, the varied company, the rapid motion, the bustle of the inn-yard, and the loveliness of England, ample compensation for the occasional mishaps and discomforts they encountered on their way.

[1] *The Torrington Diaries.*

77 The Farmer and Parson lead the Harvest Home

From a print by Thomas Rowlandson

78 A Merry-go-Round at a Village Fair

From a print by J. B. Pyne

79 An Eighteenth-Century London Hospital: Guy's Hospital for Incurables, *c.* 1770

Chapter XIII

DISEASE AND ITS CURE

ONCE the Georgian child had weathered the perils of his infancy, he stood a much better chance than his predecessors had done of living to a ripe old age. Ignorance and prejudice still stood between him and health in many directions but on the whole he was far better tended and led a much more natural life. Infectious diseases ravaged innumerable homes, rickets and tuberculosis were all too common, and jaundice, ague, diphtheria and gout are constantly mentioned in contemporary letters and diaries. Even in well-to-do families whose members could afford to pay for the best medical advice, children perished from fevers of all sorts; many young wives died in childbirth, and surgical operations remained the perilous undertakings they had always been, only slightly alleviated by a better knowledge of anæsthetics, and still overshadowed by the fear of gangrene and collapse. Amongst the poor, matters were often much worse. In the congested slums of the larger towns, smallpox and typhus raged like destroying demons, while the unspeakable filth of overcrowded prisons made a term of imprisonment almost equivalent to a sentence of death by gaol-fever. Unhappy prisoners frequently brought the disease with them into court and infected those about them; it was not as a pretty custom but as an elementary precaution that judges carried bouquets of sweet herbs into the tainted atmosphere of the court-house.

In the country, purer air and an outdoor habit of life protected the cottager from the worst evils of the town, but even here undrained marshy lands, inadequately protected wells, and the custom of keeping windows tightly shut throughout the winter encouraged agues, typhoid, and tuberculosis. Rickets bent the limbs of many children and rheumatism those of the old, "vapours" or the spleen afflicted the wealthy, and young people of all classes were frequently carried off by vaguely diagnosed diseases described as "low" or "putrid" fevers.

Yet in spite of all these ills, life was on the whole much healthier than it had been in earlier years. In all but the poorest homes the standard of cleanliness was rising and more attention was paid to sanitation and diet. Sash windows admitted light and air more freely than their mullioned predecessors, the rooms in most houses above the rank of cottage were of fair size and

height, and there was less overcrowding in the sleeping arrangements. Generous feeding defeated the onslaughts of deficiency diseases, though it sometimes had unpleasant effects in the form of gout, indigestion, and excessive corpulence. The very fact that children were no longer forced into the schoolroom when they were little more than babies probably gave them a better start in life, since for two or three years at least they could run free in field and garden and so build up a reserve of strength unknown to the hard-worked Stuart child.

Medical science also was rapidly emerging from the darkness of former centuries. The work of such men as Stark and Cullen, Erasmus Darwin and John Hunter, was slowly but steadily lifting it from the bog of superstition and ancient practice in which it had struggled for so long, and adding enormously to the chances of saving life. There were many more hospitals both in London and the country and these, though they were primitive enough when judged by modern standards, were no longer places of horror which only the destitute and friendless could be persuaded to enter. Their wards were often dark, crowded, and none too clean, their nurses poorly paid women without proper training and with far too much to do. But here too the cleansing winds of new ideas were blowing strongly, and it was in such institutions that many early experiments were tried which eventually led on to the great advances of the nineteenth century.

The best physicians were, of course, to be found only in London and the larger towns. In the country most people depended upon the services of the local apothecary who rode from house to house in the gown and bag-wig that were the marks of his profession until a changing fashion caused him to discard them and dress like other men. Very often he was a man of little knowledge and practically no training, whose only qualifications were common sense and experience, coupled with a real desire to alleviate suffering. He was not obliged to have any regular degrees, and there was nothing to prevent anyone with a slight smattering of learning and a taste for giving advice from setting up as an apothecary wherever he liked. He was not supposed to charge for his services as such. His remuneration came from the gifts made to him by grateful patients and from the sale of drugs and other things necessary for his treatment. The surgeon was somewhat better placed since he could make a definite charge for his work but, except in the case of really well-known practitioners, his social position was little better than the apothecary's, and both alike were despised by the established physicians of the time.

Quacks naturally flourished in an age when even the squire was content to be treated by a man without any sort of diploma or degree. Labourers often preferred to give a few pence to a cheap-jack at a fair for some "infallible" remedy rather than call in the apothecary for whose drugs they might not be able to pay. Most villages had their own "wise-woman" or "cunning man" to whom the cottagers turned, as their ancestors had turned to the white witch in the days when medical science was at its lowest ebb. Such healers were usually a great deal more honest than the professional quacks, charging little or nothing for their services and undertaking only such work as, rightly or wrongly, they felt competent to do. Many of them were not without some rough and ready knowledge of herbal medicine, and their cures, though lavishly trimmed with magic, were often based upon sound common sense. In any case they had a reputation to maintain since, like the doctors, they practised in a given area where their past failures could be remembered and held against them. The poorer people of the district had far more faith in them than in any outside physician, and they probably did more good and less harm than might at first be supposed.

A few were known outside the boundaries of their own village and were visited by hundreds of people from the surrounding districts. The *Gentleman's Magazine* in 1748 described the work of Bridget Bostock, a servant in Church Coppenhall, who cured disease and cast out devils by prayer and the use of her own spittle. This woman refused all payment for her work, though she had no money of her own besides the meagre salary paid to her as a housekeeper. In the height of her fame she was visited by people of all classes and we are told that she sometimes treated as many as a hundred and sixty patients in the course of a week.

Blacksmiths were sometimes consulted by sufferers who remembered the ancient magical associations of their trade, and veterinary surgeons were not above prescribing for human ills whenever their advice was sought. Midwives also were usually considered capable of dealing with many diseases other than those caused by complications in childbirth. The midwife in any community was an important and busy individual whose help was sought alike in cottage and manor-house. Lying-in hospitals existed in many towns and were usually better run and served by a higher type of nurse than the ordinary hospitals for the sick. But most women preferred to be confined at home and to be tended by local midwives whom they knew and trusted, and who could lighten their convalescence with all the news and gossip of their own countryside.

The housewife was still the principal nurse and healer of the family. The apothecary might come round regularly to attend the master when he was troubled with gout, or to let blood from those who required the operation; in serious cases a London doctor might be hurriedly sent for to deal with fevers or broken limbs, but there was always the chance that bad roads and foul weather might delay either or both until it was too late. Every woman had to have some knowledge of nursing and first aid and such matters formed an essential part of any girl's education. In their household books wives and mothers wrote out the simple remedies for coughs and colds, for cuts, burns and bruises, the receipts for drinks to cool fevers, cordials, ointments, and poultices, that they had received from their mothers or their friends. When their children were fretful they dosed them with herbal decoctions of their own making, or with Daffy's Elixir, a curious compound of senna, jalap, aniseed, caraway seeds and juniper berries steeped in alcohol and mixed with treacle and water. Spring rashes were treated with an infusion of ground-ivy leaves or stinging-nettle tea; houseleek or burdock leaves were laid upon a burn, and ointments made of primrose roots upon a cut. If any member of the family suffered from an internal upset, doses of black nightshade and water were prepared, or chopped goose-grass served in a mess of water-gruel, while if an emetic was needed the patient was given an infusion of chamomile heads which, as the writer of an old herbal book delicately puts it, "will do all that is necessary".

More serious ailments called for more drastic measures. "My Boy Jack had another touch of the Ague about noon," wrote Parson Woodforde in 1779. "I gave him a dram of gin at the beginning of the fit and pushed him headlong into one of my Ponds and ordered him to bed immediately and he was the better after it and had nothing of the cold fit but was very hot."[1] James Clegg's remedy for the same trouble was less heroic but apparently less efficacious. "I took powdered sulphur and Balsam of sulphur," he notes in his *Diary*, "mixed with conserve of roses, drinking after it whey and small liquers but had a very bad day."[2] Almost every household had its own remedies for this disease which constantly appeared in single cases or sudden epidemics in every part of England. John Wesley recommended the leaves and blossoms of July flowers beaten together with salt and applied to the head, Mrs. Delany a paste of ginger and brandy spread on a sheep's leather and laid upon the stomach.

[1] Woodforde, *op. cit.*
[2] *Extracts from the Diary and Autobiography of the Rev. James Clegg*, ed. Hy. Kirk, 1899.

Doctors fought it chiefly with quinine. Parson Woodforde gives us a detailed account of Dr. Thorne's treatment in 1784, which consisted of an emetic followed by a rhubarb draught and then, when the actual fever had gone, diminishing doses of quinine taken during several days, with laudanum drops added "if at the beginning of taking the Bark it should happen to purge."

Jaundice was another common trouble which country people treated with barberry tea or ground-ivy roots boiled in water. It seems to have been a somewhat elusive ailment, not always easily diagnosed by the doctors of the time. "I went to Sherborne," wrote Claver Morris on one occasion, "and saw Mr. Shirley, who was very ill of a jaundice, and his physician Dr. Bull not discerning rightly his disease, and prescribing very languid medicine for what he thought it to be, he desired mine assistance and I prescribed."[1] In a letter to Lord Fermanagh, Ralph Palmer described the death of Peregrine Bertie in 1721. "The Doctors did not find out his distemper," he wrote, "he had all the great ones, and as soon as the Jaundice did appear it hurried him away at once in a trice." Poor Mr. Palmer must have been rather troubled by this news, for at that moment his own wife was seriously ill with a variety of troubles, amongst which jaundice was included. "Sir Hans Sloane has been with my spouse," he told his correspondent, "and after a thoro enquiry (of above half an hour's continuance) gives me great hopes he will put a stop to a complication of ailments, that are making ther advances against her precious health, no fewer I think than Dropsy, Rheumatism, Cholic, Stone and Jaundice."[2] Sir Hans Sloane was a very famous physician who could be relied upon to cure his patients if it was humanly possible in the existing state of medical knowledge; but not every sufferer could call in such a man, and there must have been many who perished from jaundice and other diseases which their apothecary, "not rightly discerning" their true nature, had treated as something else.

Much heavy eating and drinking made most well-to-do families all too familiar with the pains of gout. For these a variety of remedies were prescribed. Verjuice was used for both inside and outside application, and hemlock roots roasted in wet paper until they were soft were sometimes laid upon the afflicted part to ease the pain. Many patients went to Tunbridge Wells or Bristol to drink the waters there. "My complaint has been very obstinate, tho' never dangerous," wrote Miss Iremonger in 1783, "& Dr. Nott is convinced that it does not arise so much from weakness as from an undetermined flying Gout in my constitution,

[1] *The Diary of a West Country Physician.*
[2] *Verney Letters.*

for which he tho't the Tunbridge Wells and the Islington Spas (for they are exactly similar) more suited to me than any other to perfect my present cure." The poor lady must surely have been anxious to conclude the matter, since for months she had been dosed with steel and angostura bark, "habited in flannel next the skin", forbidden all wine and allowed only a very restricted choice of food. "Meat and plain boiled Rice has been my invariable diet," she wrote to her friend, Miss Heber, "nearly for a Twelvemonth past till I am sick of the sight of the latter, for I never loved it."[1] It does not sound a very exciting regimen, and it is pleasant to note that after a fortnight at Tunbridge Wells she declared herself much better, "tho' still obliged to be very cautious and prudent."

Blood-letting remained a favourite remedy for many indispositions, as it had been in the previous century. Claver Morris "was let blood to 16 ozs by Mr. Lucas in the right arm" when suffering from what he took to be spotted fever. His illness lasted for three weeks, during which time he was not only blooded but subjected to all the usual course of sweating, purging, and emetics. "I sweat in the sweating chair," he notes on the third day, "and continued it for three hours after."[2] When Lady Fermanagh had an apoplectic fit the first thought of her attendants was to draw off blood, and as soon as her physician arrived he ordered it to be done a second time, with the unfortunate result that she fainted before half an ounce had been taken away and was very ill indeed. Men of full habit often had recourse to bleeding as a precaution. Surgeons visited their patients for this purpose at regular intervals, usually when the moon was waxing, since an ancient and persistent superstition declared it dangerous to perform the operation when she was on the wane. "I was bleeded this morning by Mr. James Clarke," wrote Parson Woodforde in 1767, "and had two ounces of blood taken from me, for which I gave him 2.6. N.B. My blood was very rich and therefore proper to be bled."[3]

Teeth and eyes both gave trouble now and then. Housewives used the distilled waters of borage or fennel, and lotions of their own making to strengthen the sight; when matters had gone too far for home treatment they bought spectacles which varied in price from one to thirty shillings according to the material of which the fittings were made. Herbal nostrums of all sorts were tried for toothache, from cinquefoil roots boiled in vinegar and hog's fennel juice mixed with wine to the vapour of henbane

[1] *Dear Miss Heber . . .* [2] *The Diary of a West Country Physician.*
[3] Woodforde, *op. cit.*

seeds smouldering on hot coals. The end of the story, however, was generally extraction. The art of stopping teeth with lead or gold had been known even in the seventeenth century, but few ordinary dentists rose to such heights. Decaying teeth were usually left in the head until their owner could bear them no longer and then they were removed. It was possible to have them replaced by artificial teeth of bone or ivory fixed in the mouth with wire, or by real teeth taken from other heads. The latter custom was too unpleasant, even in that far from squeamish age, to be really popular, and it died out rapidly when the manufacture of false teeth improved. Nevertheless, the fact that some "resurrectionists" in the early nineteenth century found it worth their while to rob graves solely for the sake of the teeth they contained suggests that it persisted in certain circles to a comparatively late date. Dentistry was then far from being the separate and honourable profession it has since become. Teeth were usually extracted by the local surgeon and, amongst poorer people, by the veterinary surgeon or a cheapjack at the fair. Yet even the woman dentist of to-day is not, after all, quite so startlingly modern an innovation as is usually supposed. One at least flourished at Wapping in 1754, for Fielding tells us that when he was waiting for a favourable wind to take him to Lisbon,

> my poor wife after passing a night in the utmost torment of the toothache resolved to have it drawn. I dispatched, therefore, a servant to Wapping to bring in haste, the best toothdrawer he could find. He soon found out a female of great eminence in the art; but when he brought her to the boat at the waterside they were informed that the ship was gone.[1]

Infectious fevers of all sorts were common and made the more so by the very casual notions of isolation which then prevailed. Little attempt was made to keep the sufferer from diphtheria, measles, influenza, or smallpox, away from his fellows and those with comparatively mild attacks usually continued to receive visitors as long as they felt well enough to do so. When Claver Morris already had the sickness he believed to be spotted fever upon him, he left his bed to go to Colonel Berkley's house, "it being our mutual entertainment", and came back much worse than he went. Whether Colonel Berkley or any of his household took the disease we are not told, but no one seems to have thought of this danger, though Morris himself was a doctor and should have known something about infection. In a really serious epidemic fear acted as a check upon the indiscriminate mingling

[1] H. Fielding, *The Journal of a Voyage to Lisbon*, ed. A. Dobson, 1907.

of the sick and the healthy, but where only single cases were concerned few people troubled much about the perils of contagion. Friends were freely invited to stay in houses where one member of the family lay ill, or were asked to come and cheer the patient, and no physician seems to have frowned upon the practice. It was usually easier for a servant to find a place if he or she had already had smallpox, and in some advertisements this was made a necessary condition of engagement. But precautions of this kind were by no means universal and were used only in the case of the disease which was the worst scourge of the eighteenth century and annually carried off hundreds of victims and disfigured many more. Less dangerous but equally contagious troubles were more lightly regarded, and even the dreaded smallpox did not always produce the caution that might have been expected.

Plague had disappeared from England after the last great outbreak in 1665. In 1760 a rumour that it had broken out in St. Thomas's Hospital sent the price of rue and wormwood rocketing upwards for a few days in London, but it proved to be a false alarm. Smallpox, however, had increased in virulence and was almost as dangerous as the plague until vaccination was introduced. In 1717 Lady Mary Montagu, whose husband was then Ambassador to Turkey, noticed the custom of inoculation practised there and sent home a long account of it. She described how

> there is a set of old women who make it their business to perform the operation every autumn, in the month of September, when the great heat is abated. People send to one another to know if any of their family has a mind to have the smallpox; they make parties for this purpose, and when they are met (commonly fifteen or sixteen together) the old woman comes with a nutshell full of the matter of the best sort of smallpox, and asks what veins you please to have opened. She immediately rips open that you offer to her with a large needle (which gives you no more pain than a common scratch) and puts into the vein as much venom as can lie upon the head of her needle, and after binds up the little wound with a hollow bit of shell; and in this manner opens four or five veins. . . . The children or young patients play together all the rest of the day, and are in perfect health till the eighth. Then the fever begins to seize them and they keep their beds two days, very seldom three. . . . Every year thousands undergo this operation; and the French embassador says pleasantly, that they take the smallpox here by way of diversion, as they take the waters in other countries.[1]

To Lady Mary, who had lost her only brother when he was a young man and whose own face had been marred by the loss of

[1] *Letters of Lady Mary Wortley Montagu.*

her eyebrows through smallpox, the custom offered something more than a diversion. "I am patriot enough to take pains to bring this useful invention into fashion in England," she wrote in the same letter, "and I should not fail to write to some of our doctors very particularly about it, if I knew any one of them that I thought had virtue enough to destroy such a considerable branch of their revenue for the good of mankind." She was bold enough to experiment upon her own son. "The boy was ingrafted on Tuesday," she wrote to her husband on 23 March 1718, "and is at this time singing and playing, very impatient for his supper. I pray God my next may give you as good an account of him."[1] The risk was fully justified by the results, and as soon as she returned to England in 1720 she embarked upon the arduous task of converting a conservative people to this novel and revolutionary practice.

At first she met with very strong opposition. Doctors heartily disliked this irruption of the laity into their own cherished preserves, the clergy preached against the suggestion as a violation of God's laws, unscrupulous people did not hesitate to revile her as an unnatural mother who risked her children's lives for her own glorification. There were times when she was driven to regret that she had ever undertaken this crusade. Nevertheless, she persisted, and before long gained the powerful support of the Princess of Wales, who, with great courage, allowed two of her children to be inoculated after the same operation had been successfully performed on Lady Mary's own daughter in the presence of four physicians chosen by the government.

Thereafter the acceptance of the new remedy was only a question of time. The general public were slowly but surely won over to a practice thus openly sponsored by royalty, and though many doctors remained doubtful, the more progressive became its enthusiastic supporters. Indeed, a too great willingness to experiment brought with it almost as many difficulties as the previous reluctance. Unqualified men sometimes operated upon unsuitable patients, with serious and even fatal results, and now and then matter taken from an unhealthy person carried other troubles with it. The attack produced by inoculation was too mild to be dangerous and left no marks behind it, but it was quite as infectious as the ordinary variety and sometimes helped to spread the disease in districts which had been free before. Nevertheless, while vaccination was still hidden in the future, it was the only preventive available, and it did a great deal to check the

[1] *Letters of Lady Mary Wortley Montague.*

widespread mortality from smallpox. In 1796 Mrs. Penyston expressed a fairly general opinion when she wrote of

> . . . the inoculation of our three eldest dear children, who have had the disorder in quite a satisfactory, yet most favourable way. Our youngest dear little Boy being about his teeth & then not a year old, we thought it most advisable to separate & am rejoiced to tell you we are now again one party as he has returned to us a little time, & charmingly well during the whole anxious time, which even in the lightest cases must be a great trial to *Parents*, whose duty it certainly is to alleviate this frightful disease by the methods now used.[1]

Yet something more effective was already on the way. In the very year in which Mrs. Penyston wrote, Dr. Jenner announced his discovery of vaccination, performed for the first time upon a boy named Phipps. If Lady Mary Montagu had had to face opposition and personal abuse, it was as nothing to the chorus of vituperation which greeted Dr. Jenner's first attempts. His enemies were not content with hurling against him the usual charges of blasphemous interference with divine ordinances; they accused him also of introducing bestial diseases into the human frame and even of changing human characteristics by inoculating men with animal matter. Cartoons appeared showing people with cow's heads and horns growing upon them, and one doctor declared that a child at Peckham was so brutalized by vaccination that he ran upon all fours, bellowing like a cow and butting with his head like a bull. But this hysterical denunciation was both short-lived and useless. Vaccination had come to stay and by the middle of the nineteenth century had entirely ousted its predecessor and early rival, inoculation. In 1840 the older practice was forbidden by Act of Parliament. Henceforward Jenner's method was the only permitted surgical preventive of a disease which, thanks to him and perhaps a little to Lady Mary also, had ceased to be the terrifying scourge it had been for a hundred years before. Her method was by then outdated, but it is possible that, had it not been for her courage and persistence in paving the way, Jenner's discovery might not have been so quickly or so universally accepted, and smallpox might have had a longer reign as an almost unconquerable death-dealer.

[1] *Dear Miss Heber . . .*

80 The Quack Doctor

From the painting by William Hogarth

81 In St. Andrew's, Plymouth, *c.* 1800

82 As seen by William Hogarth in a London Church, *c.* 1750

SUNDAY MORNING SERVICE

Chapter XIV

TO CHURCH ON SUNDAY

THE eighteenth century, or at least that part of it between the death of Queen Anne and the coming of the Evangelical Revival, is usually regarded as a period of great religious and moral laxity, when the ardent faith of the Stuart age had burnt itself out and religion had sunk to be a matter of Sunday church-going rather than a strong light to guide the daily footsteps of all men. In many ways this is a substantially true judgement, but not perhaps in all. There was a sharp decline of fervour in the first years of George I's reign and a general loosening of the rigid moral standards that had once been preached by churchmen and dissenters alike. Compared with his grandfather, the early Georgian was but a tepid Christian where worship was concerned, and if he was moved to greater ardour he was often restrained by the fear of being thought "enthusiastic". As a rule he was not so moved. He saw little necessity to deny himself the good things of life for religion's sake or to spend much time in church. If he was so disposed, he gambled, drank, and swore, without a twinge of conscience, and as long as he did his duty as he saw it "in the state of life to which it had pleased Providence to call him", he was rarely troubled by higher spiritual aspirations.

All this did not mean that he was an unbeliever or that he doubted any of the doctrines taught him in church or chapel. Deep down in the hearts of most men the old fire still glowed, for almost everyone believed sincerely in God and all but the most neglected and ignorant were loyal members of one faith or another. But the outward manifestations of their beliefs were much cooler and more temperate than they had once been. The fierce controversies of the past had died away and left men free to follow their own way of thought without fear of persecution or the hatred of their neighbours. Tolerance was all the fashion and, though lingering prejudice and laws as yet unrepealed still placed the Dissenter and the Roman Catholic at a disadvantage in public life, no one was called upon to suffer martyrdom for his creed or to fight for his views upon the battlefield. This was an immeasurable gain but, like most good things, it was not achieved without cost. Much of the vivid faith that inspired the intolerant, harsh, but nevertheless heroic professors and martyrs of Stuart times had gone. God was no less real to the ordinary

eighteenth-century man and woman than He had been to their forebears but He was farther off. His hand was no longer seen in every trivial occurrence nor His will consulted with prayer and fasting before every important decision. Religion had become more a matter of weekly duty than of daily feeling; most people went regularly to church on Sunday and received Holy Communion two or three times in the year, but beyond this they were not conspicuously devout, and no special ardour was demanded of them by the majority of their ministers.

It was an age when balance in all things was greatly admired and enthusiasm in spiritual matters suspected as a form of fanaticism. A temperate morality was more highly prized than religious fervour. Excessive devotion was feared as a sign of fanatic or popish tendencies, and any claim to divine inspiration or a special call regarded as consciously false or at best unbalanced. Such an outlook produced only a tepid piety, but its existence, especially in the early years of the Georgian period, is not altogether surprising. Men who could remember the Sacheverell riots or the looting and violence at the beginning of William III's reign, and whose grandfathers had endured all the horrors of unbridled sectarian bitterness during and after the Commonwealth, could hardly be blamed if they dreaded religious excess of any kind. If they went too far in the opposite direction and sank occasionally into an arid formalism, that was but the natural result of an inevitable reaction—a reaction hastened by increasing scientific knowledge which made miracles less easily acceptable, and a general weakening of authoritarian claims which affected the Church no less than the secular government of the country.

In Queen Anne's reign a strong wave of religious feeling had swept over England and produced a number of voluntary societies whose members devoted themselves to leading a godly life and spreading Christian knowledge. It was at this time that the Society for the Propagation of the Gospel was founded and that the fund known as Queen Anne's Bounty was started by the generosity of the Queen. Young men banded themselves together to stamp out swearing and gambling and to encourage by their example daily attendance at church and frequent celebrations of Holy Communion. But this wave of fervour was short-lived, and when it receded it left behind it a somewhat denuded spiritual territory over which blew the desiccating winds of Deism and Latitudinarianism. The former, with its insistence on natural religion rather than Christian revelation, had comparatively little effect upon English belief and hardly survived its refutation by

Joseph Butler's *Analogy*, but it was not without its influence. Latitudinarian tendencies were more powerful since at their best they were founded upon tolerance and a genuine desire to connect Christianity more closely with the new scientific notions of the age. But in far too many cases they produced an uninspired and unhelpful teaching which was of little value in times of temptation or stress and slid all too easily over the boundaries of Christian doctrine into a morass of vague morality unsupported by any clear-cut creed.

The Church itself was not without its difficulties, of some of which it was dangerously unaware. After its many fierce battles for survival and its final victory over its rivals, it tended towards an undue complacency. The missionary spirit was almost dead. Little or no effort was made to convert those outside the fold, and those within were often offered the minimum of service and teaching. The poorer townsman, the slum-dweller, the isolated miners of Durham and Cornwall, were hardly reached at all, and in some remote villages of the north and west Wesley and the pioneers of the Sunday School Movement were later to find appalling ignorance which no ordained clergyman had attempted to modify. "As the bells rang out in 1714," says one historian of the Church, "to welcome the accession of George I, they sounded the death-knell of her high ideals and vigorous life for more than a century."[1]

Pluralism was rife, with its inevitable consequences of absentee clergymen and neglect of parish interest. Numerous parishes had no resident incumbent and depended upon visiting pastors who weather and bad roads might keep away from their duties in the depth of winter. Many were served only by underpaid curates put in to do the work by ministers who held a variety of livings and grossly neglected all but one of them. This combination of livings was often made necessary by the inadequacy of the tithes, and where minister and curate were men of goodwill and conscience it did not greatly matter. But all too often a pluralist rector paid scant attention to his parishes and was content to leave them in the hands of a deputy chosen more because he was willing to live on the miserable stipend offered than because he was fitted for the task. Few men of ability were prepared to accept a wage that was rarely more than £50 a year and might be as low as £20 or £30. Even in those days, when money went so much farther, stipends of this kind reduced the unhappy clergyman to a life of extreme poverty which in its turn adversely affected his social position and influence. In some villages the

[1] H. O. Wakeman, *History of the Church of England*, 1908.

curate's circumstances were very little better than those of the labourers to whom he ministered, and his spiritual authority over his more educated parishioners practically non-existent. Many did noble work in the face of these financial and social disadvantages but, inevitably, there were others who took the easier path and did as little work as possible in return for the meagre sums received.

In such parishes the church was often the worst-kept building in the village, cold, damp, and badly cleaned, its walls covered with dirty whitewash, its pews rotting, its altar poorly furnished, and its aisles and chapels used to store parish goods, or even the ill-gotten kegs of smugglers. Where there was a resident incumbent or a conscientious squire this was not the case but in the more neglected places the care of the church was nobody's business. On Sundays the congregation might be of respectable size, but few went to church at other times, and those who were willing to do so not infrequently found the doors locked against them. Parson Woodforde recorded in his *Diary* for 1777 how he read prayers and preached at Weston on Good Friday, a practice hitherto unknown in that village. "I gave notice this morning at Church," he writes on 23 March, "that there would be Prayers on Friday night being Good Friday—there used to be none that day, which I think was very wrong."[1]

Yet in spite of all this it would be incorrect to regard the eighteenth century as a completely irreligious age, even before the bright flame of the Evangelical Revival came to warm old truths to new life. If religion had sunk a little below the surface, it had gone no farther. Sceptics, unknown in Stuart times, existed here and there, but they were rare birds, distrusted by the vast majority and with but little influence on their fellows. The great bulk of the people were sincere, if not very ardent, Christians who never doubted the truths of their religion and ordered their lives as far as they could upon its precepts. If some parishes were neglected by their rectors, many more were not. It is true that Church livings were often given to younger sons whose chief qualification for the ministry seemed to be that they were the sons of patrons, but even these usually tried to do their duty, and there were scores of truly devout and conscientious clergymen scattered up and down the country who cared for their flocks in secular as well as religious matters. The kindly Mr. Woodforde and his friend, Thomas Du Quesne, were quite as typical of their age as any Parson Trulliber or the frivolous divines depicted by Crabbe. A century such as our own, which

[1] Woodforde, *op. cit.*

83 A Country Bride and Bridegroom

From a painting by Francis Wheatley

84 John Wesley preaching in the Open Air

From a painting by J. P. de Loutherbourg

85 Whitefield preaching at Moorfields, London

From a painting by John Collet

THE EVANGELICAL REVIVAL

has seen so great a decline in worship, has little right to criticize the simple piety of countless thousands who regularly discharged their obligations of faith and morals as these were taught to them by their pastors. And certainly it has no right to describe as irreligious an age which produced such giants as Wesley (84) and Whitefield (85), Elizabeth Fry and Hannah More, or the strong faith of such diverse believers as Dr. Johnson and Lady Huntingdon.

Sunday was strictly observed everywhere as a day of devotion. In the early part of the century no one travelled then who was not constrained by the most urgent reasons. Public coaches did not run on Sundays before the middle of the century, and even when they began to do so, there was a strong lingering prejudice against any unnecessary travel on the Lord's Day. Almost everyone went to church at least once, and usually twice if two services were held in the parish (81, 82). According to modern ideas, the demeanour of the worshippers was not always very reverent, but allowance must be made for the more casual notions of the age. Service and sermon were both long, too long, very often, for the bursting energies of children or the precarious wakefulness of the aged. Those who talked, fidgeted, or nodded too obviously, were liable to receive a sharp tap from the wand wielded by the dog-whipper, an official whose principal duty was to evict the dogs that strayed through the open doors in search of their masters. The gentry frequently had refreshment brought to them by one of their servants just before the sermon—a glass of sherry or some other drink and a little food to keep them awake during the long homily to follow. All this suggests a somewhat more workaday atmosphere in the house of God than would be tolerated there to-day. Yet if attention sometimes wilted under the strain of a too-lengthy discourse, or drowsiness proved too strong on a warm summer morning, few people ever thought of staying away from the service altogether, and no one dreamt of coming in late or leaving before the end.

Every householder had his own appointed seat in a country church. In towns pew rents were sometimes paid, but in rural districts the seats were free and went with the house in which the worshipper lived. At the west end there was usually a gallery for the village musicians who accompanied the psalms and hymns with their fiddles, flutes, oboes, and horns. The servants of the manor-house sat all together under the stern eye of the housekeeper; the children of the charity-school, where one existed, were placed where their occasional lapses from grace could be most conveniently observed and corrected by beadle or sidesman.

In the squire's large box-like pew, cushions and carpets did something to mitigate the hardness of wooden seats and stone floors, and in some churches it even contained a small fireplace where burning logs struggled with the intense winter cold of the unheated building.

Now and again the congregation stared to see some unhappy woman doing penance for immorality or publicly recanting some slander against a neighbour. "One Sarah Gore came to me this morning," wrote Parson Woodforde on 3 February 1768, "and brought me an instrument from the Court of Wells, to perform publick Penance next Sunday at C. Cary Church for having a child, which I am to administer to her publickly next Sunday after Divine Service."[1] Such bitter ordeals, however, were becoming rare, though they had been common enough in the previous century. Sometimes a betrayed girl charged a man with the fatherhood of her child, and then the local Justice could order him to marry her or go to prison, unless he was able to offer sufficient security to indemnify the parish. Forced marriages of this kind had to be performed by the clergyman of the parish, for there were then no weddings except in church. Parson Woodforde was called upon to unite several couples thus. He describes one case where the unwilling bridegroom could hardly be persuaded to the altar and behaved very badly when he was at last induced to come there. The good old rector tells us that he greatly disliked performing such unhappy ceremonies for "it is a cruel thing that any Person should be compelled by Law to marry."

No work was done on Sundays beyond that which was absolutely necessary, and in strict households no games were played nor books read other than the Bible and volumes of sermons. But except on Sundays religious observance did not impinge much upon ordinary life. Family prayers were still usual in many households but the old daily church-going had quite ceased and in most parishes the opportunity for it did not exist. Children were taught their catechism and made to learn collects, but they were no longer expected to hear long sermons during the week or give verbatim accounts of those heard on Sundays. Private fasts occurred only in the most devout families, though now and then a public fast-day was ordered, as in 1780 and again in 1782, when the military situation was very bad. Saints' days were occasionally observed; there is a delightfully human entry in Parson Woodforde's diary in which he confesses that he entirely forgot it was St. Luke's Day and so omitted the public prayers he

[1] Woodforde, *op. cit.*

would otherwise have read in church. Clergymen did not consider it incompatible with their calling to play cards, dance, or go to theatres, though they usually refrained from doing so at holy seasons, an example not always followed by their parishioners.

Certain harsh old rules still obtained. Children who died unbaptized were denied a funeral service and no bells were tolled for them. Suicides were interred in unconsecrated ground on the north side of the churchyard, or at the crossroads with a stake driven through their bodies to keep them from rising and haunting the neighbourhood. In 1781 John Bitten, of Fawley in Hampshire, was so buried at Hardley Lane Ends. His resting-place is still locally remembered, but there must be many other crossroads over which the motorist now passes, all unaware that he is driving over the forgotten grave of some unhappy wretch who once found life intolerable. The last of these semi-pagan funerals took place in 1823 when a murderer and suicide was buried in St. John's Wood, after which such interments were forbidden by law. Yet even in the case of avowed suicides a kinder attitude of mind often prevailed, and every effort was made to afford them Christian burial if the law could anyhow be stretched to admit of it. When Sarah Fletcher died by her own hand at Clifton Hampden in 1799, driven to despair by the discovery that her husband was attempting to arrange a bigamous marriage with another woman, the kindly local jury brought in the only finding that would permit her to be laid in consecrated ground. "After a full investigation of the previous conduct of the deceased," says the account in *Jackson's Oxford Journal* for 15 June 1799, "and the derangement of her mind appearing very evident, as well as many other circumstances, the jury, without hesitation, found a verdict—Lunacy."

Besides the churchmen who formed the majority of the population there were large numbers of dissenters who were allowed to worship in peace though they were debarred from certain public offices and privileges. But they too had lost a little of their former ardour. Like the Church of England, they suffered somewhat from the disease of comfortableness, though the political disadvantages under which they laboured kept them, perhaps, rather more on the alert. Unitarianism was spreading, especially amongst Presbyterian families, but its tenets made little appeal to ordinary people and its followers were regarded by some as dangerous enemies of Christianity. When Elisabeth Ham was converted to this faith by Dr. Southwood Smith, she had to suffer for it afterwards in her profession. She gave up one position as a governess because the children mocked her religion and their

mother refused to reprove them for it, and she was denied another as soon as she acknowledged that she was a Unitarian. "I have such a horror of those who presume to deny our Lord and Saviour Jesus Christ," said her prospective employer, "that I would not admit such a person into my family on any consideration."[1] Except where Unitarians were concerned there was little bitterness against dissenters and much less proselytizing zeal amongst them. The Quakers who had caused so much scandal in Stuart times had quietened down and were now principally prosperous business men who led exemplary lives but kept themselves strictly to themselves. The Baptists and Congregationalists had their own chapels and followed their own rule of life devoutly enough, but it was sufficient for them to do this and no more. They no longer produced fiery revivalist preachers as they had once done, nor cared very much about the conversion of outsiders.

It was upon this quiet and somewhat pedestrian religious world that the fire of Methodism burst towards the middle of the century. For John and Charles Wesley, with their strong belief in the possibility of salvation for all men and the necessity for stern spiritual discipline, the easy contentment of the age savoured too much of complacency to be borne. Revolting fiercely against apathy and formalism wherever they found it, they provided the inspiration that was lacking in the religious teaching of the day and, by their own preaching and example and those of their more energetic followers, they accomplished in a comparatively short time what was little short of a revolution both within and without the Church.

When John Wesley (84) began his missionary journeys up and down the country, he intended only to revivify his own church, not to found another, but in the end he did both. Trained by a deeply religious and intelligent mother and a father constantly at odds with his apathetic and unfriendly parishioners, he came very early in his career under the influence of the mystical William Law and, later, under that of the Moravians. At Oxford he gathered round him a few like-minded young men who established for themselves a strict rule of life, spending much of their time in prayer, in visiting the sick and those in prison, and in other works of charity. From this small beginning the Methodist movement was to spring after an interval during which its leaders were preaching and working in Georgia. In a few years it spread rapidly throughout England and Wales and finally, though against the original desire of its founder, became the nucleus of a new and separate church.

[1] *Elisabeth Ham, by Herself.*

At first it was regarded by many with deep and sincere distrust, a distrust that was natural enough when we consider some of its early manifestations and the general temper of the age. We hear a great deal of the extravagances of the eighteenth century, of the wild young men who drank, gambled, and indulged in riotous pranks, of "Hell-Fire Clubs", and other excesses of young bloods and even of some who could not plead the excuse of youth. Such things undoubtedly existed and made a great noise, but they were confined chiefly to the more frivolous members of the wealthy classes, as scepticism was confined to the more rarefied intellectuals. For ordinary citizens, for the country gentry and their tenants, the merchants, clergymen, schoolmasters, and sober householders, decency and decorum in all things were cardinal virtues. It was against these that some of the early Methodists seemed to offend and by so doing alarmed many who might have sympathized with them. It was primarily the hysterical outbursts, the fainting, weeping, and loud cries, the sensational conversions which took place at Methodist meetings, that frightened away those who would otherwise have been drawn to the new movement. Whitefield's violent eloquence and his dark Calvinistic teachings sometimes moved his audience to a pitch of fervour that bordered upon frenzy, and even the more temperate Wesleys often produced hysteria amongst their hearers.

John Wesley himself realized how alarming all this seemed to many people. "We understood," he wrote in his *Journal*, "that many were offended at the cries of those on whom the power of God came," and he goes on to relate how one physician went specially to observe what passed at these gatherings and stood by a woman who "broke out in strong cries and tears . . . till great drops of sweat ran down her face and all her bones shook." He tells us also how at one meeting a Quaker "was not a little displeased at the dissimulation of those creatures, and was biting his lips and knitting his brows, when he dropped down as thunder struck. The agony he was in was even terrible to behold. We besought God not to lay folly to his charge, and he soon lifted up his head, and cried aloud, 'Now I know thou art a prophet of the Lord.'"

Such scenes repelled the fastidious and excited hostile mobs to violence. Many clergymen refused to allow Wesley to preach in their churches, and their attitude finally drove him to ordain his own ministers and thus create a separate sect. Methodist meetings were constantly broken up by angry crowds, the preachers attacked and hustled and the congregation insulted. Once at Walsall Wesley was very roughly handled by a furious mob who

rushed him from one end of the town to the other, and there were many similar riots in the course of his long career. Much of this violence was due to nothing more than hooliganism, but some of it sprang from a deep-seated fear of fanaticism. The daily discipline required by the Methodist rule was distinctly puritanical in tone and to those untouched by revivalist fervour it seemed cold and unnatural. Certainly it had one unfortunate effect, more deplored perhaps to-day than at the time, inasmuch as it obliterated much that was valuable in folk-art, especially in Wales where so many lovely old songs and ballads have been forgotten because the early Methodists were taught to regard them as ungodly. When Wesley was haled by the mob to the house of a Justice near Wednesbury, all his accusers could find to say against him or his followers was: "Why, an't please you, they sing psalms all day; nay, and make folks rise at five in the morning."[1] These cannot be considered very heinous crimes; but the confused statement of the mob-leader probably expressed the vague misgivings of hundreds of unthinking people who saw in the new movement the beginnings of another attack upon their normal pleasures and liberties, such as that which the Puritans had made all too successfully in the time of the Commonwealth.

More educated people resented the Methodist habit of exhorting all and sundry to a godly life, regardless of the degree or age of their hearers and the circumstances in which they met them. It was perhaps a little startling to be suddenly questioned by a total stranger as to the state of one's soul, and many objected to it strongly. Wesley, however, considered it his clear duty to bring up the subject whenever he got into conversation with any one at an inn, in a coffee-house, or on the highway. When he failed to do so, he reproached himself bitterly, and once, when a heavy shower of hail followed such an omission, he regarded it as a direct punishment from God. His strongly superstitious habit of mind also alienated some who feared that his teachings would foster undue credulity amongst the ignorant. He was a firm believer in witchcraft and demoniac possession, and a convinced opponent of the Witchcraft Act of 1736 which put an end to the legal persecution of so many poor wretches. He accepted without question the curious tale of Elizabeth Hobson who alleged that her grandfather had returned from Hell to haunt her with the sole purpose of making her evict her aunts from the house which he had left her in his will. This story, with all its evidences of hysteria, he continued to believe in spite of the

[1] *Journal of John Wesley*, Standard edition, III.

openly expressed doubts of his less trusting brother Charles. He was not, however, always so easily deceived. When a certain woman claimed prophetic powers and deeply impressed some of those present by her supposedly inspired utterances, Wesley wrote very coolly in his *Journal*

> The motion might be either hysterical or artificial. And the same words any person of a good understanding and well versed in the Scriptures might have spoken. But I let the matter alone; knowing this, that "If it be not of God, it will come to nought."

Nevertheless, no doubts or misgivings, no mob riots or unseemly happenings at Methodist meetings could quench the light of the Evangelical Revival once it had been lit. In the later years of the eighteenth century there was a great awakening of the spirit both within and without the Church. Wesley's tireless missionary journeys took him to places where religion had scarcely penetrated before. His open-air sermons brought the Gospel to thousands whom the Church had hitherto failed to influence, and gave a new purpose to the lives of the roughest and most ignorant. A new seriousness made its appearance in many circles not consciously touched by Methodist teachings. The careless parson became much rarer, the neglected church a less common sight. Even in the novels of the time the general tendency was evident, for we hear constantly of men and women being judged by their principles rather than their accomplishments or charm. Good morals and religious observance were now demanded of heroes and heroines; and if equality of wealth and station was always insisted upon in the marriages described in these tales, so also was equality of character.

Much of this revival of religious feeling flowered in an active philanthropy which drove shy women like Elizabeth Fry to face all the difficulties of public life in order to help the unfortunate, and led others, like the More sisters, to forsake a comfortable and leisured existence to bring education to the poor. In 1773 John Howard, then High Sheriff of Bedfordshire, began his great work in the prisons, and early in the nineteenth century Mrs. Fry opened her famous school for the children of Newgate prisoners. In 1763 Theophilus Lindsay, a clergyman, founded one of the first Sunday Schools at Catterick, and six years later Hannah Ball, a Methodist started another at High Wycombe. At Styal in Cheshire the daughters of Samuel Greg, the mill-owner, gave up their Sundays after church to teaching their father's child-apprentices in the old building still known as the Prentice House. Mrs. Trimmer, whose educational books were once to be found

in almost every schoolroom, devoted all the spare time left from her writing and the care of her own twelve children, to the organization of schools and the clothing of the impoverished pupils who came to them.

When Hannah and Martha More drove one day to see the beauties of the Cheddar Gorge, they were so horrified by the barbarous and uncivilized appearance of the people that they started schools in thirteen villages. In this work they were strongly opposed by the local farmers who feared that education might make their labourers unwilling to work, and even the curate of one parish threatened them with legal proceedings for teaching without a licence. Their instruction was of the most limited description and did not include reading or writing, but such as it was, it was more than the children of the district had ever received before. It was at this time that some of the worst evils of the growing factory system were beginning to appear. Yet side by side with the indifference and cruelty of some employers, the child-labour, the long hours, low wages, and appalling housing of thousands of workers, went a deepening sense of responsibility towards the poor and needy. It produced a generous crop of voluntary workers, drawn from widely differing circles, and their efforts, limited and unimaginative as they sometimes were, paved the way for the legal reforms introduced by Lord Shaftesbury and others in the following century.

Not every religious person, naturally, had the courage or the opportunity to follow the lead of the great pioneers. But the work of these leaders was generally admired, and there were many whose names have not come down to us who were inspired by the Evangelical Revival to give whatever help they could to those in need around them. In her *Diary* Fanny Burney tells us of the impression made upon her by one Sunday School which she visited in 1791. "Such a number of poor innocent children," she writes in sincere admiration, "all put in the way of right; most taken immediately from every way of wrong, lifting their little hands in these prayers and supplications for mercy and grace, which even if they understood not, must at least impress them with a general idea of religion, a dread of evil, and a love of good."[1]

The Georgian period was in many ways a coarse and cruel age in which drinking, gambling and immorality flourished and extremes of wealth and poverty created a host of horrible abuses. But, for all its faults, it was alive and vigorous and essentially well intentioned. Its cruelties sprang mostly from lack of vision,

[1] *The Diary and Letters of Madame d'Arblay*, 1778–1840, ed. C. Barrett, 1891.

its kindnesses from genuine warmth of heart. Under all the extravagances and excesses of the upper classes, all the brutalities of the rough and ignorant, lay a fundamental strength of character and, in most people, a deep-seated if sometimes inarticulate religious feeling. For the vast majority the basis of life was the family, with all its steady, cheerful virtues, and the sober, decorous teachings of church or chapel. These were the enduring roots of the nation's strength, however overlaid they might be on occasion by frivolity and crime. "A nation of honest men", the Duke of Wellington called the men of his time, and this in general they were; but they were usually the possessors of something that went deeper than honesty. A few weeks before he died, Lord Malmesbury wrote in his *Diary* his own reflections upon his life, and in so doing put on record the inner feelings of many thousands of his compatriots who lacked his gift of expression. In sober thankfulness and an unclouded consciousness of God he wrote:

> Thou has completed thy seventy-fourth year, having been permitted to live longer than any of thy ancestors as far back as 1606. —Thy existence has been without any great misfortune and without any acute disease, and has been one for which thou ought'st to be extremely grateful.—Be so in praise and thanksgiving towards the Supreme Being, and by preparing thyself to employ the remnant of it "wisely and discreetly".—Thy next step will probably be the last.—Strive not to delay the period of its arrival, nor lament at its near approach.—Thou art too exhausted, both in mind and body, to be of service to thy country, thy friends or family.—Thou art fortunate in leaving thy children well and happy; be content to join thy parent earth calmly and with becoming resignation. Such is thy imperious duty.—Vale.[1]

[1] *Malmesbury Diaries and Correspondence*, ed. J. H. Harris, 1844.

BIBLIOGRAPHY

ASHMOLE, ELIAS — Diary and Letters. Ed. R. T. Gunther. 1927

ATKINSON, J. C. — Forty Years in a Moorland Parish. 1892

AUBREY, JOHN — Brief Lives. Ed. A. Clarke, 1898
Miscellanies upon Various Subjects. 1696
Remaines of Gentilisme and Judaisme 1686-7

BAMFORD, E. — Dear Miss Heber . . . 1936

BARNARD, E. A. — A Seventeenth Century Country Gentleman. 1944

BEALE, C. H. — Reminiscences of a Gentlewoman in the Last Century. 1891

BELL, W. G. — The Great Plague in London.

BERESFORD, J. D. — The Diary of a Country Parson; the Rev. James Woodforde. 1924–31

BLUNDELL, M. — Cavalier. 1933

BOORDE, ANDREW — A Compenydous Regyment, or a Dietary of helth. 1542

BRETON, NICHOLAS — The Courtier and the Countryman. 1618

BRINSLEY, JOHN — Ludus Literarius, or the Grammar Schoole. 1612

BROME, JAMES — Travels over England, Scotland and Wales. 1700

BRYANT, ARTHUR — England in the Reign of Charles II. 1934
Postman's Horn. 1936
The Years of Endurance. 1942

BURNEY, FANNY — The Early Diary of Fanny Burney. Ed. A. R. Ellis. 1906
The Diary and Letters of Madame d'Arblay. Ed. C. Barrett. 1891

BYROM, ELISABETH — The Diary of Elisabeth Byrom. Chetham Society

CALVERLEY, SIR WALTER — The Diary of Sir Walter Calverley. Surtees Society

CAMDEN, W. — Brittania: Newly Translated into English with large Additions and Improvements. Published by Edward Gibson of Queen's College, Oxford. 1695

CAMPBELL, MILDRED — The English Yeoman. 1942

CHAMBERLAYNE, EDWARD — Angliae Notitia: or the Present State of England. 1669

CLARKE, W. K. LOWTHER — Eighteenth Century Piety. 1944

CLEGG, JAMES — Extracts from the Diary and Autobiography of the Rev. James Clegg. Ed. H. Kirk. 1899

CORRY, J. — History of Macclesfield. 1817

COX, J. C. — The Household Books of Sir Miles Stapleton, Bart., 1658–1705. (In *The Ancestor*, July, 1902)

DALTON, MICHAEL — The Country Justice. 1618

DEFOE, DANIEL — A Tour through the Island of Great Britain. 1724

D'EWES, SIR SIMMONDS — Autobiography and Correspondence of Sir Simmonds d'Ewes. Ed. J. O. Halliwell. 1845

DICTIONARY OF NATIONAL BIOGRAPHY

DRUMMOND, J. C. AND WILBRAHAM, ANNE — The Englishman's Food. 1940

EDEN, SIR FREDERICK — The State of the Poor. 1797

EGMONT, THE EARL OF — Diary of Viscount Percival, Earl of Egmont. H.M.C., Vol. I. 1920

ERONDELL, P. — The French Garden. 1605

EVELYN, JOHN — The Diary of John Evelyn. Ed. W. Bray. 1859

EYRE, ADAM — The Diary of Adam Eyre. 1646–48. Surtees Society

FALKLAND, LADY — The Lady Falkland, her life, by her daughter

FANSHAWE, LADY — Memoirs. Ed. Sir M. H. Nicholas. 1829

FARINGTON, J. — The Farington Diary. Ed. J. Grieg

FIELDING, H. — The Journal of a Voyage to Lisbon. Ed. A. Dobson. 1907

FIENNES, CELIA — Through England on a Side Saddle in the Reign of William and Mary. Ed. Hon. Mrs. Griffiths. 1888

FLETCHER, J. S. — Memorials of a Yorkshire Parish. 1917

FULLER, DR. THOMAS — Good Thoughts in Bad Times, Together with Good Thoughts in Worse Times. 1649
The Holy State and the Prophane State. 1642
Worthies of England. 1662

GALE, WALTER — The Diary of Walter Gale. Sussex Archeological Collections, Vol. IX

GENTLEMAN'S MAGAZINE LIBRARY

GIBSON, T. ELLISON — Crosby Records. 1895

GODFREY, ELISABETH — Home Life under the Stuarts. 1925

GOTCH, J. A. — The Growth of the English House. 1909

HALKETT, LADY ANNE — The Autobiography of Lady Anne Halkett. Camden Society, N.S. No. 13

HAM, ELISABETH — Elisabeth Ham, by herself. Ed. E. Gillett. 1945

HANWAY, JOSEPH — An Essay on Tea, by Mr. Hxxxx. 1757

HARLEY, LADY BRILLIANA — Letters of Lady Brilliana Harley. Camden Society, No. 58

HARRISON, WILLIAM — A Description of England. 1577

HENTZNER, PAUL — Travels in England. 1588

HEYWOOD, OLIVER — Autobiography, Diaries, Anecdotes and Event Books, 1630–1702. Ed. J. Horsfall Turner. 1872–85

HOBHOUSE, E. — The Diary of a West Country Physician. 1934

HOLLYBAND, C. — Campo di Fior. 1583
The French Littleton. 1566
The French Schoolmaister. 1573

HUTCHINS, J. — History of Dorset

HUTCHINSON, MRS. LUCY — Memoirs of the Life of Colonel Hutchinson. Ed. C. H. Firth. 1895

JOSSELYN, R. — Diary of the Rev. Ralph Josselyn. Ed. E. Hockcliffe. 1908

JOYCE, H. — History of the Post Office, 1893

LECKY, E. H. — The History of England in the Eighteenth Century. 1883

LEE, W. H. MELVILLE — A History of the Police in England. 1901

LEWIN, WILLIAM — Her Majesty's Mails. 1864

LYSONS, DANIEL — The Environs of London. 1811

MACHYN, HENRY — Diary of Henry Machyn. Camden Soc. 1848

MALMESBURY — Malmesbury Diaries and Correspondence. Ed. J. H. Harris. 1844

MARCHAND, J. — A Frenchman in England. 1933

MARKHAM, GERVASE — The English Hus-wife. 1615

MARTINDALE, ADAM — Life of Adam Martindale. Ed. R. Parkinson. Chetham Society, No. 4

MISSON, J. — Memoirs and Observations of M. Misson in his Travels over England. Trans. J. Ozell, 1719, from the French of 1697

MONTAGU, LADY MARY — Letters of Lady Mary Wortley Montagu

MORITZ, C. P. — A Journey to England. Ed. P. E. Matheson. 1924

MORYSON, FYNES — An Itinerary. 1617

NEWTON, LADY — The House of Lyme
Lyme Letters. 1925

NICHOLS, JOHN — The Progresses, Processions . . . of Queen Elisabeth. 1823
The Progresses, Processions . . . of King James I. 1828

NORTH, ROGER — Lives of the Norths. Ed. A. Jessop. 1890

OSBORNE, DOROTHY — Letters of Dorothy Osborne to Sir William Temple. Ed. G. A. Parry, 1914

PARKES, JOAN — Travel in England in the Seventeenth Century. 1925

PASTON, G. — Sidelights on the Georgian Period. 1902

PEACHAM, HENRY — The Compleat Gentleman, 1622. Ed. G. S. Gordon. 1906

PEPYS, SAMUEL — Pepys' Diary. Ed. H. B. Wheatley. 1893–9
Correspondence of Samuel Pepys. Ed. J. R. Tanner, 1926
Further Correspondence of Samuel Pepys. Ed. J. R. Tanner. 1929

PIETTE, MAXIMIN — John Wesley in the Evolution of Protestantism. 1937
PLATTER, THOMAS — Thomas Platter's Travels in England, 1599. Ed. Clare Williams. 1937
PORTER, ENDYMION — Letters of Mr. Endymion Porter, Gentleman of the Bedchamber to King Charles I. Ed. Dorothea Townshend. 1897
PUREFOY — Purefoy Letters, 1735–53. Ed. G. Eland. 1931
RAWDON, MARMADUKE — Life of Marmaduke Rawdon. Camden Society, No. 85
ROWSE, A. L. — The English Spirit. 1944
Tudor Cornwall. 1941
RYE, W. — England as seen by Foreigners in the Days of Elisabeth and James I. 1865
SALZMANN, L. F. — England in Tudor Times. 1933
SELDEN, J. — Table Talk of John Selden. Ed. S. H. Reynolds. 1892
SHUTTLEWORTH — The House and Farm Accounts of the Shuttleworths. Chetham Society
SLINGSBY, SIR HENRY — The Diary of Sir Henry Slingsby. Ed. Rev. D. Parson. 1836
STOW, J. — The Survey of London. Ed. Rev. J. Strype. 1755
STRUTT, JOSEPH — The Sports and Pastimes of the People of England. 1801
STUBBES, PHILIP — The Anatomie of Abuses. 1583
THACKER, F. S. — The Thames Highway: A History of Inland Navigation. 1914
THOMSON, GLADYS SCOTT — Life in a Noble Household. 1937
The Russells in Bloomsbury. 1940
THORNTON, ALICE — Autobiography of Mrs. Alice Thornton. Ed. C. Jackson. Surtees Society. 1875
TORRINGTON, VISCOUNT — The Torrington Diaries. Ed. C. Bruyn Andrews. 1934–5
TRAILL, H. D. — Social England. 1895
TREVELYAN, G. M. — English Social History. 1944
TROTTER, ELEANOR — Seventeenth Century Life in a Country Parish. 1919
TUER, ANDREW — The History of the Horn-Book. 1896
TURBERVILLE, A. S. — English Men and Manners in the Eighteenth Century. 1926
TURNER, T. H. AND PARKER, J. H. — Domestic Architecture in England. 1877
TYERMAN, L. — The Life and Times of John Wesley. 1870
VERNEY, P. AND M. — Verney Memoirs. Ed. P. and M. Verney. 1904
Verney Letters. Ed. P. and M. Verney. 1930
WAKEMAN, C. — History of the Church of England. 1908
WESLEY, JOHN — The Journals of John Wesley. Standard Ed. 1910
WHITE, GILBERT — The Natural History and Antiquities of Selborne. 1789
WILSON, F. P. — The Plague in Shakespeare's London. 1927
WOOD, ANTHONY — The Life and Times of Anthony A. Wood. Coll: A. Clarke. 1904
Atheniae Oxoniensis. 1681
WYNNE — The Wynne Diaries. Ed. A. Freemantle. 1935–40
YOUNG, ARTHUR — A Six Month's Tour through the North of England. 1771
A Six Week's Tour through the Southern Counties of England and Wales. 1772. (3rd ed.)

The Cheshire Sheaf
Devonshire Association Transactions
Gloucestershire Notes and Queries
Hampshire Field Club Proceedings
Kent Archæological Society's Publications. (Archæologia Cantiae)
Lancashire and Gheshire Antiquarian Society's Transactions
Lancashire and Cheshire Historical Society's Transactions
Leicestershire Notes and Queries
Lincolnshire Notes and Queries
Newcastle Society of Antiquaries' Transactions (Archæologia Aeliana)
The Suffolk Garland. 1818
Somerset and Dorset Notes and Queries
Somerset Record Society's Publications
Surrey Archæological Collections
Sussex Archæological Society's Collection.
Sussex Record's Society's Publications
Yorkshire Archæological Collections
Yorkshire Notes and Queries

INDEX

(The numbers in heavy type refer to the *figure numbers* of illustrations)

Agriculture, *see* Farming
Ague, 68, 72, 73, 155, 158, 159
Anglicans, 82, 83, 84
Ale, 15, 21, 23, 62, 76, 77, 86, 97, 108, 113, 114, 152
Apothecaries, 13, 52, 156, 157, 158, 159; **26**
Apsley, Lucy, *see* Hutchinson, Lucy
Archery, 29, 30, 47, 135; **16**
Architecture, *see* Houses
Aromatic Waters, 16, 103
Ascham, Roger, 27, 43
Ashmole, Elias, 64, 68, 72, 90
Astrology, 66, 90
Atkinson, J. A., 99, 123
Aubrey, John, 3, 32, 42, 73, 90
Austen, Jane, 60, 97, 115, 120, 126, 141

Baiting: Bear, 32, 33, 133, 136
  Bull, 32, 33, 136
Bakehouse, 10
Bakewell, Robert, 94
Banns of marriage, 62, 127, 128
Bath, 36, 128, 133, 141, 142, 143, 144
Bathrooms, 11, 97
Baths: at home, 11, 98
  public, 11, 142, 143, 144
Bedford, Duke of, 56
  Earl of, 57, 58
Bedrooms, 4, 5, 6, 7, 8, 95, 97, 98, 99, 100; **32**
Beds, 3, 5, 6, 7, 8, 74, 97, 100
Betrothals, 56, 60, 61
Bills of mortality, 73
Blood-letting, 66, 67, 158, 160: **27**
Blundell, Nicholas, 33, 136
  William, 65, 80, 84
Books, 25, 28, 47, 48, 94, 140, 141, 175
Boorde, Andrew, 8, 30, 71
Bowls, 24, 30, 135
Boxing, 135, 136
Brandy, 113, 152, 158
Breakfast, 20, 108, 144
Breton, Nicholas, 23, 48, 49
Brewhouse, 5, 10, 97
Brewing, 10, 15, 97, 103
Bridal dress, 60, 61, 128
Bride-ales, 61, 62
Brighton, 147; **71**
Bull-running, 136
Burial in woollen, 74
Burney, Fanny, 141, 176
Buttery, 5, 97
Buxton, 142
Byng, John, *see* Torrington, Lord
Byrom, Elizabeth, 92

Calverley, Sir Walter, 74, 77
Cambridge University, 52, 85
Candles, 6, 9, 15, 47, 71, 100, 101, 102, 103, 152
Card-games, 24, 28, 50, 83, 138, 144; **45**
Carpets, 3, 4, 5, 7, 100
Carr, Anne, 57, 58
Carriages, 37, 38, 39, 96, 107, 122, 145, 146, 148, 153; **7**
Carriers, 25, 36, 37, 140, 141
Chapels: private, 19, 80, 86, 95; **30, 31**
  unlicensed, 127, 128
Chaplains, 18, 19, 80, 86
Charity, 47, 74, 76, 77, 115, 124, 130, 131, 175
Charles, I, 58, 84
Charles II, 20, 36, 66, 67, 84, 85
Charms, 40, 41, 42, 57, 61, 69, 88, 89, 90
Cheltenham, 142, 144; **72**
Chester, 36, 70, 137
Child-labour, 123, 124
Children, 16, 17, 18, 20, 30, 40 *et seq.*, 55, 56, 57, 58, 67, 72, 73, 75, 76, 80, 81, 83, 87, 88, 100, 104, 107, 108, 115, 117 *et seq.*, 129, 131, 155, 156, 163, 164, 169, 170, 171; **18, 19, 24**
Children, training of, 16, 18, 30, 42 *et seq.*, 80, 81, 104, 115, 118 *et seq.*, 129, 170
Chimneys, 1, 2, 3, 6
Chocolate, 20, 23, 108, 109
Christening, 41, 42, 77, 83, 85
Christmas, 21, 28, 31, 50, 83, 115, 130; **42**
Church-ales, 32, 83
Church of England, 63, 79, 80, 82, 166, 167, 168, 169, 171, 172, 175
Circulating libraries, 141, 144
Civil war, 31, 65, 70, 84
Class distinctions, 18, 19, 32, 53, 59, 60, 93
Clegg, J., 158
Clergy: position of, 167, 168
  stipends of, 112, 167
Clocks, 9
Clothes, 8, 9, 15, 18, 25, 42, 60, 61, 71, 72, 74, 75, 105, 128, 139, 144, 145, 146; **1, 2, 22, 23, 33, 36, 75, 76**
Coach fares, 38
Coaches: private, 37, 38, 71, 148
  stage, 38, 39, 148, 149, 150, 151, 153, 169
Cock-fighting, 33, 133, 136
Coffee, 20, 23, 108, 109, 112
Coffee houses, 23, 52, 109, 141
Coke, Thomas, 94, 132
Common rights, 29, 93
Cooking, 9, 10, 16, 101, 109
Corals, 42
Correspondence, 25, 26, 139
Coryat, Thomas, 23
Cosmetics, 8, 16
Cotswold games, 31
Cottages, 10, 12, 93, 98, 99, 101, 132, 133: **40**
Coursing, 27, 31, 135
Coverley, Sir Roger, 130
Cradles, 42
Cricket, 123, 133, 135: **69, 70**
Culpeper, Nicholas, 68
Cures, herbal, 12, 13, 68, 69, 73, 139, 157, 158, 159, 160, 161
  household, 15, 16, 68, 158, 160

Dairy, 5, 9, 95, 98, 103, 124: **10**
Dancing, 9, 24, 31, 32, 61, 62, 138, 139, 143, 144; **11, 34, 43**
Death, moment of, 73, 74
Dee, Dr., 18, 90, 105
Defoe, Daniel, 34, 70, 148
Deism, 166
Dentists, 68, 161
D'Ewes, Sir Simmonds, 52, 81
Derby, Countess of, 65
Dice, 24, 28, 50, 83

Dining-out, 111, 112
Dining-rooms, 5, 95, 97, 98, 99, 108
Dinner, 20–2, 108, 110–11, 112, 115
Disease, 2, 11, 13, 40, 66 *et seq.*, 79, 104, 117, 155 *et seq.*
Dissenters, 82, 91, 92, 165, 171, 172–5
Divorce, 63, 129
Doctors, 16, 66, 67, 68, 72, 118, 156, 157, 159, 160, 161, 162, 163
Domestic Routine, 15 *et seq.*, 103 *et seq.*
Dowries, 58, 59, 126
Drawing-room, 5, 95, 97, 111
Dress, *see* Clothes
Dressing-room, 95

Eagle-stones, 40, 41
Easter, 98; **67**
Eden, Sir Frederick, 110
Education, 24, 25, 42 *et seq.*, 120 *et seq.*, 138, 158, 175, 176
Edward VI, 46, 75
Egmont, Earl of, 129
Elizabethan settlement, 78
Elopements, 127, 128
Elyot, Sir Thomas, 43
Enclosures, 27, 29, 93, 114, 132
Epidemics, 13, 68, 69, 70, 71, 72, 81, 161
Epsom, 36, 137, 142
Evangelical Revival, 165, 168, 175, 176; **84, 85**
Evelyn, John, 14, 37, 44, 73
Eyes, care of, 160
Eyre, Adam, 18

Fairs, 106; **78**
Falkland, Lady, 64, 87, 88
Family prayers, 17, 80, 81, 170
Family, size of, 40, 117
Fanshawe, Lady, 65
Farington, Joseph, 107, 152
Farmers, 4, 21, 48, 53, 60, 93, 98, 106, 115, 122, 130, 133
Farmhouses, 7, 10, 98, 99, 101, 157
Farming, 27, 29, 93, 94, 132; **8, 77**
Fast-days, 81, 112, 170
Fielding, Henry, 136, 141, 161
Fiennes, Celia, 11, 13, 33, 34, 36
Fireplaces, 2, 3, 5, 6, 8, 98, 100, 101; **50**
Fish-days, 20, 21, 81
Fishing, 24, 27, 135; **15**
Fitton, Francis, 7
Fives, 135
Floor-coverings, 4, 98, 100
Flowers, 12, 15, 16, 21, 68, 73, 75, 110
Food, 5, 13, 15, 20, 21, 22, 36, 76, 94, 95, 107, 108 *et seq.*, 139–40, 152
Football, 30–1, 135
Forks, 22, 23
Forty-five, The, 92
Fowling, 27
Franking letters, 25, 26
Fruit, 12–14, 15, 21, 111
Fry, Elizabeth, 169, 175
Fuel, 15, 100, 101
Fuller, Dr. Thomas, 22, 56, 73
Funerals, 74–7, 171
Furniture, 2, 3 *et seq.*, 22, 25, 42, 74

Gale, Walter, 123
Gambling, 28, 137–8
Game-laws, 27, 114, 133, 135
Games: indoor, 24, 28, 50, 83, 138; **47, 48**
outdoor, 24, 27, 28, 30, 31, 51, 83, 123, 135; **68**
Gamekeepers, 133–4
Gardens, 1, 2, 11–14, 30, 95, 96; **6**
George III, 146, 147
Gerard, John, 68
Gin, 113, 118, 158
Girls, education of, 24, 25, 44, 46, 47, 48, 123, 124–6, 138, 158
Golf, 135
Gout, 155, 156, 158, 159
Governesses, 46, 124, 127
Grand Tour, 97, 121–2
Graves, situation of, 76
Great Chamber, 5, 8, 50, 74, 97
Grey, Lady Jane, 46

Hackney cabs, 39
Hairdressing, 50, 60, 105, 144, 145; **74**
Halkett, Lady Anne, *see* Murray, Anne
Hall, 1, 2, 3, 5, 6, 10, 95, 97; **3**
Hall, John, 68
Hallowe'en, 31
Ham, Elisabeth, 147, 171–2
Hangings, bed, 3, 4, 6, 7, 74, 100
wall, 4, 5, 8, 74
Hanway, Joseph, 110, 145, 148
Harington, Sir John, 10, 11, 138
Harley, Lady Brilliana, 65
Harrison, William, 2, 3, 4, 7, 12, 20, 29, 36, 52, 53
Harrogate, 36, 142
Hawking, 24, 27, 28, 51, 135; **14**
Henry VIII, 30, 33, 71, 79
Herbal Remedies, 12, 13, 68–9, 73, 139, 157, 158–9, 160
Herbs, 11, 12, 13, 15, 68, 71, 73, 155, 162
Hermitages, 96
Heywood, Oliver, 81, 82
Highwaymen, 30, 33, 34, 35, 151–2
Honeymoons, 62, 128
Horn-books, 45
Horse-litters, 37
Horse-racing, 36, 137
Hospitals, 69, 156, 157, 162; **28, 79**
Hospitality, 17, 25, 60, 97, 107, 115, 138, 147
Household books, 16, 155
Houses, 1 *et seq.*, 12, 13, 14, 94 *et seq.*, 103, 122, 155–6
Housewives, duties of, 13, 15, 16, 17, 62, 101, 103, 108, 138, 158
Howard, John, 175
Hunting, 24, 27, 28, 29, 133, 134; **17, 20, 66**
Hurling, 31
Hutchinson, Lucy, 44
Hutton, Catherine, 112, 121, 154

Infant feeding, 41, 73, 117–18
Infant mortality, 40, 67, 117
Infection, 11, 40, 66, 67, 69, 71, 117, 155, 161–2, 163
Inoculation, 162–4
Inns, 36, 112–13, 141, 148, 150, 151, 152–4
charges at, 112–13, 152

Jacobites, 91, 92
James I, 7, 12, 37, 52 ; **25**
Jaundice, 155, 159
Jenner, Dr. 164
Jesters, 19
Johnson, Dr., 136, 169
Josselyn, Ralph, 79
Justices of the Peace, 36, 62, 63, 85, 106, 114, 131, 170, 174

Kitchen, 5, 9–10, 15, 95, 97; **12, 44, 46**
Kitchen utensils, 9

Labourers, 8, 93, 98, 101, 106, 110, 114, 115, 116, 123, 124, 133, 157
Landowners, 13, 28, 29, 32, 53, 59, 86, 96, 115, 130 *et seq.*, 142, 144
Latitudinarianism, 166–7
Laundry, 5, 15, 16
Legh, Francis, 49, 51, 58
Piers, 58
Sir Peter, 19, 51, 58, 74, 75, 121
Library, 5, 95, 140
Lighting, 6, 15, 100, 101, 102
Linen, household, 3, 6, 7, 8, 15, 16, 36, 60, 72, 154
Lodge, Dr. Thomas, 68, 69

INDEX

London, 4, 10, 20, 23, 28, 30, 33, 36, 37, 39, 58, 60, 61, 69, 70, 73, 80, 128, 133, 144, 153, 162
Long Gallery, 5, 8, 9, 95; **4, 5**
Lotteries, 138
Luncheon, 109
Lyon, John, 47

Machyn, Henry, 31
Magazines, 140–1, 157
Maiden Garlands, 75
Malmesbury, Earl of, 177
Manningham, John, 81
Markham, Gervase, 17, 28
Marriage, 49, 55 *et seq.*, 126–9, 170, 175; **83**
  age of, 49, 56, 57, 119, 127
  arrangements for, 55–6, 59, 60, 126
  banns of, 62, 127, 128
  ceremony, 56, 60, 61, 77; **62**
  customs at, 60–2, 77, 128, 139; **21**
  during Commonwealth, 62–3, 83
  for love, 55–6, 127
  preparations for, 8, 60, 77
  settlements, 64
Martindale, Adam, 34
Matches, 101
May-day, 31, 32, 38, 83, 98, 139, 149
Meals, 6, 20, 24, 62, 95, 107, 108 *et seq.*, 152, 153–4
  hours of, 20, 21, 23, 108
Medical science, 40, 66–9, 72, 156, 157
Merry meal, 139
Methodists, 138, 172–5
Midsummer, 31
Midwives, 41, 157
Milton, John, 44, 64
Mirrors, 8, 100
Misson, J., 21, 23, 62
Montagu, Lady Mary, 124, 125, 138, 162–4
Months, Mind, 76
More, Hannah, 169, 176
Moritz, C. P., 109, 111, 140, 153
Morning calls, 109, 138, 144
Morris, Claver, 108, 122, 127, 159, 160, 161
Morris dancing, 31, 32, 83
Moryson, Fynes, 35, 36
Mourning, 74
Murray, Anne, 63, 80
Music, 9, 24, 46, 133, 139; **35**
Musical instruments, 9, 24, 31, 99, 139
Musicians, 19, 24, 31, 32, 36, 62, 75
Muslin, introduction of, 146

Nash, Richard, 143
Needlework, 5, 9, 24, 25, 99, 124, 138–9; **60, 61**
Negro servants, 104–5
Nevinson, William, 30, 35
Newcome, Henry, 40, 79
Newmarket, 36, 137
Newspapers, 140–1
North, Roger, 39, 89
Novels, 141, 145, 175

Open-field farming, 27, 29, 94
Osborne, Dorothy, 55, 57, 72
Oxford University, 20, 49, 50, 52, 121

Pages, 19, 104
Panelling, 4, 5, 8, 100
Pantry, 5, 97
Parks, 13, 14, 29
Parlour, 5, 6, 74, 95, 97, 98, 99
Passing bell, 74, 171
Peacham, Henry, 43, 49, 50
Peachey, Dr. J., 68
Pedlars, 103, 104, 107, 146; **41**
Pennant, Thomas, 148
Pepys, Samuel, 13, 19, 20, 38, 39, 70, 81
Pest-houses, 69
Pets, 24, 136–7
Picnics, 39, 109, 142
Plague, 13, 67, 68, 80, 81, 83, 106, 162
Plate, 2, 3, 4, 5, 6, 22
Platt, Sir Hugh, 16
Players: private, 19
  touring, 138
Plays, 52, 83
Plough Monday, 31
Poaching, 114, 133–4; **49**
Poor: burial of, 75
  care of, 76–7, 114–15, 130, 131, 175, 176
  education of, 46, 52, 53, 122, 123, 124, 131, 175, 176
  food of, 21, 73, 94, 100, 111, 114–15
  pastimes of, 27, 134, 139, 140
  state of, 93, 94, 110, 114–16, 155
  weddings of, 55, 62
Porter, Endymion, 40, 56, 65
Post-chaises, 148, 153
Post-horses, 36
Postal services, 25–6
  charges of, 25–6
Potatoes, introduction of, 13
Preachers, unlicensed, 82
Presbyterians, 40, 82, 171
Prices: food, 23, 94, 109–10, 112–13, 114, 147
  magazines, 141
  muslin, 146
Priest-holes, 84, 85, 91
Priests, Roman Catholic, 20, 84, 85, 86
Privacy, desire for, 2, 13, 100
Privies, 10, 11, 97
Puritanism, 82–3
Puritans, 25, 31–2, 40, 52, 82, 88, 174

Quack Doctors, 157; **80**
Quakers, 73, 82, 172, 173
Queen Elizabeth, 10, 20, 30, 46, 64, 79, 90
Quintain, riding at, 31

Raikes, Robert, 124
Ranelagh Gardens, **73**
Rawdon, Marmaduke, 19
Recusants, 85, 86
Reformation, 46, 49, 60, 61, 77, 78, 142
Religion, 17, 47, 62–3, 64, 76, 77, 78 *et seq.*, 91, 92, 119, 130, 131, 165 *et seq.*
Renaissance, 1, 52
Rickets, 73, 155
Riding, 28, 33, 36, 38, 51, 144, 148
Rings: engagement, 61
  wedding, 61, 82
Rising, hours of, 20, 108
Roads, 15, 33, 131, 132, 133, 140, 149, 150
Robin Hood Bowers, 32
  Plays, 31
Roman Catholics, 20, 46, 64, 79, 82, 84–7, 88, 91, 92, 165
Royal Society, 66
Russell, Lady Caroline, 118, 121
Russell, Lord, 57, 58
Rushlights, 100, 101–2

Sanitation, 10, 66
School Fees, 120–1, 122
Schools: Boarding, 47, 125–6; **59**
  Charity, 122–3, 131, 169
  Dame, 48, 122; **54, 57**
  Free, 48, 122–3
  Grammar, 46, 48, 53, 120, 122
  Private, 120, 125–6; **51, 56**
  Public, 46, 47–8, 120, 121, 122; **52**
  Sunday, 123–4, 175, 176
Scot, Reginald, 42
Scurvy, 11, 68
Sea-bathing, 146–7
Sermons, 47, 61, 75, 81, 82, 140, 169, 170, 175
Servants, 5, 6, 7, 10, 16, 17, 18, 19, 20, 22, 25, 28, 36, 37, 60, 97, 98, 99, 100, 103 *et seq.*, 110, 111, 121, 122, 133, 152, 154, 162, 169; **13**

INDEX

Servants' dress, 18, 105, 106
  hall, 5, 97
  wages, 17, 18, 104, 105–6
Shooting, 28, 133, 135; **65**
Shorthand, 47
Silhouettes, **38, 39**
Skating, 31
Slingsby, Sir Henry, 19, 45, 119
Sloane, Sir Hans, 159
Smallpox, 67, 69, 72, 155, 161–4
Smoking, 12, 52
Smuggling, 110, 113–14, 168
Soap, 11, 15, 103
Somerset, Countess of, 57
Spinning, 6, 8, 15, 60, 103; **9**
Sport, 24, 27 *et seq.*, 32, 33, 51, 133 *et seq.*
Squires, *see* Landowners
Stables, 5, 95
Stairs, 2, 74, 98
Stalking, 27
Stapleton, Sir Miles, 86
Statute Fairs, 106
Steeplechasing, 137
Stillroom, 5, 16, 97, 103, 124
Stow, J., 33, 60, 61, 76
Stubbles, Philip, 31, 32
Suicides, burial of 76, 117
Sunday Observance, 47, 85, 130, 165, 166, 168 169, 170; **81, 82**
Supper, 23, 61, 107, 108, 111, 112
Surgical operations, 66, 155; **29**
Sydenham, Thomas, 67, 72

Table Manners, 22, 23, 111
Tavistock, Lord, 118, 120–1
Taxation, 94, 105, 110, 114, 133
Tea, 23, 106, 108, 109–10, 111, 112, 113, 115, 147; **87**
Teeth, care of, 11, 160–1
Tennis, 24, 30, 51, 135
Thames as highway, 39
Thames watermen, 39, 143
Theatres, 143, 144
Throckmorton, Sir Francis, 85
Tinder boxes, 101
Tobacco, 12, 13, 69, 114
Toothbrushes, introduction of, 11
Torrington, Lord, 112, 142, 144, 147, 148, 154
Toys, 118–19; **58, 64**
Tradesmen, 12, 28, 103
Travelling, 33 *et seq.*, 148 *et seq.*, 169
  cost of, 36, 38, 148
Tunbridge Wells, 133, 142, 144, 159–60
Turner, Anne, 57
Tutors: private, 19, 43, 44, 46, 81, 87, 120–1, 122, 124: **55**
  University, 50, 51

Umbrellas, 144–5
Unicorn's Horn, 71
Unitarianism, 171–2
Universities, 36, 48, 49 *et seq.*, 85, 91, 120, 121; **53, 63**
  age of entry, 49, 121
  classes of students, 52–4, 121
  discipline at, 49, 50, 51, 52
  expenses at, 51, 53, 121
  tutors at, 50, 51
Upholstery, 5, 25, 99

Vaccination, 117, 163, 164
Vails, 17, 105
Vegetables, 13, 15, 109, 111
Verney, Edmund, 51, 62
  John, 35, 97
  Mary, 40, 56, 57, 65, 73
  Ralph, 35, 44, 47, 50, 56, 83, 119, 121

Wages, 17, 18, 77, 93, 105, 106, 114, 115, 124, 133
Waiting Gentlewomen, 18, 59, 104, 127
Wakes, 32, 33
Wallpapers, 4, 100
Watering-places, 36, 128, 133, 137, 141, 142 *et seq.*, 159, 160
Weapons, 6, 28, 29, 30, 47
Weaving, 15
Wesley, John, 119, 148, 158, 167, 169, 172–5
Wet-nurses, 41, 117–18
Weymouth, 146–8
White, Gilbert, 101, 102
Whitefield, John, 169, 173
Whitsuntide, 31, 32
Wigs, 100, 144, 156
Wills, 3, 7, 22, 48, 75, 76, 131
Windows, 1, 2, 3, 5, 8, 96, 98, 105, 155
Wine, 23, 24, 61, 63, 73, 76, 86, 109, 112, 113, 152, 154, 160
Wise-women, 157
Witchcraft, 41, 42, 57, 88, 89, 90, 174
  Acts, 89, 174
Wives, position of, 17, 59, 65
Women, careers for, 58–9, 127, 161
  pastimes of, 24–5, 134, 135, 138
Wood, Anthony, 23, 38, 52, 53
Woodforde, Rev. James, 105, 107, 112, 113, 114, 115, 136–7, 145, 148, 153, 158, 159, 160 168, 170

Yeomen, 4, 21, 28, 47, 48, 59, 104, 123, 133, 139
Young, Arthur, 112–13, 120, 148, 149, 150